MICHA~~EL BURNS~~

ALL
THINGS
— TO —
ALL
PEOPLE

THE POWER OF CULTURAL HUMILITY

All Things to All People
The Power of Cultural Humility
© 2019 by Michael Burns

ISBN: 978-1-948450-54-6. Printed in the United States.

Illumination Publishers cares deeply about the environment and uses recycled paper whenever possible.

All Scripture quotations, unless indicated, are taken from the Holy Bible, New International Version, (NIV), Copyright © 2011, 2015 by Biblica, Inc. Used by permission. All rights reserved.

Cover design by Roy Appalsamy of Toronto, Canada. Interior layout by Toney Mulhollan. Copy editing by Amy Morgan.

Illumination Publishers titles may be purchased in bulk for classroom instruction, business, fund-raising, or sales promotional use. For information please email paul.ipibooks@me.com.

About the author: Michael Burns  is a teacher in the Minneapolis-St. Paul Church of Christ. He is a graduate of Wesley Seminary of Indiana Wesleyan University (MA). He taught high school history in the central city of Milwaukee for nearly ten years. He is a national and international biblical teacher at churches and workshops. He is the founder and director of the Ministry Development and Training Academies centered in Minneapolis, Minnesota, and serves as an instructor in the Ministry Training Academies in Africa. He is the author of the C.O.R.E. series of books. He married his wife, MyCresha, in 1997. They have two sons and reside in Roseville, Minnesota.

LUMINATION
PUBLISHERS

www.ipibooks.com
6010 Pinecreek Ridge Court
Spring, Texas 77379-2513

CONTENTS

Foreword

April 26, 2019 marked my forty-fourth year as a disciple of Jesus and a member of the churches of Christ. Over these years I have read many spiritual books and heard hundreds of sermons on diverse topics addressing a multiplicity of needs. I can't think of any that have addressed the cultural challenges we face as Michael Burns does in his book *All Things to All People.* Reading it has been enlightening and has helped me to see in a greater way God's plan for a multicultural body of believers to change the world.

Michael takes us on a biblical, historical, and cultural journey that is educating and inspiring. This is a serious book. As a church leader in the family of God, I have gained from it greater perspective and insight on how we can be one in Christ. As an African American disciple who believes God wants all people from all nations to be saved and to work together as one in Christ, I see this book as an effective tool for educating fellow church leaders and members on how to achieve God's dream of a united church family. Michael does more than just highlight the challenges of building a multicultural church in these turbulent times, he also offers many solutions and insights on how we can do so. If you are serious about the mission to build a truly unified church of all nations, this is a must-read.

I was initially reticent to write a foreword, as I do not consider myself a writer naturally. My friend, Scott Kirkpatrick, who is the chairman of the International Churches of Christ Diversity Team, convinced me to read the book and write a short introduction. I believe that this book will help any disciple and any church wishing to grow in their cultural humility. The text itself, the resources, and the activities in its companion devotional workbook, *A Crown That Will Last,* will guide groups to greater understanding and growth in the complex areas of cultural communication and life together in a diverse group.

I will turn the rest of the foreword over to Scott to introduce the Diversity Team and its relationship to this book.

—Sam Powell, Evangelist, New York City Church of Christ

God, in his incredible creativity, brought a diverse human population into existence. Everything that our God has created is beautiful, especially the human race. When sin entered the world, it cast this beautiful creation, including humankind, into a fallen state. This caused humanity to divide from one other and our creator. Over the millennia, the divisions between one another have only seemed to deepen.

Racial and cultural division plague our society here in America, as well as around the world. There is only one remedy to this enormous problem, and it is found in Jesus Christ through the word of God, the Bible. Disciples of Jesus, through the Bible, can bring Jesus' power of reconciliation to these deep divisions.

Jesus destroys the barrier of hostility, and only he can permanently bring down the walls that separate. I'm a part of diversity team that focuses on reconciliation between races and cultures for the sake of Christ. This US-based

Diversity Team is made up of leaders from around the United States, which includes evangelists, elders, teachers, and lay leaders. We plan to soon expand this team to have international arms as well.

The purpose of the team is to research, discuss, identify, and inform churches and leaders on how to navigate racial and cultural issues within our churches and communities. The goals of this team are as follows: (1) creating oneness in Jesus in our fellowship of churches, (2) assisting churches and leadership to live up to the biblical calling of being a light to the world, and (3) modeling this in efforts to reproduce within the church and community the reconciliation that Jesus taught throughout the Bible.

Michael Burns, the author of the extraordinary work *Crossing the Line: Culture, Race, and Kingdom*, has done it again. His book, *All Things to All People: The Power of Cultural Humility* is exhilarating. It was nearly impossible for me to put it down. While *Crossing the Line* focuses more on the "why," *All Things to All People* focuses more on the "how," which has been immensely helpful to me in the practical sense of dealing with racial and cultural issues.

Michael eloquently challenges the reader to embrace the Scriptures, which the Apostle Paul used to challenge disciples of Jesus to "become all things to all people" for one reason only: to win as many as possible for our Lord and Savior Jesus Christ. This book helps us to practically and spiritually understand God's calling for his creation and his people, from image bearers of God to the family of God. Michael challenges us to bridge the gap and fight for common ground and unity, even through the difficulties.

All Things to All People is a spiritual masterpiece and challenges the heart and mind while also bringing the reader closer to the Savior. The attention to grace when addressing the battle to fight for selflessness instead of selfishness is refreshing and inspiring.

The goal of the book is to enable its readers, including church leaders, to teach with confidence and conviction on sensitive issues such as racial and cultural diversity. It is the hope and goal of the Diversity Team that every church that takes seriously the call to be the diverse family of God would work through this book and the resources contained within it. It will serve as a curriculum for any group that wants to go deeper in its cultural competency and answer the biblical call to be all things to all people.

This book can stand alone, or it can be accompanied by *Crossing the Line* as curriculum for a church, Bible school, or individual. Together, these two books provide a complete arsenal for accurately and confidently educating people about the opportunities that face us in terms of race and culture.

I thank God that Michael was inspired to produce this amazing piece of work. I hope you are as motivated and challenged by it as I am, and I hope you will decide to make a difference in the world for true diversity. But more importantly, I hope you remember that there will be no major change without Jesus Christ being at the very center of it. I hope and pray that God will inspire more works like this to help people bring him glory through reconciliation.

—Scott Kirkpatrick, Evangelist, Columbia, South Carolina

Introduction

I lay deep asleep in my bed, exhausted after another long day of teaching high school history and coaching the boys' basketball team. I had finally succumbed to my fatigue and surrendered to the day just before midnight. My wife was laboring on an overnight shift at the hospital in her role as a registered nurse. Just short of 4 am I was shaken from my slumber by a noise. Dazed and a bit startled, I tried to connect what I was hearing with something that I could recognize or categorize. It took but a few seconds to realize that it was my older son, stumbling up the stairs into our bedroom.

I could only barely make out his silhouette as he tottered past the window. As he staggered toward the bed, I heard him weakly force out a "Da-a-a-ad." The ghostly timbre of his utterance, along with his gait, which resembled more that of a drunken man walking through wet cement than an eight-year-old boy, came together on my parent radar in an instant. I sprang straight up in the middle of the bed to a sitting position with my legs still under the covers. At the same time, I mustered all the force I could and attempted to shout out, "Don't you dare!"

But it was too late. He was positioned at the foot of the bed, aiming straight at me. I thought I might be able to grab him and stop the assault that was about to be unleashed, but my reflexes were slowed at that time of the morning, and he transitioned from the slow stagger to a lighting quick cannon as the projectile vomiting began to stream at me like angry water that had been penned up in a dormant fire hose far too long. It went all over the bed, the sheets, the pillows, and of course me. Did I mention that it was not even four in the morning yet?

I spent the rest of the morning cleaning and getting him settled back in bed, complete with a bucket next to him, as well as cleaning myself up, changing all the bedding, and starting an unexpected load of laundry.

Just a few days later, I was hurrying to get ready to leave for school. That morning I had the task of getting our then eighteen-month-old out of his crib and dressed and ready to go to daycare. On occasion, my wife would leave a special cookie for him on the dresser in his room and tell him that if he went to sleep quickly, he could have the cookie when he woke. No, we were not above bribery. When I opened the door to his room, I was irritated to see that he had apparently played the role of expert cat burglar in the night and somehow gotten hold of the cookie. Not only that, but he had made a mess of it, and the chocolate from the chips in the cookie was smeared everywhere. A bit frustrated by this new inconvenience to my morning, I momentarily wondered how that much chocolate could have been in one cookie.

You may already see where this is going, but as I neared his crib, I began to be overtaken by the sharp odor of what was clearly not the aroma of chocolate. It was then that I noticed that this special brownish substance was smeared on several of the slats of his crib. Further investigation of the wall next to his crib revealed something of a work of art that could rival some of the masterpieces of the great impressionists. Another glance down at my grinning son and I now saw the full glory of his foray into the world of art. His organic brown paint had leaked out of his diaper, and he had not just worked on the wall, but perhaps his magnum opus of finger painting was all over the sheet of his crib. Another memorable morning. Another impromptu hosing off and unscheduled load of laundry.

WHATS AND WHYS

If someone had come to my bright-eyed, the world-is-my-oyster, fifteen-year-old self and told me that I would willingly sign up for and continue to be part of projectile vomiting and scat art, I would have been certain that this person had fallen violently off several rockers, not just their own. There is no way I would have agreed to such a life.

What could possibly make someone buy in to such a thing? Although your first suspicion might be mental disease, that's not the case. In fact, millions of rational and well-functioning adults around the world submit to such indignities every day and do so willingly.

The reason is simple. Your "why" becomes bigger than your "what." Why would you allow such things to repeatedly happen? Because you meet these little humans and without fully understanding it, you love them—more than you could ever explain. You are willing to lay your life down for them. That is your "why." And that "why" becomes far greater than heat-seeking vomit or little pants full of human mud could ever be. You are willing to deal with an unbelievable and unfathomable amount of "whats" because the "why" has become so overwhelming.

In this book, we are going to talk about some very big "whats." If our "why" is not established and maintained as far bigger than our "whats," then we will fail at perhaps the greatest and most important task that God has ever entrusted to his people. What are these "whats" and what is our "why"? We'll get to that in due course.

A DIFFERENT WORLD

Have you ever traveled outside your home country? I'm not talking about a few days at some resort in a country that caters to foreign visitors and seeks to make them feel at home while enjoying a dash of luxury and being spoiled. Have you ever spent several weeks in a country that was far away and totally different from your home? Imagine doing that for several months. It can be fun, exhilarating, and exciting, but it also comes with numerous challenges.

Traveling away from home is difficult, especially for an extended time. Various researchers have demonstrated that spending time in a new environment is quantifiably taxing, both mentally and physically. It wears you down and tires you out, because your system is constantly under stress. Even if you're having a great time, enjoying the food, and adjusting well to a different time zone, being outside a familiar location is exhausting.

But if you're enjoying the location, savoring the food, and sleeping well, what is it that could be so demanding on your system? Believe it or not, it is most likely some level of culture shock. Culture shock is a very real and challenging thing to overcome. It grinds most people down.

When you are immersed in a different culture, there are many elements that demand concentration and a new level of understanding. You can rarely, if ever, put your mind on cruise control and relax. At every turn is something you don't fully understand, something unfamiliar, and you aren't exactly sure how to navigate.

"Why are they standing so close to me?"

"Why are they all standing so far apart when far more people could get in there?"

"Why are people lining up like that? That's not how I've ever seen it done before."

"Why did that airport worker not seem to care about what was right and fair in that situation?"

"What did they mean when they said that?"

"Why did everyone look uncomfortable when I said that?"

"How on earth did anyone find that joke funny? It made no sense at all!"

"Why do they allow that kind of behavior?"

"Why would they dress like that on such a hot day?"

"Does no one seem to care what time it is or respect anyone else's time?"

"Why does everyone seem so uptight about what time it is?"

"Why would they do that?"

"How could they think that way?"

"Why would they believe that?"

The list is nearly endless. The point is that there is much to learn when entering another culture. There are many things that cause stress because we don't understand and are constantly in fear of making a mistake, offending someone, or just looking clueless. Merely listening attentively and paying careful attention to someone for an extended period of time, something that is often required when you are outside your cultural norm, can by itself be mentally and physically draining.

What might seem like an adventure at first quickly becomes less than fun. You start to feel irritated and tense more often. You grow increasingly judgmental of behavior that seems odd and inexplicable. After a while, you start to long for home. You want to hear familiar music. You want comfort food. You want to be around people who make a little more sense and don't tire you out just being around them. We have a term for that feeling in my country. We call it homesick. What it actually is, though, is culturesick. We want to be home because we want to be surrounded by a culture that is comfortable, that makes sense to us, and that we know how to navigate with little effort or thought.

I have traveled extensively outside my own culture in this last decade or two, and I enjoy the adventure and excitement of interacting with other cultures in new parts of the world. But I would be lying if I said it wasn't exhausting at times. I've found places that I visit regularly that are still different, but close enough to my cultural comfort zone that they feel pretty comfortable and have become a home away from home. But even in those places, after a while, I find myself longing to be back at home surrounded by what I know best. Those feelings come on even quicker when I'm traveling in a place with cultures that are profoundly different from my own. Learning the customs, picking up on what things mean and what's going on, trying to make sure I don't do something offensive—I love it, but even so, it's taxing.

I have seen many people move to other countries to share the gospel and advance the mission of the kingdom, and they have been used by God in amazing ways. But most of them that I have talked to have found it difficult and stressful to live in a place where they are surrounded constantly by a culture foreign to their own. The majority of those faithful souls eventually make their way back to their home culture at some point, as though a powerful magnet were pulling them back to the land of familiarity. Some stick it out and begin to embrace a new culture as their own, but for most, they enjoy their time away but then are thrilled to be back "home."

My point here is not to discourage anyone from traveling or moving to another country to minister. Those are amazing opportunities that I would wholeheartedly encourage you to embrace if God calls you to such adventures and opens the doors for you. Rather, I want you to think about how demanding it can be to be immersed in another culture. Now imagine what it would feel like if you were part of a church family in your own city where the default culture was not your own. How exhausting would that become over time?

CHALLENGES AHEAD

Cross-cultural encounters are difficult. There's really no way around that. And if we are truly embracing the gospel of Jesus Christ, our lives will be cross-cultural affairs. They just will. In this book I will make the case that the gospel itself involves the call to gather up people under the rule of Jesus the King from every people group and culture. We have been given the mission to gather the nations into one family, and that means that our life in Christ will be intercultural. I will also make the case that it is far too easy for multiracial churches to slip into utilizing one culture as its default, making it quite comfortable and homey for one group but a constant grind and effort for all others.

Being a truly multicultural church brings challenges. That's what this book is about. How do we navigate those challenges? Can you imagine a church that never taught about biblical manhood or womanhood? How about a church that never mentioned, taught, or gave any attention to the topic of marriage? A church that held no marriage retreats, never did premarriage counseling, never mentioned the subject of marriage or married life from the pulpit, and skipped over biblical passages focused on marriage or applied them to other topics. What would be the state of marriages in that church? I think it's safe to say that it would be abysmal.

But what about the body of Christ, which should be full of people from varying backgrounds, perspectives, ethnic groups, nations, and cultures? In your time as a Christian, how many sermons or teaching days have you heard that walked the church through the challenges of cross-cultural living or intercultural communication? How many lessons have focused on the many scriptural passages that teach cross-cultural competency and how to navigate these difficult issues within the body?

The more diverse a group is, the more difficult it will be to find unity and harmony. That is as true in Christ as anywhere else. It would be easier to join a church that is culturally homogenous, where everyone's culture was strikingly like your own. That is far more comfortable. Therefore, there will be a consistent and strong pull on a diverse church to break into more comfortable groups of like-minded folks. It's simply naïve to claim anything other than that.

And this is where it gets serious. Throughout recent history, at least in my country, the United States of America, there have been many attempts at multiracial and diverse churches. Many of those groups have prospered and multiplied quickly. At least they did so for a time. They heard the call of Christ to gather the nations and they answered it. But history also shows that most of those groups crumbled within a generation or two, and either disappeared or went back to segregated groups.

There were brief moments of multiracial churches in the 1700s in the United States that included African American preachers such as the Baptist William Leman and the Methodist Henry Evans, but most of the diverse congregations were limited to blacks and poor whites and were still typically dominated culturally by whites. But these efforts quickly faded by the Civil War, and there is little to no evidence that they extended beyond those two racial groups.

Following the Civil War, there was a brief appearance of interracial churches, but most whites found that unacceptable, and even those who did not rarely fully accepted their black comembers as true equals. These postwar groups eventually separated the races in all areas of church life, including seating, and it wasn't long before most parted ways altogether. This phenomenon really began in 1787 when Richard Allen and Absalom Jones left the Methodist Episcopal Church and would eventually form the African Methodist Episcopal Church (AME), but the process of interracial groups splitting into separate organizations continued through the post–Civil War generation. The Congregationalists were the last major group to resist that split, but they eventually gave in and split in the 1880s.

In the early 1880s a movement in the Midwest of the United States called the Evening Light Saints began in earnest with a heart toward gathering the nations into one multiethnic community. This movement would eventually come to be known as the Church of God, and they embraced a nondenominational instinct, though they would eventually become a denomination. Their early leader was a white minister named Daniel Warner. He formed a powerful partnership with AME preacher Julia Foote. This movement was deeply committed to racial reconciliation and was so countercultural that they faced intense opposition, including one of their camp meetings in Alabama being dynamited in the late 1890s. Following Warner's death, other Church of God preachers began to back off the message of racial and cultural solidarity, especially in areas of evangelism, fellowship, and marriage. By 1909, congregations in Pittsburgh and New York split racially, and most of the rest of their churches soon followed suit. To this day, the Church of God can still claim to be more diverse than most denominations, but it is largely a false diversity, as most of its congregations are segregated into one race or another.

In 1906 in Los Angeles, what would come to be known as the Azusa Street Revival began as a gathering of the nations and would develop into the Azusa Street Apostolic Faith Mission. The leader of this multiracial group was a black preacher, William Seymour. Although they were deeply committed to full racial inclusion and reconciliation, once the excitement of the initial revival meetings wore off, they eventually slouched back toward segregated worship. The same could be said of the Assemblies of God, which started as a cross-racial gathering around the turn of the century, but by 1920 saw most of their Hispanic congregations leave to start their own groups. They too would fall back into racial homogeneity for the most part, as would almost every other group in the first three centuries of American history.[1]

I think that this largely has to do with the dynamics of culture. If we do not understand cross-cultural dynamics, and we ignore what the Bible has to teach us about this topic, we will be doomed to repeat history. The early church thrived in diversity for hundreds of years, and I believe it is because they paid careful attention to the biblical teaching on cultural competency. In short, they took seriously the task of being all things to all people.

Pious-sounding Christians may say that we don't need to worry about culture, or that it is a worldly topic being smuggled into the church. That couldn't be further from the truth. Culture is a God-given human trait, and we all bring our own with us. To ignore the power of culture is to invite the seeds of division into our fellowship. Coming to Christ does not take away your culture any more than coming to Christ takes away your individual personality. It's still there, and it can be honed to help bring unity or, if left untouched, can cause much irritation and conflict.

My hope is that in reading this book, we will agree that the gospel mission is to gather the nations together as one people. Once we grasp that, we can turn our attention to the task of being all things to all people. If we don't get the mission right, we will fail to become what God desires his family to be. And if we don't get the task right, we will squander and splinter the mission that God has given us.

Let me be clear: there is nothing in this book about being culturally hip, cool, or relevant. That is not what we are talking about. In many ways, we are moving in the opposite direction. Typically, those who are obsessed with being relevant to the culture are picking one segment or target audience and attempting to be relevant within the context of that microculture. Valuing someone's culture, recognizing its dignity, and at times participating in it for the purpose of including all people in worship of God has nothing to do with being cool.

The work of being all things to all people and truly being the diverse group that God desires to have as his family is full of exceedingly difficult "whats"—more than we can list and discuss here. There is much that can divide and separate us. There is much that can stress us out and cause us to want to give up and go back to the far easier life of being around people more like us. The "whats" are numerous and daunting.

As we will see, being all things to all people is our "what." But it is God's call for his people to gather the nations as the fulfillment of his most ancient promises that will serve as our "why." It is this mission to gather the nations and the task of making the church all things to all people that are not only our "why" and "whats" but will be the focus of *All Things to All People*.

A WOLFPACK, NOT A LONE WOLF

As we approach these topics, we need to be realistic; they can easily cause passions to boil. If we are to be victorious in Christ, it is vital to work together as a community. Being a lone wolf leaves one vulnerable to becoming a victim of deep-seated hurts and bitterness. When we dive into these waters together, we can help keep one another afloat and throw a life preserver if we see someone drowning. For this to work, individuals must not become obsessed with issues of race and culture.

The goal is for an entire church community to work together as family to grow in their humility and love for one another. That will take all parts of the body pitching in and using their strengths. Leaders will need the help of other members to see their blind spots. The spiritually young will need wiser and more mature Christians to navigate them through the choppy waters of being all things to all people. Those with knowledge in the subjects addressed in this book will need the fresh eyes of those who are encountering these concepts for the first time. Those who can easily become overzealous will need the steady hand at the wheel of a seasoned mentor. In other words, we need each other. To be a Christian is to bond with people who are not like us and to become family. This will take all of us working together in love and humility to continue to be something that truly stands out in the world.

REPETITION

I don't know about you, but I don't remember things like I used to. If someone tells me their phone number and I can't immediately write it down or enter it in my phone, I have to repeat it in my head fifty times in order to recall it when I need it. Or someone will tell me their name and five seconds later, before we even finish the conversation, I've already forgotten it. I often need to hear someone's name several times before finally committing it to the storehouses of my memory. Throughout this book you will see things repeated, topics restated in slightly different ways, and areas returned to multiple times from different angles. That is not a mistake. It is designed to help us become familiar with the unfamiliar and to cement some of the ideas and concepts from this book into our minds, so that we will be able to recall and use the information when needed.

Additionally, in a companion workbook, *A Crown That Will Last*, you will find discussion questions and activities for each chapter to help reinforce and facilitate practical applications of the material in the chapter. These activities are designed for groups and churches to go further in their understanding and begin to weave the concepts of cultural humility into their community life.

Finally, before moving on, I want to finish the introduction with some important definitions that will help ensure that we are operating with the same word meanings.

Culture—A group of people who share a similar learned set of customs, beliefs, values, arts, social institutions, social practices, assumptions, traditions, and way of thinking.

Ethnocentrism—Evaluating and judging other cultures according to preconceptions and assumptions that the standards and norms of one's own ethnic group are ideal and superior.

Bias—Prejudice in favor of or against a person, group, or thing, typically in an unfair manner.

Bigotry—The intolerance of a group, creed, opinion, belief, lifestyle, or worldview other than one's own. Whereas prejudice is a feeling, bigotry is putting that feeling into action.

Cultural competency—The ability to interact humbly, intelligently, and effectively with people of cultures other than one's own, showing respect and appropriate responsiveness to their cultural practices and needs.

Discrimination—The unjust or prejudicial treatment of differing categories of people or things.

Ethnicity—Belonging to a social group that shares a common language, religion, nation, or culture.

Ethos—The characteristic culture and spirit of a group or community that is demonstrated in their beliefs, actions, and aspirations.

Race—A group of persons related by common descent or heredity; the traditional divisions of humanity, the most common and broad being the Caucasian, Mongoloid, and Negroid groups, categorized by alleged distinctive physical or biological characteristics.

Racism—A system of domination or oppression of one ethnic or racial group over another based on differences that are believed to be hereditary and unchangeable. For racism to exist, a group must have the power to enforce their dominance through either overt or hidden means.

Prejudice—A negative or unfavorable opinion or feeling formed about another and based on preconceived notions rather than fact, thought, or reason.

Chapter 1

The Purpose: Image Bearers

Shortly after moving into our new house, I had the task of hanging all the pictures and mirrors. This not being the most technically demanding of jobs, I finished quickly despite being possibly one of the least handy people alive. I have long accepted that in the aftermath of some sort of apocalypse that sends humanity hurtling back toward the dark ages, I will be among the first to get voted off the island, having no useful skills in such a regressive world. Even though I thought I had completed my task, a few days later I discovered a picture I had failed to hang. I didn't want to go to the trouble of trekking into the garage for a hammer, so I decided to use a handy kitchen knife to bang the nail into the wall. Holding the knife backward by the handle, with the blade aimed at me, I took the first few whacks with the butt of the knife. My plan was working, as the nail began to bite into the wall. So, I decided to hit it a little harder, but on the next swing, the knife slipped off the nail head rather than driving it in more. As it slid, my hand continued to grip the knife solidly—which caused my hand to slide down the nail toward the wall. The nail now became the aggressor rather than the victim and tore into the flesh of my hand, ripping an inch-long gash. It wasn't that deep, but it hurt like crazy. I learned a valuable lesson that I should have learned long ago.

It is a bad idea to use a tool for something other than its designated purpose. In this instance, it was my hand that became the casualty. Quite often, though, it is the tool that succumbs to misuse. I have broken the tips off two of my favorite kitchen knives while using them as crowbars. (I'm at a loss as to why I didn't learn my lesson after the first broken blade.) It has long been purported that the number one cause of broken tools or household items is misuse. Whether damage comes to the tool or the human using the tool, using something for an inappropriate purpose inevitably leads to trouble.

IN OUR IMAGE

When it comes to humanity, we often ponder what we are for. What is the meaning of life? Why are we here? Even those of us who recognize the existence of a creator are left to wonder why exactly God made us and what our purpose is.

These are vital questions to ask and to work toward answering as we begin a study of the dynamics of culture in the human experience. If we don't understand our purpose as human beings, we will certainly get off track in understanding and creating culture, and most definitely will get lost in our cross-cultural interactions and conflicts with others.

A friend of mine recently sent me a link to an online article in which a religious author was making the case that Christians often don't read the Bible well and instead use it to suit their own desires. It's difficult to disagree with that. That wasn't the lynchpin of the article, though. The author went on to make the case that the ultimate purpose for which humans were made is to do what is helpful to other human beings and not what is hurtful. He then used that assumption as the foundation from which he built the rest of his article.

Does that sound right to you? Is it the highest virtue and purpose of human beings to do what is helpful and not hurtful? I would argue that this is quite dangerous, both because it is wrong and because it sounds so good.

In Genesis 1, God comes before his divine council and for the first time during the creation of the universe makes a statement of intent about an element within his great creation project. "Let us," he says in verse 26, "make mankind in our image, in our likeness." Verse 27 confirms that God does just that, crafting humans in his own image.

The important question for us is, What does it mean to be made in the image of God? At times it has been asserted that this passage transmits the idea that human beings resemble God in form and function. The most common explanation I heard growing up is that this doesn't so much mean that we look like God in physical appearance but that we have intellectual and spiritual abilities that open possibilities that other species do not have, so in that sense we are like God. While that may be true to a certain extent, biblical scholars have pretty well established that it is unlikely that this is what an ancient author or audience would have taken from the term "image."

In Numbers 33:52, God encourages the Israelites to "destroy all their carved images and their cast idols." The word translated "image" here is the Hebrew term *tselem*. This is the same word used in Genesis 1:26–27. It had much more to do with an image or idol of a divine being rather than simply looking like someone.

This makes perfect sense, because much of the language and imagery of Genesis 1 seems to be alluding to the concept of a temple. In the Ancient Near Eastern context in which it is written, it appears that the author of Genesis very much intended to communicate that the creation itself was a temple of sorts. Temples were crafted as the dwelling place of the gods and would only be complete when the image of the god was set into the temple. It seems that there was typically some sort of "opening of the mouth" ceremony in which life was breathed into the god and he began to rule in his temple through this image.

That doesn't mean that our ancestors thought that these statues made of wood or precious metals were gods in themselves. Rather, they believed that the essence of the god inhabited the image. Once life had been "breathed" into it, the statue reflected the will, rule, and authority of the god into their territory, which for most deities was a limited area. The image was the tangible representative of the god, mediating his or her rule in his or her temple and domain.

With that in mind, the point of Genesis becomes clearer. There is none other like the creator God. His domain is not a limited corner of creation; it is the entire cosmos. The whole world is his temple. But he too, had an image bearer. Unlike the pagan gods, it was not a lifeless statue. God made humans to be his imagers. They would work together in community, just like their Creator, who is in himself a perfectly unified community.

Let's break this down into the practical. Human beings were made for the specific purpose of operating as a unified community to mediate the will and rule of the Creator into his creation. We would be the physical, tangible presence of the rule of God in his temple. We would run things the way he would. And he wanted this rule to be spread to the entire creation, every corner of it. We weren't intended to be in only one portion of the globe. No, humans were to reflect the purposes of God into every part of this amazing world. The intent of creation, then, is to be a picture of a world brought into submission and subdued by unified imagers working together to facilitate God's character and desires into his creation.

What would that have looked like? We can't say for certain, but surely it would have included bands of imagers living together in unity and spreading out around the globe, subduing and ruling over it the way God would have himself. Each of those human groups would have lived in harmony with one another as they worked toward the same goal as God's imagers. Humanity would have reflected the same unity in relationship as does the Trinity.

DOMINATED INSTEAD OF HAVING DOMINION

This was the vocation of humans had they continued in submission to God and reflected his will into the world. But something goes very wrong in Genesis 3. We seem to be given an ironic picture of a rogue member of God's divine council coming to the first humans. He is described in terms of a serpent. His main objective becomes clear to the reader. He seeks to convince the humans that they are made for more than being an imager. They do not have to be limited to merely doing God's will; they can know it for themselves. They can become divine beings, capable of shining their own light and not just reflecting the Creator's. Suddenly part of the creation is taking dominion over the humans—the exact opposite of the way it was supposed to be, with humans having dominion over the created order.

The humans quickly fall for this divine-being line of thinking, and I can't judge them too harshly. I'm not convinced that I wouldn't have fallen for the same line had I been in their place. They exchange the glory of image bearers for the illusion of being self-determining entities. They decide to do their own will rather than God's. And in that moment, they stop being useful for the purpose for which they were made. They become broken, and this affects the entire creation. God did not make the world to operate entirely on its own lest it become something like a runaway train. Again, we can't know all of what that means, or what the alternative would have been, but it is enough, I think, for us to understand that the entire creation is negatively affected. The farmer's plow has broken, and the field will not be plowed properly.

Humans were not created with the primary purpose of doing good or being helpful. How would we even know what that is? We could easily think we are helping or doing good but be doing just the opposite. No, that's not our purpose. We were made to reflect God's will as his image bearers; and failure to do that has huge ramifications.

Genesis 5:3 shows us just how severe this is. Adam and Eve have a son, but we should not miss the dire repercussions of the fall seen in this verse. They had a son who would be God's image bearer? No, that's exactly not what the text says. Adam had a son in his own image and likeness. At best, the son could obey and do the will of his earthly father, but he was no longer God's imager as humans were intended to be. The life of humans was still to be considered sacred because they were made with the capacity to be God's image bearers (Genesis 9:6), but they were no longer fulfilling that calling.

What happens when humanity rejects our purpose as image bearers? The Bible uses startling imagery to get that point across. One of the primary tasks given to the human imagers was to govern the animals and care for them, but that is one of the most shocking points of Genesis 3. The beast now has the upper hand. This rogue member of the divine council has used the image of a lesser creature to tempt humans away from their vocation. The ruler has become the ruled. Roles have been symbolically reversed, and the humans have now taken the role of the beast, creatures that were made with no capacity higher than following instinct and acting in their own self-interest.

This theme is picked up again in several key junctures in the biblical narrative. Nebuchadnezzar, for example, rejects his role as image bearer and embraces his own self-glorification. God responds by relegating him to the function of a beast. He will be what he was acting like. In Daniel 7, horrifying beasts are running amuck until the messianic figure, one "like a son of man," appears and defeats the beast, offering a new path to the holy people of the Most High, who can once again reflect his image and enter his kingdom. This theme of the battle between man and beast pops up briefly again in Mark 1, after Jesus has resisted the temptation from presumably that same rogue divine council member we saw in Genesis 3. Jesus did what humanity failed to do. He acted the way a human should act. He did God's will rather than his own, and in response, Mark depicts him fulfilling the archetypal role of a human: "He was with the wild animals, and angels attended him" (Mark 1:13). But the beast is not entirely gone. The final battle will come in the book of Revelation when the picture of humanity in full rebellion against God is described as a beast; and as Daniel 7 predicted, the beast is taken down by the Son of Man.

Humans were made to rule together, but they abdicated that responsibility, as Psalm 8 so poetically describes:

> What is mankind that you are mindful of them,
>   human beings that you care for them?
>
> You have made them a little lower than the [divine council][2]
>   and crowned them with glory and honor.
> You made them rulers over the works of your hands;
>   you put everything under their feet:
> all flocks and herds,
>   and the animals of the wild, the birds in the sky,
> and the fish in the sea,
>   all that swim the paths of the seas.
>
> Psalm 8:4–8

Humans are still made with the capacity to bear God's image, but sin, the exaltation of our own will over that of God, has distorted that and caused us to go offline as reflecting images. We are fragmented. In fact, after Genesis 9:6 we will not encounter the phrase "image of God" again until the New Testament. Countless generations come and fade away with no one able to pick up the mantle of being a true imager. That is, until the Messiah comes. That is why Mark depicts him as the one at peace with his role as ruler over the wild animals. It is he who is the image of the invisible God (Colossians 1:15; 2 Corinthians 4:4). Jesus came to do God's will (John 6:38) and enable us to do it by entering into him (Romans 8:29; 1 Corinthians 15:49; 2 Corinthians 3:18; Colossians 3:9–10; Ephesians 4:24).

Rebellion against being image bearers is seldom obvious, at least to us. We don't have to be serial killers or Satan worshippers with fresh goat's blood dripping from our knifepoints to be in rebellion against God. In fact, we can look like decent, upstanding, loving people, and in many respects, we are all those things. But subtle rebellion lurks just under the surface. Adam and Eve flipped their true purpose by allowing a member of the created order that they should have been ruling over to gain the upper hand. They were fooled by this member of the divine council into believing that they could exert their own will rather than reflecting God's. In so doing, rather than exercising God's rule over the beast, they became like the beast.

What does all this mean? God made humanity for the purpose of being his imagers, to reflect his will and his rule into his creation. We were to work together in unity as a collective image-bearing group that would spread around the world and introduce God's order and reign. We abdicated that position by seeking to exercise our own will rather than God's. But rather than raising our status higher, we lowered ourselves from our intended purpose. Instead of being a united class of rulers, we became violently divided into separate tribes and people groups. That's not truly human behavior; it is reflective of the beast.

Just three chapters into the book of origins that we know as Genesis, God's selected representatives have already rebelled and gone offline. In the subsequent chapters, humanity shatters, and God's plans for his creation seem to be in shreds. How could God possibly resolve this terrible situation?

Chapter 2

The Mission: Gathering the Nations

Let me start off this chapter with a bit of honesty. Being around new people is typically not easy for me. There are several factors that work together to make this statement truer than those who only know me casually might suspect.

First, I'm an introvert. That means primarily that being around most people in a social setting drains my energy rather quickly. The closer I am in proximity, the more that becomes a factor. If I'm in a room teaching a group, I'm insulated from that personal give-and-take that saps me so quickly. But smaller social situations and one-on-one interactions with most people is difficult. It's not that I don't like being around or talking to people all the time, but it is a challenge. And because I'm an introvert, I usually find my own inner world of thought more interesting than any outside stimuli, so being alone is a process that recharges me and is usually what I prefer if left to my own devices.

Second, I'm shy. Like, really shy. It is painful to start a conversation with people I don't know. Apart from the power of God, I don't know how I do it. Again, it's not that I feel unfriendly or don't like people, but for reasons that I can't fully explain, it is monumentally difficult to strike up interactions with people I haven't had a chance to become comfortable with. When I enter a room full of people, my first instinct is to turn around and walk out. Most of the time I know I can't do that. My second instinct is to immediately find a familiar face that feels safe and comfortable and go to that person. Other people can easily mistake this as me not liking them or being aloof, or some such thing, but most of the time it is closer to sheer panic and simply not knowing what to say in those situations.

Adding to those two elements is the fact that for whatever reasons, I've always felt like a bit of an outsider and like I don't belong. That's even true of places where others might consider me to be a leader and certainly part of the community. Part of this is the uncertainty about how to get into conversations. Once I'm in, I can figure it out most of the time, but I never know how to start, and that adds to the feeling that I don't fit in and would rather be anywhere else. I'm not asking for you to feel sorry for me in all this, I'm just keeping it real and making a point.

You take a shy introvert who never feels at ease or like he fits in and often doesn't know what to say to people, and you have the perfect formula for a recluse. I'm certain that if I wasn't a follower of Jesus, I would go do my job and then sit at home reading by myself all night, interacting with the smallest number of people possible outside my immediate family. That's what I feel like doing.

But the joke is on me. I became a disciple of Jesus and suddenly I had this large extended family. That was anxiety inducing enough. Then God called me to be a teacher who travels around the world, going from church to church and constantly meeting and talking to people that I don't know or don't know well. Even when I'm in my hometown, meetings of the body are no picnic in the park. It's a challenge for me to be around and talk to that many people each week. Constantly being called to interact with others, reach out to people I don't know or who are barely acquaintances, talk on the phone with any and everyone, and much more, is consistently painful. Paul asked for his thorn in the flesh to be removed three times. I'm pretty sure I've passed the three million mark, but to no avail.

It's a constant struggle. It is never easy. So, why do I do it? It's simple. My "why" is bigger than my "what." It's the difference between running a marathon for no particular reason and running one to raise money for kids at the children's hospital. The first scenario will likely not carry you through the most painful stretches, but the thought of helping those kids is much more likely to motivate you to keep those legs moving.

If you've ever had a conversation with me, then there is solid evidence for you that the power of God is real in the lives of his people. It is the power of the Spirit and the desire to be part of God's family, as he has called me to be, that helps me push past my own inadequacies and my innate desire not to interact with very many other human beings.

WHY DIDN'T THEY SEPARATE?

When the going is tough, we need strong motivations to keep us driving forward. As we will see throughout this book, building and maintaining a diverse church is tough sledding. It is easier to surround ourselves with people who think like us, act like us, look like us, and approach the world with a mindset like our own. There will be many times of struggle and conflict when it will be easier to throw our hands up and quit.

In Acts 15, Paul and Barnabas head up to Jerusalem some fifteen years or so after Paul's conversion and several years into his ministry mission to the Gentiles. A great controversy had developed over just what it would mean for Gentiles to join the family of God through Jesus the King. Would they need to become Jews culturally to be accepted into the family? This was an ongoing and apparently contentious debate, and Christian leaders were now gathering in Jerusalem to talk through the issue and come to a final decision. They eventually decided that peoples from the Gentile nations would not need to culturally become Jews to be accepted as Christians. No, the body of believers would not be limited to one culture, one nationality, and one ethnicity. It would encompass and embrace people from all cultures. The gospel would adapt to every culture rather than demanding that the cultures adapt to the gospel.

But if you read Acts 15 carefully, it might jump out at you that the apostles and leaders present in Jerusalem missed the easiest and most efficient solution. That's right, I said the apostles missed it. I'm not setting myself up as greater than the apostles by any stretch. But if we take an honest assessment of the situation, they missed the easiest resolution of the problem.

Why didn't they just separate into two churches, Jewish and Gentile? That would have solved the issue painlessly. There would be no need for cultural concessions and no need to suffer through the ongoing challenges, conflicts, and strife that would follow. Why didn't they split? In fact, they could have employed the separation model as early as Acts 6 when controversy broke out between the Hebraic and Hellenic Jews. As separate groups, they could have continued to work toward a global mission of gathering the nations without the pesky hassles of a multicultural community.

In the early 2000s a church-growth theory called the homogenous unit principle (HUP) caught on in many parts of the evangelical world. Its basic premise was that individual churches should focus on a specific section of society in which all the members have a common characteristic. This typically means that everyone in a church shares a common culture, socioeconomic status, ethnicity, or some other important group identifier. The reason it caught on so quickly is that it works. It resulted in churches exploding in growth as they focused on catering to the needs, likes, concerns, and worldview of the population they wished to serve. It meant that their church community was tailored to what the homogenous members wanted and preferred. It meant that the people around them understood them, and they were, in turn, understood by those in the seats next to them. Visitors tended to be like-minded people, and they often stayed because everything felt so right to them. It's quite straightforward, really. You find your target audience and then give them what they want.

It is easier and less stressful to be part of a church where everyone is like you and shares your culture. It dramatically cuts down on the number of conflicts and misunderstandings. It keeps stress levels at manageable lows. It makes life far more comfortable than being surrounded by people who are different.

If the church in Acts had had access to the HUP theory, they surely would have had the wisdom to split into a Jewish church and a Gentile church. As time went on, they might have found it advantageous to split into Hebraic Jewish churches, Grecian Jewish churches, Greek Christian churches, Scythian Christian churches, Barbarian Christian churches, Cretan Christian churches, churches for the freeborn, churches for the freedmen, churches for slaves; the possibilities are nearly endless. There is little doubt that they would have grown faster and had far fewer conflicts to work through.

A quick look around the world today will demonstrate that for the most part, this is what we have done in Christendom. In the United States, for example, most studies have shown that less than five percent of evangelical churches are multiracial. And it's not just in the US. Whether it is split along tribal lines, ethnic lines, social status, or some other unit of commonality, we have shattered Christianity into countless tiny fragments of homogeneity. It's easier and it works.

So, why didn't the apostles think of this solution? Could it be that their theories of church growth and principles of ecclesiological dynamics simply hadn't progressed far enough yet to reach the enlightened levels of our day? Or is it that they had a different motivation than mere growth?

Before I answer that, I'm going to make a bold statement. Jesus did not give a command to his followers to "go and make disciples." He didn't order that. You might be screaming at me in your head right now, because you know Matthew 28:19 well; maybe you have it memorized and you know for certain that Jesus did give that directive. Some churches have built their entire identity around that saying, so how could I claim that Jesus never gave that order? Simple—that's not what he said. Of this I assure you.

THE ENTIRE COMMAND

Let's take a look at the passage in question, which we have come to know as the "Great Commission."

> Then Jesus came to them and said, "All authority in heaven and on earth has been given to me. Therefore go and make disciples of all nations, baptizing them in the name of the Father and of the

Son and of the Holy Spirit, and teaching them to obey everything
I have commanded you. And surely I am with you always, to the
very end of the age."

Matthew 28:18-20

That's powerful communication. Communication is an interesting phenomenon. Consider the following examples.

> Today, I plan to shoot my sons
> I am going to smother my wife

Hopefully both of those sentences come off as dark and starkly inappropriate. That's because they are incomplete. If you take half of a sentence and isolate it, the result can be something startlingly different from what is intended. So, let's complete those two sentences and see if they take on different meaning.

> Today, I plan to shoot my sons a text and invite them to go out
> for a special dinner this evening.
> I am going to smother my wife with love, affection, and atten-
> tion next week on our anniversary.

Suddenly you're no longer wondering how much prison time is looming in my future. If I had written the full sentences, but you then repeated the shortened versions from above, you would have changed what I said to something I had not said at all.

Let's consider one more example, a command this time.

> Send out an invitation to disciples around the world to have
> a conference

That seems straightforward, right? But is it? When you take an extra moment to look at that sentence, you will realize that it could have different interpretations. Let's finish the sentence and see if it brings more clarity.

> Send out an invitation to disciples around the world to have
> a conference, coming together in one location to celebrate our
> diversity around the world and get focused on the same vision.

Without the rest of the sentence, we could easily have a hundred or more different conferences spread out around the world. The remainder of the sentence clarifies the command to one specific event.

What's the point of all this? Consider this phrase from the Great Commission:

Go and make disciples

Books have been written on that phrase. Philosophies have been constructed. Churches have been created and then multiplied, thanks to those four little words in this English translation and others like it. It's a good thing to go and make disciples, isn't it? Our mission is to go out and spread the gospel through discipleship. We are on an assignment from the King himself to multiply. We need to be ever vigilant about growth and making more and more disciples. If something stands in the way of growth, then we should overcome it and keep expanding. In fact, if we're not increasing as fast as we could, then something is probably wrong. Based on this, perhaps the apostles should have considered the HUP theory because it accelerates and makes easier the command to make disciples. And it's all about multiplication, baby. Imagine how fast the first-century church could have grown.

But Jesus did not say "Go and make disciples." He simply did not, any more than I proclaimed that I was going to shoot my sons. What did he say?

Go and make disciples of all nations

Do you see the difference? I hope so, because it is monumental. Jesus did not just command growth and expansion. He was calling us to a specific mission, one that God had been promising for a very long time. God gave humanity the commission of being fruitful and multiplying to fill his creation. But in Genesis 11 we find that they come up with an alternate plan. They will stay together and manipulate the deity to bend to their wishes. God comes to the nations, who share a common language, and confuses them by giving them multiple languages. Now God's plan of a unified humanity spreading around the globe but also united can only happen through him. The differences that God gave us quickly became divisions, and only God could put the nations back together as one people. That's the message of Genesis 11. When the nations come back together as one people, that is a sign that God has solved the problem that only he could. At weddings, we often talk about not letting what God has joined together be torn asunder. But the opposite is also true. What God has separated, let no human try to join together. Humanity has tried many times to come together in the thousands of years since Babel and experienced nothing but failure. We cannot and never will do it on our own.

GOD'S PROMISE TO GATHER THE NATIONS

In Genesis 12, God reveals his plan in broad strokes, at least to one man, who would eventually take the name Abraham.

> "Go from your country, your people and your father's household to the land I will show you.
> > "I will make you into a great nation,
> > > and I will bless you;
> > I will make your name great,
> > > and you will be a blessing.
> > I will bless those who bless you,
> > > and whoever curses you I will curse;
> > and all peoples on earth
> > > will be blessed through you."
>
> Genesis 12:1-3

Through Abraham's descendants, God would bring blessing and reconciliation to the nations. He would continue to hold out that promise as his goal for humanity throughout the Hebrew Scriptures. Consider this partial list.

> All the ends of the earth
> > will remember and turn to the LORD,
> and all the families of the nations
> > will bow down before him.
>
> Psalm 22:27

> May God be gracious to us and bless us
> > and make his face shine on us—
> so that your ways may be known on earth,
> > your salvation among all nations.
>
> Psalm 67:1-2

> "He will not falter or be discouraged

till he establishes justice on earth.
    In his teaching the islands will put their hope."
"I, the LORD, have called you in righteousness;
    I will take hold of your hand.
I will keep you and will make you
    to be a covenant for the people
and a light for the Gentiles."

Isaiah 42:4, 6

He says:
"It is too small a thing for you to be my servant
    to restore the tribes of Jacob
    and bring back those of Israel I have kept.
I will also make you a light for the Gentiles,
    that my salvation may reach to the ends of the earth."

Isaiah 49:6

See, darkness covers the earth
    and thick darkness is over the peoples,
but the LORD rises upon you
    and his glory appears over you.
Nations will come to your light,
    and kings to the brightness of your dawn.

Isaiah 60:2-3

"And I, because of what they have planned and done, am about to come and gather the people of all nations and languages, and they will come and see my glory.

"I will set a sign among them, and I will send some of those who survive to the nations—to Tarshish, to the Libyans and Lydians (famous as archers), to Tubal and Greece, and to the distant islands that have not heard of my fame or seen my glory. They will proclaim my glory among the nations."

Isaiah 66:18-19

LORD, my strength and my fortress,
    my refuge in time of distress,
to you the nations will come
    from the ends of the earth and say,
"Our ancestors possessed nothing but false gods,

worthless idols that did them no good.
Do people make their own gods?
Yes, but they are not gods!"
"Therefore I will teach them—
this time I will teach them
my power and might.
Then they will know
that my name is the LORD."

Jeremiah 16:19–21

"Many nations will be joined with the Lord in that day and will become my people. I will live among you and you will know that the LORD Almighty has sent me to you."

Zechariah 2:11

The Apostle Paul well understood that God had promised the gathering of the nations as the sign of the coming of the Messiah and that the Messiah was the beginning of God's plan to bring humanity back together as one family of all nations. In his letter to the Romans explaining to them why they must stay together as one church and work through their thorny cultural conflicts, he wrote:

For I tell you that Christ has become a servant of the Jews on behalf of God's truth, so that the promises made to the patriarchs might be confirmed and, moreover, that the Gentiles might glorify God for his mercy. As it is written:
"Therefore I will praise you among the Gentiles;
I will sing the praises of your name."
Again, it says,
"Rejoice, you Gentiles, with his people."
And again,
"Praise the Lord, all you Gentiles;
let all the peoples extol him."
And again, Isaiah says,
"The Root of Jesse will spring up,
one who will arise to rule over the nations;
in him the Gentiles will hope."

Romans 15:8–12

Jesus did not just say, "Go and make disciples," because by itself that would not be the fulfillment of God's promise. He said, "Go and make disciples of all nations." That is the mission of the gospel: to gather the nations into one family. Paul confirms this in his letter to the Galatians where he explains that "Scripture foresaw that God would justify the Gentiles by faith, and announced the gospel in advance to Abraham: 'All nations will be blessed through you'" (Galatians 3:8).

The sign of the Messiah's kingdom would be the launch of the mission to gather the people of all nations back together as one. The earmark of the true King would be that people from all the nations would come to him and find peace with one another. No longer would they be scattered and at odds with one another. God would piece back together what was shattered at Babel as peoples from every nation were melded as one. This is what Micah (and Isaiah 2:2–4) foresaw.

> In the last days
> the mountain of the LORD's temple will be established
>   as the highest of the mountains;
> it will be exalted above the hills,
>   and peoples will stream to it.
> Many nations will come and say,
> "Come, let us go up to the mountain of the LORD,
>   to the temple of the God of Jacob.
> He will teach us his ways,
>   so that we may walk in his paths."
> The law will go out from Zion,
>   the word of the LORD from Jerusalem.
> He will judge between many peoples
>   and will settle disputes for strong nations far and wide.
> They will beat their swords into plowshares
>   and their spears into pruning hooks.
> Nation will not take up sword against nation,
>   nor will they train for war anymore.
>
>   Micah 4:1–3

IN EVERY COMMUNITY

At this point, some might stop me and say, "Yes, but there are Christians all over the world in every nation. That doesn't mean individual churches must be diverse." I would be so bold as to argue that the apostles would disagree with that. That was, in essence, the question before them at the Jerusalem council in Acts 15. Would there be separate strains of Christianity that diverged and left each other to their own unique cultural practices and preferences?

At every opportunity, the apostolic church described in the New Testament rejected separation and homogeneity because they understood that they must be the visible display of God's great project to gather the nations.

If God said that he must separate humanity at Babel, then Pentecost (Acts 2) is the great moment when he declared that the time had finally come to fulfill his promises to Abraham. Since Genesis 3, we see a humanity that has lost access to God's presence and is acting out the desire to regain it in many ways, including their ineffective attempt at Babel. As Peter stands up to proclaim the kingdom of God, he does so to Jews "from every nation under heaven" (Acts 2:5). This is undeniably the work of the Holy Spirit. At this point it is just a start. It includes Jews from every nation, but make no mistake: the gathering of the nations has begun. From the very first day, the church was diverse and was indeed the gathering of the nations.[3]

This gathering of the nations is without question the work of the Spirit. It is he who brings us into sonship in the Father's family (Romans 8:14-17). If we don't keep at the forefront reliance on the work of the Spirit in this great project, it will quickly devolve into human effort and will fail. It is easy to start efforts with a desire to please God and then slowly drift off until we are relying almost exclusively on our own flesh and strength. There is no mistake that in Acts 1, just before Pentecost we find the church devoting themselves to prayer and to the work of the Spirit. At every step of the pursuit of cultural humility and competence, we must seek God's direction and guidance through prayer. This is not an easy road and will have more than its share of challenges.

In Acts 6 we see the challenges of that diversity already taking shape. Rather than taking the easier route and allowing Hebraic Jewish churches and Hellenic Jewish churches to form separately, the leaders entrusted the minority Hellenic Jews with power over one of the most important elements of church life, ensuring that they would take the more difficult step of staying one body.

In the multiethnic city of Antioch, Paul confronted Peter directly and publicly when Peter began to pull away from table fellowship with Gentile believers to placate some who had come from Judea. This is a particularly interesting case given the setting.

Antioch was an extremely diverse city in the ancient world. But it was not unified. There were as many as eighteen separate ethnic boroughs in

Antioch, and in the first century it was marked by regularly occurring sectarian violence and ethnic riots. It was diverse but deeply divided. Apparently, the church stuck out. Acts 11:26 tells us that the disciples were called Christians first in Antioch. It has long been repeated that the term "Christian" here was used to mock the believers for their association with Christ. While there may be truth to that, there is no hard evidence that this was the case. It is speculative. Rather, what seems to better fit the situation is an explanation that has to do with this ethnic divide in Antioch. We can tell by the lists of names from the church in Antioch in Acts that it was an ethnically and nationally diverse church. There were people from all different ethnicities worshipping and living together as family. It is likely that the people of Antioch didn't know what to do with that. What ethnic group were these people? They weren't Jewish. They weren't Greek. They weren't any one group. They didn't fit into any of the boxes with which they normally categorized people. With no clear ethnic name available for such a strange gathering of people, the citizens of Antioch gave them a social name. It is quite possible that they hung the name "Christian" on them because of their incredible diversity.

This is why Paul was so quick to confront Peter and wrote about it in his letter to the Galatians (2:11–18). This was bigger than who Peter sat with in the cafeteria. Peter's actions were a threat to the diversity of the church. They would have resulted in a split between cultures and surely have led to separate groups based along the fault lines of culture, ethnicity, and nationality. Paul knew that such a body of Christ would not reflect the gathering of the nations.

In his letters to the churches in Galatia and Rome, for example, Paul addressed deep cultural divides that were taking place between Jews and Gentiles. In Corinth he addressed philosophical and economic divisions. Each time the possibility of separation arose, Paul and the other leaders rejected it as a viable solution. It wasn't enough to have a universal body of Christ that was, in theory, diverse. The gathering of the nations had to be on display in the churches in Rome, Galatia, Antioch, Ephesus, and in every community that was claiming to follow Christ.

THE MYSTERY OF CHRIST

I believe this is at least partly what Paul was gently reminding his readers of when he penned what we know as the letter to the Ephesians. He praises them in chapter 1 for their faith in the Lord and for their "love for all God's people" (Ephesians 1:15). It might be tempting to think of that phrase in a generic way, but I don't think the context of the rest of the letter, especially the next two chapters, allows us to do that.

Paul reminds them that all of us, despite our religious or cultural background, are the beneficiaries of escaping the kingdom of darkness thanks to Jesus the King. He won't let the Gentiles forget that they were once excluded from citizenship in Israel, God's family, but the "dividing wall of hostility" (Ephesians 2:14) has been destroyed. In other words, the nations have been gathered together at last in Christ. This is the effect of the gospel.

He goes on in chapter 3 to teach that the nations coming together as one is the mystery of Christ. When Paul uses that term "mystery," he means something that had been previously concealed that is now being revealed through God's work. How would God fulfill his promise to bring the nations back together as one? This is how. The church itself is the gathering of the nations. It can be nothing less.

Not every local church can be diverse in every way. It would be exceedingly difficult for a church in Guangzhou, China or Abuja, Nigeria to be racially diverse. But every church can be committed to the gathering of the nations. Churches can be ethnically diverse, tribally diverse, socioeconomically diverse, diverse in age, and so on. Like the first century church, we should strive to reflect the great gathering in every location. A church that is in a diverse area and is not itself diverse, is, at the very least, not reflecting God's grand mission of nation gathering.

God's mission, from the book of Genesis forward, has been to reconcile all of humanity to himself. The plan has always been to gather the nations. This would be one of the major visible signs that God's kingdom had broken into the present age. The sign would be the love for one another that transcends all nationalities. Even well into the second century, the church was still citing this as one key sign that they stood apart as God's true people.

> We who valued above all things the acquisition of wealth and possessions, now bring what we have into a common stock, and communicate to everyone in need; we who hated and destroyed one another, and on account of their different manners would not live with men of a different tribe, now, since the coming of Christ, live familiarly with them, and pray for our enemies.[4]
>
> Justin Martyr, c. AD 165

The early church believed that a central piece of their identity was the gathering of the tribes and nations into one family because Jesus had clearly given them that undertaking.

This must be our theological foundation. This is our "what." We are not just called to make disciples and grow. That is not our mission. That is part of the mission, but only a part. We are to gather the nations. This is precisely why the picture of God's restored humanity in the book of Revelation includes a "great multitude" of people "from every nation, tribe, people and language" (Revelation 7:9).

As we progress through the pages that follow and delve into the intricacies of culture, culture clashes, and cultural competency, there will likely be times when we will begin to suspect that it would easier and more efficient to simply go our separate ways and carry the work of the gospel on in different directions. You'll get no argument here. It is easier. It is. But that's not the mission that we have been given. Jesus envisioned God's people as a "house of prayer for all nations" (Mark 11:17) and gave us the mission of making disciples of all nations. That is our theological foundation, of which we can never lose sight. It must continue to inform and guide the decisions we make and the direction we take in serving as citizens in God's kingdom.

But the mission to gather the nations is just the start. There is a great task that we are called to in response to this mission.

Chapter 3

The Task:
All Things to All People

I can still remember going to see *Star Wars* for the very first time in 1977 with my mom and dad. I was so proud of the brown Chewbacca shirt I was wearing, and even though I was only six, I was certain that everyone in attendance that day was looking at that shirt and wishing they had one just like it.

That started a bit of a love affair for me with all things *Star Wars*. I began to collect action figures, trading cards, and anything else I could get my hands on. The pride and joy of my collection was a fully functional AT-AT, also known as an elephant walker, featured in the opening scene of *The Empire Strikes Back*. I took phenomenal care of all my action figures, keeping them in a special case and being very careful when I took them out to play. The AT-AT stayed in the original box, and I was incredibly careful with that too. It took much effort, but I maintained those things and kept them in impeccable condition even long after I stopped playing with them.

By the mid-2000s I had children of my own and thought that it was time to pass on to them the mission of being guardians of this special collection. A new round of movies had come out in the series, and surely, they would care for these treasures as wisely as I had.

That was my first mistake. They enjoyed that I had given them these new toys, but they never appreciated the work that would go into properly maintaining and caring for them. One day I walked in and much to my horror discovered that my favorite Luke Skywalker figure, known as the "early bird" because it was a bit rare and worth a nice little sum of money, had been beheaded. Several of the weapons from different figures were missing in action. And you may want to sit down for this next one, but one of the laser guns from the head section of the AT-AT was broken off.

That was that. They had been given the mission of caring for these toys as I had and of passing them on to their sons one day, but they had not done their part. Inherent to the mission of caretaking these toys was the task of keeping them in good working order, which included keeping them cleaned, stored properly, and not decapitated. They had been handed the work of the mission, which was primarily already completed. All they had to do was keep it in good order.

THE MISSION AND THE TASK

In his letter to the Corinthians Paul spends a great deal of his time addressing the many forms of division that were threatening the body of Christ. Paul understood that a small band of disciples who were claiming to the world that they were the subjects of the true King of creation, who had called the nations and people groups to live together as one family, must not have divisions that could cause separation in the future. If they broke into separate groups dictated by culture, ethnicity, nationality, or anything of the like, he knew that they would fail to be the proclamation to the world that God was finally gathering the nations together under his kingdom rule.

In chapters 1–4, Paul lays out the many reasons that they simply cannot allow themselves to be divided for any reason. In chapter 6 he directs the believers away from taking one another to Roman courts to resolve disputes between one another. In that culture, you settled most disputes through the courts, except with family members, whom you would rather allow to rip you off than leave judgment in the hands of the court. Paul knows that having lawsuits within the Christian community sends the message to the world that they are not really family after all. It is better to lose some property than to damage the truth and message of the gospel.

In chapter 8, Paul delves into some deep and potentially divisive cultural waters. Is it okay to eat meat sacrificed to idols? To some it felt like sin and capitulating to cultural practices without discernment. For others, they wanted to show their disdain for the whole idea of the pagan gods by not giving them any power over their life. Why not eat meat that was sacrificed to a powerless vapor? The apostle carefully navigates through the shoals of exercising one's rights while still making the interests of others a priority. He calls them to consider one another first to help determine their actions in these situations. If it will truly harm a brother or sister, then the action is not worth taking.

In chapter 9, Paul illustrates this by teaching that as an apostle there are rights that he has but will not exercise, because it would damage the unity of the new society that they are building in Christ. He has laid down his rights for the benefit of others and even says that he would rather die than not have that basic and necessary element of the kingdom on display (1 Corinthians 9:15).

Underlying Paul's constant call for unity is the gospel itself. In the first century Roman world, gospel was a proclamation about a king or ruler. In the Old Testament tradition, a gospel message was a message about God, typically about him coming through on his promises to bring salvation to all humankind. For Paul, the gospel was an intentional combination of those two streams. It was the proclamation that Jesus was the true King of all creation and also the fulfillment of God's promises to gather the nations. The gospel, then, was the declaration that God was, at long last, inaugurating his long-awaited kingdom for all the nations and tribes. The gospel is the mission to gather the nations. That's precisely why Jesus commanded that his people not just go make disciples but go make disciples of all nations.

Paul understood an important fact that we often seem to overlook. Yes, if we follow Jesus' call to bring the nations together, the Spirit will empower us. That's true. The early church was incredibly diverse in every way imaginable, and there have continued to be multiracial and multi-tribal movements of Christianity over the centuries. But this amazing diversity is not automatic. The Spirit will not do the work for us. We can take half the gospel and just make disciples, ignoring the important element of "all nations." We can universalize the call and consider it mission accomplished, resting in the knowledge that the universal body of Christ is diverse if we were to consider all believers across the globe. We can also come together as the gathering of the nations, as I believe God intends, and then lose it if we're not careful, devolving into segregated communities of worship that do not reflect God's full mission and plan for the world. That can happen and has.

Yes, the mission is God's. But he has given us a role in that mission that we can either embrace or neglect. Paul describes it for the Corinthian believers, writing:

> Though I am free and belong to no one, I have made myself a slave to everyone, to win as many as possible. To the Jews I became like a Jew, to win the Jews. To those under the law I became like one under the law (though I myself am not under the law), so as to win those under the law. To those not having the law I became like one not having the law (though I am not free from God's law but am under Christ's law), so as to win those not having the law. To the weak I became weak, to win the weak. I have become all things to all people so that by all possible means I might save some. I do all this for the sake of the gospel, that I may share in its blessings.
>
> 1 Corinthians 9:19-23

Let's be clear on this. Paul is not giving them a quick evangelism technique that will help them get their conversion numbers up quickly. He is describing the task that the body of Christ must embrace if it is to fully and effectively engage in the gospel mission. An ethos is the collection of values or spirit of a group that is manifested in their beliefs and practices. To be all things to all people must be the ethos of a community of disciples.

It is not easy to implement what Paul is describing here. He is like a master violinist calling us to his craft when we barely know how to play. The "all things" ethos demands four highly challenging elements that we will simply describe here and then spend the rest of the book unpacking and wrestling with.

First, we must become familiar with our own cultural practices and preferences. Most of us don't spend much time thinking about the things we do that are simply cultural preferences and tendencies. That can be a problem, because if we're not aware of these things, we won't be very good at the remaining three steps. What actions do I inherently think are respectful versus those that seem disrespectful to me? What style of communication is best, direct or indirect? What makes for good humor? What are the best ways to worship God? What does it mean to be family to one another? These are just the tip of the iceberg.

Knowing our own cultural tendencies is a necessary first step on our journey toward cultural competence. Paul was such an effective community builder because he first knew himself. He knew the values with which he was raised and conditioned. He could discern between the absolutes of the life in Christ and his own cultural practices, which could be bent and molded to the situation.

Second, to be all things to all people, Paul implies that we must be willing to give up our rights and preferences for the benefit of others. Ethnocentrism, the tendency to prefer our own culture and see it as superior to others, is the biggest obstacle when it comes to our willingness to engage at this level. To overcome it, our "why," which is to further the gospel message, must remain preeminent to the "whats" of cultural expressions.

To be blunt, most people are not willing to do this. They may explore a few surface elements of other groups and cultures, but few are truly willing to become a blank slate. It is uncomfortable and stressful to learn new ways of doing things and see the world from a different perspective. It is easy to look down on what others do, and once we accept that view of the world, we see no need to change or do things that don't feel natural just so that others feel welcomed, valued, and accepted. When Paul says he will enmesh himself in whatever culture he is engaged with, he makes clear that he is willing to give up his natural way of doing things. It is required of us to be willing to do the same if we want to set up effective cross-cultural communities as the early church did. We cannot have ministries like Paul's apart from the methods of Paul.

Third, we must become students of other cultures. How could Paul become like the other groups he mentions without knowing them well? Wherever Paul went, we see that he knew the beliefs, philosophies, and values of the people he encountered. When in Athens, he could speak to the people of their practices toward an unknown God and craft a gospel message that reached their culture. This takes time and effort. It does not mean that we must get a PhD in intercultural communications to be a Christian. Rather, it means that we should be willing to maintain an awareness and sensitivity to the dynamics of culture and be receptive to learning from others whenever we can.

A word of warning here, though. We will not be effective at this vital aspect of being all things to all people if we attempt to skip the first two steps. We have to know ourselves and be willing to sacrifice our preferences if we are to imitate Paul as he imitates Christ.

Finally, we must intentionally bring ourselves to a state of cultural flexibility. This is what Paul is calling Jesus' people to. This is one of the most distinctive aspects of the Christian faith. Islam, for example, comes with a culture that you must embrace and hold to in order to truly be a faithful Muslim. There is little adaptability or wiggle room.

Christianity is quite different because of the principle that we are discussing. Following Christ is not limited to one cultural group or nationality. This is what was so clearly declared in Acts 15 when the leaders of the young movement decreed that Gentiles need not become Jews to fully enter the faith. Christianity is not a prisoner to culture, and we should not try to make it so. It must be free to encompass all people and adjust to the expressions, customs, and practices of all the nations.

Since the gospel is the announcement that Jesus is the King of the gathered nations, this is exactly what we should expect. To come to Christ, you do not need to become a first-century Jew, a third-century Roman, a fourth-century Alexandrian, or a twenty-first-century white American (although we often unwittingly send the message that you do need to do this last). The mission and our task become paramount and take precedence over any specific culture. We are commissioned with being cultural free agents, ready to acclimate and constantly reach out to all groups so that they feel understood and valued. This is what Paul called the Corinthian believers and all others after them to do.

GREATER THAN TOLERANCE

When it comes to the beliefs and cultural preferences of others, the world has largely settled on the concept of tolerance. The word "tolerance" finds its roots in the Latin term *tolerare*, which implies enduring, suffering through, and forbearing As a philosophical idea, it goes back as far as Socrates, but in the modern context it was developed by European philosophers in the seventeenth century as they urged society to recognize the limits of knowledge and the certainty of human fallibility, which should lead to a tolerance of the actions and practices of others.

By the twentieth century, philosophers were urging tolerance as a pragmatic response to diversity. Each group, they argued, had its own identity, experiences, and truths; no one group could claim that they had cornered the market on absolute truth. So, the only reasonable response was to tolerate the truths and lifestyles of other groups and individuals.

As we moved into the twenty-first century, tolerance had become a virtue of the highest order. So much has this been the case that it is fair to say that one of the greatest sins that a person or community can make in the eyes of society is to be intolerant. And our definition of tolerance has expanded to include acceptance. It is not enough to suffer with or bear with alternative practices and worldviews, you must accept them as valid and not critique them in any way.

The problem with this kind of tolerance is that it cannot stand up under its own weight. It continues to keep groups and cultures separate while demanding that they embrace and validate one another. In the end, it maintains separation, all the while striving for unity. Additionally, there is a logical fallacy in the concept that everyone should be tolerant of everyone else, in that it never includes being tolerant of those who are intolerant. They become the devil in the religion of tolerance and are themselves not tolerated. Additionally, the definition of what constitutes intolerance is subjective and thus a moving goalpost, which means that nearly anyone can be grouped in the aberrant intolerant group on a whim.

The more the world tries to be tolerant, the more it seems to fail at true unity. Tolerance, in limited fashion, can be a wonderful thing and should be practiced, but when taken to the extremes that it has been today, it can cause more division than it solves, and it eventually becomes the tool of the tyrant. "See the world as I do," says the tyrant, "or you will be labeled as intolerant and cast out of the ranks of the accepted."

Paul wanted to build communities around Christ that went well beyond mere tolerance. They were taught to be all things to all people. The best the world can do is tolerance; the kingdom calls for participation. It calls us to cultural flexibility and the willingness to constantly venture outside our comfort zone for the sake of the community God is building that is rooted in oneness. This is well beyond mere tolerance and diversity. It is a level that I don't believe human societies can consistently reach without the Holy Spirit guiding and empowering us.

Christian love for one another demands that we embrace and respect the cultural expressions of others in the kingdom community. It calls us to participate in these cultures as though they were our own. We should train ourselves until that becomes our first instinct, our default setting.

Think of this. We cannot have the diverse ministry of the apostolic age if we reject the methods they used. We will not be able to maintain the unity that the world cannot ever seem to achieve if we don't follow the scriptural call to cultural humility.

STRICT TRAINING

As we will see throughout this book, this will not be easy. It would be easier and quite arguably better for church growth in the short term to hold to the homogenous unit principle. Churches that consist of one type of person or one culture are easier to lead, it is easier for them to find their target audience and speak directly to their needs on a consistent basis, and they are more comfortable for all. But I believe that churches that either directly or indirectly hold to such principles or practices reflect Babel more than they do the kingdom.

Right after Paul calls his readers to be all things to all people, he hits them with this sobering truth:

> Do you not know that in a race all the runners run, but only one gets the prize? Run in such a way as to get the prize. Everyone who competes in the games goes into strict training. They do it to get a crown that will not last, but we do it to get a crown that will last forever. Therefore I do not run like someone running aimlessly; I do not fight like a boxer beating the air. No, I strike a blow to my body and make it my slave so that after I have preached to others, I myself will not be disqualified for the prize.
>
> 1 Corinthians 9:24–27

It is common to universalize this passage to a general description of the Christian life. And while it is true that many aspects of following Christ require the type of intentional discipline that Paul describes here, we miss an incredibly important aspect of the mission to gather the nations if we divorce this passage completely from its context.

Paul is informing his audience that being all things to all people for the sake of the gospel is not easy. It's not just something you do for a few weeks when you first meet someone, to pull them in. This is the new culture of the family of God. It is a place where everyone is learning to become part of a group that now embraces all tribes, languages, people groups, nations, and cultures. When we all work toward being all things to all, the community works the way it is supposed to. When we limit ourselves to such worldly principles as segregation or toleration, it doesn't.

This takes effort and lots of it. There is only one way to approach it, Paul says, and that is to tear down the dividing wall of hostility (Ephesians 2:14). That's one of the reasons the Old Testament law could have no place in the new covenant. By nature, it divided the nations. The commands of the law created a unique culture that kept Israel apart from the nations. Its job was to segregate. Since God's promises to Abraham were to one day bless and gather the nations back into oneness, the law could point to and help bring about that time but could never be a part of it.

No, it will not be easy. It would, in all honesty, be far easier to follow the homogenous unit principle. Intertwining our lives with others takes a great deal of intentionality, work, and effort. It will bring conflict and misunderstanding and will necessitate compromise. But it is God's plan.

DO WE HAVE TO GO THERE?

One common question that I hear often is, "Can't we stop focusing on things like culture and just get back to the gospel?" That's an interesting question, isn't it? It implies that diversity and unity have little to do with the gospel.

Let me put it this way. Very few of us would complain if our church taught a series on marriage or planned an entire weekend marriage retreat that focused on educating and encouraging married partners in our congregation. Can you imagine a church that never taught on marriage? What would it look like if they breezed past the passages in the Bible on marriage and just got back to the work of preaching the gospel? Would that be a healthy church?

I think we all know the answers to those questions. Yet if we were to survey Paul's letters in the New Testament, we might find something rather shocking. Of 2,032 verses in all of Paul's letters, he addressed the topic of marriage in about 68 verses, by my count. Now compare that with approximately 637 verses where Paul teaches the disciples about the gathering of the nations or trains them in cross-cultural life together. That's rather stunning, isn't it? That's nearly ten times the amount of marriage passages and almost one third of all of Paul's writings. That doesn't mean that marriage wasn't important to Paul, but it does give a window into how crucial the cultural unity of Christians was for the early believers, as well as how challenging it was.

Being all things to all people and learning to bring our cultures together in the family of Christ is not a side issue. It is central to the gospel. It is a necessary task if we are to be the gathering of the nations. It is integral to maintaining that gathering. And I think now more than ever, it will be one of the primary means through which the kingdom of God continues to grow.

Let me expand on that idea for a moment. In ninth grade, my younger son became focused on being able to dunk a basketball. He jumped whenever he could and kept jumping. He eventually got to the point where he could dunk, but just barely. His coaches told him that if he wanted to progress, he would have to get into the weight room. He started doing that with great vigor but soon became discouraged. The weightlifting seemed to reduce his ability to jump for a time. He almost quit, but decided to keep going with it. Once he took the time to truly create the strength needed in his legs, he began to explode off the floor. Suddenly he could dunk with ease. As I write this, he is in the tenth grade and continues to add different kinds of dunks to his repertoire. The weightlifting slowed him down for a bit, but it was because it had to tear his muscles down some to build them back up stronger than they were. Similarly, focusing on cultural awareness and competency can seem like a sidestep or added weight to a church that desires to grow and impact the community around them. Like weightlifting, it may take some time, but in the long run it will position a church to grow and to maintain that growth in a way that they could not previously attain to. We live in a world that desperately wants both unity and diversity and cannot seem to keep hold of both at the same time. The gospel has the answer that they are so fervently looking for.

But, as Paul warned us, it is not easy. It will not take care of itself. There is much left to discuss, learn, and do as we strive toward the cultural competency the Bible calls us to.

In 2018 the most well-known Christian rapper of all time, Lecrae, who has been a darling of most branches of evangelical Christianity for the past decade, announced that he was through with white evangelical Christianity. This sent shock waves through many Christian communities. His main impetus was his implication that the white evangelical world of Christians seems to want black believers around as long as they act white culturally and don't speak up about issues of racial justice.

In essence, Lecrae is saying that black evangelical Christians are seen but not heard. This is what happens when we fail to be all things to all people in the way that the New Testament describes. This is what happens when we put up a façade of spirituality, piously rejecting racial and cultural identity. The problem is that when we ignore these things and don't address them in a biblical manner, we wind up doing little more than smuggling the dominant culture of our society into the church and cementing it as the normal and right way of doing things. We then claim to only be about the gospel and not any of that worldly racial and cultural identity stuff. What sounds spiritual is actually little more than a defense of the default culture and the status quo. It's a convenient argument for those whose culture dominates and for whom church life is comfortable and familiar.

Throughout this book we will talk about cultural competence as a huge aspect of being all things to all people. There are dangers surrounding the pursuit of cultural competence, and we need to be aware of them before we go any further. Cultural competence is a constant quest and not a destination. We will never arrive and be beyond learning. Wrapped up in the idea of true cultural competence is the ever-present need for cultural humility. If we are committed to listening in humility, learning in humility, thinking of others ahead of ourselves, and being willing to sacrifice for the benefit of others, we will be well on our way toward being all things to all people and possessing true cultural humility.

Chapter 4

The Covering: Loving Others

I love my wife. A lot. I try the best I can show to her that love and be the best husband I can be, but I realize that many times, I fall short. She's very gracious and patient about it, but I would rejoice if, for her sake, I could be the perfect husband. It can be so frustrating that sometimes there's a small part of me that wants to give up. Don't get me wrong; I don't want to give up on our marriage. But there are days when I'm so aware of my shortcomings that I'm tempted to give up trying to improve. Those are the moments when it feels easier to stop running and just lay down for a while. I start to feel like, "What's the point?" It's during those flashes when I begin to believe that I don't even know how to do better in the areas where I don't measure up, so why bother? The frustration level is real, and it can be overwhelming.

Those are the times when her love toward me is incredibly encouraging. It doesn't take much, just a small gesture. But those tiny connections remind me that this is worth the headaches and the times of insecurity. Love makes up for a lot of mistakes and shortfalls.

EMBRACING THE PAIN

It is not easy to be a church that has embraced oneness and is living out the mission of gathering the nations. I've already stated that several times and will continue to restate it throughout this book, because it is a truth that we cannot forget. Multicultural communities are among the most difficult things to build and maintain in the entire world. That's not an overstatement.

We will make mistakes. We will hurt one another's feelings. We will say something embarrassing. We will get irritated and downright angry with each other. We will endure instances when we are trying really hard, only to be told that we were insensitive and still don't get it. We will sit bewildered as we are told that we need to be more culturally competent and we don't know what that means practically or even where to begin. We will feel misunderstood and that our efforts are underappreciated or never enough. We will, in other words, go through just about every daunting emotional struggle that is characteristic of any close relationship.

In a very real way, these struggles are a good sign. Let me explain why. Typically, when someone runs a marathon or any long race, they push themselves to get the best time they possibly can. That's why they are sore the day after a marathon. For runners, it's not so much the distance itself that is taxing, it's the speed they keep up. If someone finishes a marathon and is not sore the next day, that's a pretty strong indicator that they took the easy way. That's not to take away from the accomplishment of finishing the distance, especially if that was the goal. But if someone was trying to get a good time and isn't sore, it means they didn't do the hard work of pushing themselves.

If there is not some struggle and heartache in a multicultural community, then we are not going deep in our relationships. We are coasting. All those feelings of inadequacy and uncertainty, and even wanting to bag it and do something easier, are signs that we are exactly where God wants us to be.

The pain is worth it, but only under one condition: love must be present. The apostle Peter stated it succinctly and truthfully when he wrote:

> Above all, love each other deeply, because love covers over a multitude of sins.
>
> 1 Peter 4:8

We will return to this verse often in this book. What is going to be vital here is to operate with an understanding of love that is rooted in the biblical view rather than that of the modern world. Love is not an emotional response or a warm feeling, largely uncontrollable as though the heart will love whom it will. That's a popular concept today, but our world has managed to smuggle in infatuation and couch it terms of love. Infatuation is just something that happens and is mostly outside of someone's control. Similarly, we like some people while others we just don't care for—and we don't have a ton of control over those feelings. But these are liking and infatuation, not love.

Love is not strictly an emotion. It is a choice to demonstrate sacrificial loyalty to another. Affection and genuine like for someone will typically develop if you choose to love them, but they are not elements necessary for love to exist. Love is a choice.

We cannot always control whether we click with someone or we get warm fuzzy feelings when they come around, or even if something about them just rubs us the wrong way. But we can control whether we are kind, caring, committed, trusting, and loyal.

KNOWN BY LOVE

A very solid biblical case can be made that the biblical word "faith" could and perhaps should be translated "allegiance" in many instances in the New Testament.[5] If this is the case, and I think it is, then when the Bible calls for faith in Jesus, for example, it is calling us to allegiance to him as our Lord and King. It is very easy to understand why the primary identifying mark of the people of King Jesus is an unwavering loyalty to one another.

In the biblical world, then, love and loyalty to others has to do with identity. Who is our primary group? Who will we share life and resources with? Who will we embrace as our people group in which we find purpose and how we identify ourselves in the world? Who will we give our first and best to?

It's interesting that in speaking to his disciples on his last night on earth, Jesus gave them a new command to "love one another" (John 13:34). A quick reading of the Old Testament will reveal that this is not a new command in the sense of it not appearing in Scripture prior to this. So, what is new about it? "As I have loved you," he reveals, "so you must love one another" (John 13:34). Jesus loved in an unequal way. It was sacrificial. It was for the benefit of the others and not just a mutual covenant to be loyal to one another. It is a dangerous love because it is not rooted in equity. It is simply given.

The love that Jesus demonstrated throughout his life was one that made him lay down his life for others. The cross was not the first time Jesus displayed this love. He had done it right along. The cross was simply the final, grand demonstration of the love that characterized his entire life. He put the interests of others ahead of his own. That is love.

It is this kind of love to which he called us. Think of all the things that Jesus could have said would be the characteristic sign of his followers:

Everyone will know that you are my disciples if you have constant church growth.

Everyone will know that you are my disciples by how much you pray.

Everyone will know that you are my disciples by how much you give to and serve the poor.

Everyone will know that you are my disciples by how incredible your worship services are.

Everyone will know that you are my disciples by how impressive your building is.

Everyone will know that you are my disciples by how many programs and ministries you have in your church.

Everyone will know that you are my disciples if you teach flawless doctrine.

Everyone will know that you are my disciples by how powerful your sermons are.

Jesus said none of those things, though when we look at a majority of churches in the world today, we might half suspect that he must have made these statements somewhere, since so many Christians seem to find so much self-worth and identity in these very things. It's not that these aspects are bad. Some of them are very biblical, of course, but they are not the foundational characteristic or the most important thing for God's people.

No, Jesus said something far simpler and less impressive. "By this," he declared, "everyone will know that you are my disciples, if you love one another" (John 13:35). That's it. Be committed and loyal to one another. Care for one another as family. Put the interests of each other first. That's how the whole world will know that you are my people.

LOVE FOR ALL GOD'S PEOPLE

At different times in his letters, Paul used the phrase "all God's people." Sometimes he used it when sending greetings, and sometimes when addressing a group of Christians. Given the larger context of Paul's letters in which we find this language, it seems to follow that Paul didn't just use this as a generic term that meant "everyone." Oh, I'm sure it meant that too, but I believe that Paul also wanted to constantly remind them that within the diversity that they saw in each church, and as they continued to be part of the gathering of the nations, they were all God's people.

In Chapter 2, I mentioned Paul's reference to loving all of God's people. I will expand on that thought here. In Ephesians, he praises the church for the many positive reports about them that have come back to him. He has not stopped giving thanks for them, he says, "ever since I heard about your faith in the Lord Jesus and your love for all God's people" (Ephesians 1:15). They were concerned with and showed their love beyond just those who were part of their culture or ethnicity. How do we know that this is at least part of what was on Paul's mind here? In the very next chapter, he launches into a long explanation of how vital it is that they understand exactly what is happening through the power of the gospel as the Jews and Gentiles are brought together as one people and the dividing wall of hostility between them is torn down. He continues that thought into chapter 3, where he reveals that this coming together of the nations as one people is nothing less than the "mystery of Christ" (Ephesians 3:4).

Paul wanted the believers to love one another just as Jesus had called them to do, but he was particularly concerned that they were taking the uncommon step of loving beyond the usual categories. Jews were loving Gentiles, and Gentiles were loving Jews. That stood out. That showed the manifold wisdom of God (Ephesians 3:10).

They loved all God's people because they knew that they had been commissioned to make disciples of all nations, not just make disciples. They loved beyond boundaries.

THE IMPLIED PROMISES

The early Christians knew that loving beyond boundaries and loving all God's people would be hard. It is never easy to love, and it is even more difficult to love a diverse collection of souls. Any time we have deep and intimate relationships, conflict is bound to occur, but it is much more likely when we also have profound differences in background, history, and culture. Only love can cover over these differences and the sin that will inevitably materialize in our communities.

As he moves into chapter 4, Paul admonishes them: "Live a life worthy of the calling you have received" (Ephesians 4:1). He urges them to make every effort to embrace a life of unity, because they are a walking billboard for God's wisdom as they show the world what the gathering of the nations looks like. Without this, how will the world know? How will God's people look any different from any other group or religion? Paul emphasizes that there is one body and that's all there should ever be, because there is just one Spirit, just one hope of resurrection, just one Lord, just one faith, just one baptism into Christ, and just one Father of all.

So, how do we "make every effort to keep the unity of the Spirit through the bond of peace"? (v. 3). Paul answered that in verse 2. He says, "Be completely humble and gentle; be patient, bearing with one another in love."

As normal human beings, most Christians want things to be as easy as possible. We don't want conflict. We avoid trials. We'd prefer not to have struggles. We will sidestep challenges if the path allows it. We feel that we shouldn't have hard times in the church. We should be treated with love and never be hurt. But Paul knows that this is not realistic. Love is the goal, not the constant state of affairs. It will be inconsistent, but we never stop aiming for it.

Think of what Paul has not promised in Ephesians 4:2. There is no promise that we will not fall short in our love for one another as we keep striving for it. There are no promises that we will never be hurt, fail one another, let each other down, blow it, or even sin against each other. Instead, he directs them toward community choices like humility, gentleness, patience, and forbearance, and this, he says, should all be done in love. What does this promise? Disappointment. Failure. Sin. Shortcoming. Moments when we won't experience unabashed love.

Anyone could choose love in ideal circumstances. But think of what it demands to love when surrounded by unpleasant circumstances. That's difficult. That shows loyalty.

By the very fact that Paul is commanding these things, it is a promise that we will need to employ these virtues often. Count on it. We will need to be humble quite often when we feel very much like doing the opposite. We will want to be harsh because of how we are being handled, but instead should respond with gentleness. We are called to patience because we are guaranteed that there will be times when we want to be anything but longsuffering. We can take it to the bank that we will encounter circumstances that will push us beyond our normal boundaries of what we are willing to bear with.

This will all happen. You will be sinned against in the body. So will I. And we will each do our share of falling short. We will be culturally and relationally insensitive. We will make mistakes. We will hurt each other's feelings. But we are to love. It is not by lack of sin that we will show the world that we are Jesus' disciples. It is by the way we love each other despite all the reasons not to.

THE GREATEST OF ALL TIME

There was perhaps no church that underwent more direct challenges to their unity than Corinth. They were apparently dealing with community killers that would seek to divide them at almost every turn. It is no mistake that in the midst of wading through all this potential division Paul wrote what most students of the Bible agree is the greatest passage on love ever written.

Paul opens the chapter with a stunning declaration:

> If I speak in the tongues of men or of angels, but do not have love, I am only a resounding gong or a clanging cymbal. If I have the gift of prophecy and can fathom all mysteries and all knowledge, and if I have a faith that can move mountains, but do not have love, I am nothing. If I give all I possess to the poor and give

over my body to hardship that I may boast, but do not have love,
I gain nothing.

1 Corinthians 13:1–3

Imagine that I could have the most amazing spiritual gifts, know every possible fact about the Bible, understand everything God is doing in the world, possess the deepest amount of faith, and be willing to put myself on the line, even to the point of being martyred. How much would that benefit the church? If that were all true, you would definitely want me as a member in your congregation, wouldn't you? Think of the amazing lessons I could give. Think of how encouraging and enlightening that would be.

Yet if I do all those things but do not possess love, it would not benefit anyone. In fact, it would very likely be a detriment to the church because it would send us all in the wrong directions.

Impressive spiritual gifts and programs are not the goal of the Christian faith. Knowledge of God's word is not the center of the target. Even having amazing faith and enduring any persecution or hardship is not what being a Christian is all about.

The point of being a Christian is to love one another. That is it.

What does this love look like?

Love is patient, love is kind. It does not envy, it does not boast, it is not proud. It does not dishonor others, it is not self-seeking, it is not easily angered, it keeps no record of wrongs. Love does not delight in evil but rejoices with the truth. It always protects, always trusts, always hopes, always perseveres.

1 Corinthians 13:4–7

In the context of being all things to all people and embracing the cross-cultural adventure to which God has called us, think of what this passage means for us. What will it look like to be patient with others when their culture is deeply different, terribly annoying, and occasionally disturbing to your comfort zone?

How will you navigate avoiding jealousy or envy when you might be tempted to think another group is getting preferential treatment or receiving more attention than yours?

How can boasting, pride, and trusting in our cultural identity work against love and become detrimental to the community, while at the same time, we need to be constantly aware of the impact cultural identity has and the importance of paying attention to it?

What are ways that we can dishonor others, whether it be intentionally or unintentionally? Do we make every effort to discover if there are ways that we dishonor or hurt others without ever being aware? Or is that too much work?

Are we constantly seeking the good of others? How does this work out if we feel that it is our group that is being consistently marginalized? If we are not to be self-seeking, does that mean that we can never advocate for ourselves or our cultural group? How do we maintain awareness of the particularities within our group and their needs without that becoming our identity?

Are we easily angered by others' opinions or their actions? Are we willing to be as sensitive as we can to the needs of others while not being easily offended ourselves? When we all seek to be sensitive toward one another but not touchy about slights or misunderstandings that come in our direction, the community of Christ starts to become what it is supposed to be.

Do we keep a record of wrongs? We can find a lot of other reasons and justifications for keeping records of wrong without ever admitting it even to ourselves. Are we willing to explore that and ask others what they see in us?

Do we secretly like to see other groups falter or get frustrated in their efforts? Do we like to see others fail? Do we privately enjoy not liking certain cultures or revel when they are "put in their place" through some event in the news? Do we seek to embrace the implications and truth of God's gathering of the nations and let that determine how we think rather than how we were raised to think or believe?

What does it look like to always protect, always hope, always persevere?

Love is not just a challenge among a litany of other virtues. It is the preeminent value of God's people.

Love never fails. But where there are prophecies, they will cease; where there are tongues, they will be stilled; where there is knowledge, it will pass away. For we know in part and we prophesy in part, but when completeness comes, what is in part disappears. When I was a child, I talked like a child, I thought like a child, I reasoned like a child. When I became a man, I put the ways of childhood behind me. For now we see only a reflection as in a mirror; then we shall see face to face. Now I know in part; then I shall know fully, even as I am fully known.

And now these three remain: faith, hope and love. But the greatest of these is love.

1 Corinthians 13:8–13

After the soaring poetical language of the first seven verses of this chapter, many either stop right there or they get tangled in the weeds of some specific doctrinal discussions that flow out of what Paul says regarding prophecies, speaking in other languages, and just when those gifts will cease and what brings about that cessation. None of that is our concern here. In fact, I think that far too often, commentators get lost in some of those details that were hardly Paul's focus or even his concern. This is a poem about the importance of love in the community of Christ. That is what he is writing about. Granted, he uses some examples from some controversies that had arisen within the Corinthian house churches, but he is writing about love and not delivering a treatise on spiritual gifts.

Although we will not love perfectly in this age, love is the only element of the Christian life that is an eternal investment. Speaking God's words and praising him in other languages, impressive as they might be, are not qualities that will eternally be part of God's kingdom. Faith in the life of Christ and living in the settled hope of resurrection are far more important to a healthy assembly than are any gifts or abilities, but even those will fade as the present age gives way to the age to come. Love. That is what will last. That is what the body needs now, and it is also the preeminent characteristic of God's people that will continue for eternity. Love will never fail. It will never become unnecessary. It will remain and is the greatest of all qualities that we can possess.

We can only have some knowledge and some gifts. But we can pour everything we have and are into love. It is the fuel for the family of all nations because God, by nature, is love.

I have read many good books on culture and Christianity. But I do not recall any that truly stressed the importance of love as the beginning step for a multicultural community. We can have a perfectly diverse gathering of people that has all the best teaching and curriculum on cultural competency. We can have perfectly balanced cultural inclusion, flawless cross-cultural communication, and worship music that somehow appeals to every culture equally. But if we don't have love, we have nothing. That is the building block for everything else we will discuss in this book.

It's easy to say that cultural competence is built on love, because it is. But what does that mean practically? Where do we start? It starts in your living room, at your dinner table, in trips to the store, in your weekend getaways, in your backyard cookouts, and when you sit down to watch tonight's game or a new show on Netflix. In other words, it means you do life together with people of a different race, ethnicity, and culture.

I have seen countless examples of multiethnic churches where this aspect is missing. People worship together, they might be in small group together, they have consistent social interactions together at church functions, and they would even consider one another friends. But once the formal meetings of the body come to an end, they go to their own corners, live their lives, and then come back together at the next gathering of the church or their small group. Their lives are not intertwined. They don't know each other deeply. They haven't processed tragedy together or learned what life is really like for someone who grew up differently than they did and is perceived very differently in the world. They have learned each other's public church habits, but they don't know their relatives and the ins and outs of their everyday life. Families know these things about each other, and if we are called in Christ to be one family of all nations, which we are, then, well, you do the math.

Being part of a multiethnic church is still a better reflection of the gospel than being part of a monoethnic church, but we must go beyond that if we are truly going to be proficient at being all things to all people. We learn to reach out to other cultures by immersing our lives in relationship with members of those cultures. We will look at tools and concepts throughout the pages that follow that will enhance our efforts and keep us from running into too many roadblocks, but if we want to start this journey with love, then it starts with sharing our lives.

Take an honest look at who you spend the most time with outside of formal church gatherings and ask yourself the following questions:

- How many disciples of Jesus that are not blood relatives are in the "inner circle" of my life?

- Do I share life with any disciples outside my immediate household?

- With those whom I do share life, are any of them of a different:
  o Race or ethnicity?
  o Socioeconomic status?
  o Age group or generation?
  o Nationality?

- Do I really know what it is like to walk through life as the member of another cultural group? If not, am I open to learning about life from their perspective? How would I go about that?

Chapter 5

A Way of Life

In 1956 anthropologist Horace Miner released a profound and influential study on the strange cultural practices of a tribe he had monitored for years, the Nacirema. You may have learned about them in school. Miner focused his analysis primarily on the sometimes-bizarre attitudes about the body that pervaded seemingly every aspect of life among these people. He noted that while the market economy and related activities are important to the Nacirema, they spend a great deal of time each day on ritual activities involving their bodies.

The Nacirema believe fundamentally that the human body in its natural state is cursed, so they go through a great deal of trouble each day to ward off the dark forces of nature, time, and disease, which they believe are always looming through tiny imperceptible creatures that lie everywhere waiting to attack their bodies.

Each family has a shrine in their house, and wealthier families often have several, where they go each day to perform secret rituals hidden away from other members of the family. They are only shared and discussed with small children as they are being indoctrinated and initiated into the secret rituals. Once they have learned them, it is expected that they will perform them alone and not discuss them with other members of the tribe. Each shrine has a small chest where they keep many potions and charms that they receive from the traditional healer and which they believe allow them to live.

While in the shrine, each family member undergoes a ritual cleansing of the head and body, and while each person creates their own ritual order, it does appear that they undertake a cleansing of the inside of their bodies as well by symbolically cleaning their mouths with a bundle of synthetic animal hair. This part of the ceremony is considered so important to the tribespeople that once or twice a year they go to a traditional healer who pokes various sharp objects into their teeth looking for any signs of infiltration from outside forces that seek to weaken them.

Miner goes on to chronicle the cultlike belief in centers that are constructed in every village, called the *latipso*, where the sick among them are congregated both to receive special help from the traditional healers for their compromised bodies, and to keep them away from the healthy community members. This is where the love for market economy and the obsession with the body and health come together as the traditional healers turn away anyone coming to the *latipso* if they cannot provide a very rich gift for the guardian of the place. Everything is flipped upside down for those who enter the *latipso*—suddenly the very private and secret shrine rituals become public as they are stripped and given only a small robe and regularly find themselves naked, being assisted with ritual baths and even excretory functions by a vestal maiden or a young lad. This is punctuated by regular visits of prodding and manipulation by the chief healer. The Nacirema submit to this humiliating total loss of privacy because they believe that nothing is more important than preserving the body and long life.

The Nacirema, according to Miner, even have very strange practices involving "listeners." They believe that devils of a sort lodge in their heads and that going to the listener can help them rid themselves of this malady through a series of exorcism-like sessions with the listener.

Miner describes other unique practices and beliefs of the Nacirema. They have several other odd features including often obsessive attempts to not reproduce. It is also true that many women in this culture go through regular routines of torture including painting their faces and ripping the hair out of their bodies just to avoid some of the ugliness that they believe lies in the natural state of the human body.

WHAT IS CULTURE?

I was in middle school the first time I read about the Nacirema, and needless to say, I was both stunned and fascinated. It is truly amazing to study the strange and wild practices that develop from culture to culture. There was part of me that wanted to find out where the Nacirema live so that I could go experience these oddities for myself. Then our teacher blew our minds and instantly changed everything that I understood about culture up to that time. He informed us that we were Nacirema. In fact, if you haven't figured it out by now, the name of the tribe is simply "American" spelled backwards.

This highlights how easily we judge other cultures as peculiar or nonsensical. The customs of the Nacirema can sound downright repulsive until we realize that they are we; at least that's true for myself and my fellow Americans. Culture is a powerful force in our lives. So, what exactly is it?

Culture is "a socially learned system of knowledge and behavioral patterns shared by a certain group of people."[6] In other words, it is the learned set of shared attitudes, expressions, values, and beliefs that characterize an institution, organization, or group of people.

There are two powerful elements to culture, especially when speaking of a society or group in which people are raised from birth. The first is that culture is transmitted from the present generation to succeeding generations. It is passed on but rarely overtly taught. You breathe culture in day in and day out.

And that leads us to the second powerful element of culture: it is what becomes normal for an individual. Because everyone around is acting that way, we pick it up as the normal way to live or do things. We rarely question it, because it is ingrained in the way we think, believe, act, and interact with others. This is why it is so easy to dislike or look with unease at other cultures. They are abnormal and weird. Our own way of doing things is just the way they should be done.

Cultural knowledge becomes very formative to even our brain patterns. Certain aspects of our culture such as how we think logically, our ability to orient geographically, our relation to time, and social interactions with others become hardwired into our brains. For example, some cultures do not have words for left and right or up and down. Rather, they always use cardinal directions, even describing their legs as being their southwest or northeast legs. Participants in these types of cultures become oriented in their brains because of this language aspect of culture and rarely get lost, possessing an uncanny (to us) ability to orient themselves to the cardinal directions almost anytime, anywhere.

Phenomena such as this happen within numerous aspects of our cultural conditioning. They become ingrained in who we are and how we interact with the world around us. Sometimes that includes the actual pathways of our neurons so that are brains are literally formed by the culture around us. At other times it is simply in the customs and beliefs that are so drilled into us that they feel like the only normal and correct way. The process of transmitting culture from one generation to the next so that it becomes the accepted normal behavior for the succeeding generations is indeed powerful.

CULTURE IMPACTS ALMOST EVERYTHING

Believe it or not, culture is probably the most influential force operating in your life. How do you communicate with others? Does it tend to be directly and focused bluntly on truth or is it more indirect and focused on respect and not shaming anyone? How closely do you stand to someone when speaking with them? Culture influences all of this.

What is a proper and necessary amount of personal space when you are in public? If you were to enter a large room with a hundred seats and only one other person was seated in a chair, should you sit next to them or quite far away? How do you determine truth? Is family just parents and siblings or is it a much broader concept than that? Does your identity emanate from your individuality or from the group to which you belong?

What role does music play in your life? What type of logic do you use when you are thinking? What are proper ways to worship? Should you dance in church? When a tragedy happens that is in the news, one that becomes politically divisive, should it be talked about in church on Sunday or not?

How about in public? Is it okay to be loud and act in front of others exactly the way you would if they were not there, or should you dial it down and seek to not infringe upon others in any way, being very quiet and acting quite differently than you would if you were alone or with only your small group of friends or family?

Who should attend the funeral of a close family member? What sorts of things should take place at a wedding? Is it rude to show up at someone's house unannounced or does that indicate closeness of relationship?

Do you respect the authority of another person simply because they are in a certain role, or must they earn your respect and give mutual respect to you?

What do you eat? What kind of clothes do you wear? What do you consider entertainment? When you are with family and close friends do you tend to talk about people and memories of old times, or do you tend to talk about ideas and what is going on in the world?

What is the purpose of school? How should students interact with teachers?

If you are in a public place waiting in line, should you attempt to move through it aggressively and with yourself in mind, or should you work together with others to create a fair and ordered situation that equally benefits all?

We could go on, but hopefully you are starting to see the far-reaching impact of culture. From the moment you wake up until the moment you go to bed, cultural forces are at play in your life. And when you do go to bed, what do you sleep on? Do your dreams mean something profound and hold sway on the choices you make while awake, or are they just a bit of fantasy that means nothing? Yes, culture works even while you sleep.

But let me ask this important question. If culture is so far-reaching, extending into every aspect of our lives, thinking, and behavior, do you think that people of distinct cultures could be prone to misunderstanding and conflict due to the differences in their cultures? If that question seems a bit leading, it is. The answer should be rather obvious. Cultural differences and variations are one of the leading sources of conflict and confusion in our world today. Conflicts and misunderstandings are such a pervasive and powerful element in human interaction that we will spend an entire chapter looking at them, but for now, I'll simply emphasize the power of culture to create division between people. If we do not seek to understand the dynamics of intercultural communication and connection, we are doomed to become victims of the resulting battles.

CULTURE, CULTURE, AND CULTURE

To make things a bit more complex, we must recognize that we don't have just one culture being passed down to us and that is it. There are many different streams and scopes of culture.

"Culture" can refer to different things, and that can cause problems in our understanding of the topic if we're not aware of these levels of meaning and use. I was recently at a conference that was almost hostile to the topic of culture. It took me a while to figure out why. As I listened further to the speakers and classes, I realized that they were almost exclusively using the term "culture" to refer to the world and society as a whole. With this language firmly entrenched, I heard sentences such as, "We must let the Bible dictate our approach to culture rather than culture dictating how we approach Scripture." Or, "We need to strive to be an alternative to the culture rather than trying to be relevant to it." The problem with that is that people became negative and hostile to the idea of understanding culture. If you start to talk cultural competence or cultural inclusion to good people who are working with this definition of culture, you wind up getting a great deal of resistance to delving into the topic at all. Why should we learn more about the dynamics of culture when it is everything that is opposed to God's word?

So, yes, "culture" can refer to society in general, or the world. But that is not the definition of culture that we are using in this book. Culture is the way of life that a group of people adheres to. That is all. Culture in itself is not opposed to God's word nor is it negative. Aspects of culture can be closer to how God wants humans to live or directly opposed to it, but most expressions and practices of culture are neutral. There are different valid ways to approach the many facets of life, not just one way. In fact, how we approach and interact with God is largely determined by our culture. While some cultures have aspects that are more effective in some ways than others, no culture is completely superior to another. As Christians, we are not seeking to find the one, true, perfect human culture while rejecting all others.

If ever there was an opportunity for Christianity to be tied to only one culture, it would have been in the first century. Jesus was Jewish, as were most of the leaders of the first church. Would the church require a Jewish culture and way of life? That was the question that came up frequently in the first three decades or so of this new community. The loud and clear answer was, "No." As I mentioned above, there are religions, such as Islam, that tend to embrace one culture. You must accept the culture of Islam in order to truly follow the teachings of that religion, but Christianity is unique in that it can adapt to any culture.

This is good, because there are many overlapping layers of culture in your own life. You don't have just one. Countries have cultures. Regions have a culture. People groups, ethnicities, races, and tribes have cultures. Neighborhoods, workplaces, organizations, churches, and even individual families have cultures. Some of those will be more powerful influencers in our lives than others, but they all can play a role. For example, you might work at an office where there is a strong culture, but it will pale next to the culture that was passed on to you through your familial and national upbringing. A person from India and one from Idaho can share some of the same values and beliefs in the office but still have wildly divergent worldviews because of the rearing they received from their perspective national and familial cultures.

If this sounds a bit complicated, it is. We can grow up in the same country, have the same ethnicity, hail from the same city, and live on the same street as our friend. That would probably mean that we have much in common culturally. Yet there could still be profound differences simply based on the cultural influence of our families. They probably have different roots and cultural backgrounds and have developed different habits and practices.

Does that mean that the topic of culture is hopelessly complicated and unique to each person, like a personality? No. Clothing will serve as a good picture that will help bring some clarity to this. When I go to the airport in Minneapolis, I see a lot of the same type of middle-aged men traveling for business. They can be of different ethnicities and places around the country, yet all tend to dress similarly. The uniform for middle-aged US males who are traveling for work tends toward casual dress pants of some sort, button-front long-sleeved shirts with some sort of checked pattern, and brown shoes. That can shift over time, but that's the predominant style right now. Within that archetype are many different microstyles and choices, but overall, there is one broad style that is commonly seen. Conversely, if I am in an airport in West Africa, the men I see traveling on business there are dressed much differently. Again, there are small variances between individuals and regions, but overall there is a West African archetype that tends to dominate.

In the same way, the microcultures that we are part of in our city, region, or even family can lead to some variance, but we will still tend to have macrocultures that dominate our behavior. Americans can seem to have a variety of cultures, and they do in a lot of ways, until you set them next to a group of people from Southeast Asia. Then suddenly the Americans look to be much more a single cultural group.

There are macrocultural influences such as Western culture, your national culture, and in many cases, your race and ethnicity. But other streams of influence such as your region, state, city, neighborhood, social and economic status, and family will also have varying levels of influence and impact on your culture. This means that from one angle we can make some broad generalizations about "white" or "black" culture (although there will always be exceptions and anomalies in every group), or "American," "Canadian," "Honduran," "Ukrainian," or "Nigerian" culture, or a "Midwesterner" and a "Southern Californian." Yet from a different angle, cultures can be unique to small groups and even individuals, so we must be careful about making blanket assumptions that an individual will automatically possess all of the cultural proclivities of a group that you might think they belong to. You might be talking to a white person who grew up much more influenced by a Latino culture. You may find yourself interacting with a Kenyan who grew up in the UK and does not possess the cultural influence that you would assume. So, are there cultural generalizations that can be made at times? Yes. Are there many exceptions and layers of uniqueness that mean generalizations can be problematic if we're not careful? Absolutely.

When we hear people using the term "culture," we must be sure to know exactly what they are referring to. As I mentioned, it is common to go to a spiritual conference and hear people talk of standing out from the culture and being countercultural and not letting the culture dictate what we as the people of God do and believe. In these instances, the macro meaning is being thought of: society as a whole, particularly the secular aspect of society. The problem comes in when these same folks then hear of a breakout class on cultural competency at their local church and they determine not to go because they are not going to support attempts to be relevant to the culture and accept some progressive version of Christianity that waters down the gospel.

But these are very different aspects of the broad topic of culture. When we speak of cultural competency, as we will primarily in this book, we refer to the aspects of assumption and expression that we all bring with us into the body of Christ. We all have a culture and we must learn to understand, respect, and work with one another within that reality. To be culturally competent does imply that we are somehow caving in to the worldly way of life around us or embracing some trendy but unbiblical form of philosophy and worldview. Cultural competency is a deeply biblical concept that we must strive for if we are to be who God wants us to be.

VISIBLE AND INVISIBLE

Have you ever been to an ocean? I think I was about fourteen the first time I ever laid eyes on one of the oceans. It wasn't until my thirties that I got back there and got close enough to stick my toe in. I would go to the ocean many more times over the next ten years, but it wasn't until my mid-forties that I submersed myself in it. A whole new world opened up. The surface view of the ocean is beautiful; don't get me wrong. But there is an entirely different universe once you go into water that is teeming with life. It is colorful and strange, and much more challenging in many ways than above the shimmering blue surface. From the shores, though, all that is below the surface is invisible. That is, until one dives in.

Like the ocean, cultures comprise two worlds. One is visible and above the surface, and the other is invisible and below. And like the great seas, many of us only enjoy or are even aware of the visible parts of culture and remain largely ignorant of the deep and complicated trenches that lie below.

The visible or external aspects of culture are the things that can be easily observed for the most part. How does a group dress? What do they eat? What styles of art, architecture, and design do they prefer? What are common gestures and greetings? What kind of clothing do they wear? What music do they enjoy and embody within the community?

Typically, when society speaks of multiculturalism it is at this level. We can easily mix music, food, and clothing styles and enjoy these aspects of one another's culture. This is not particularly challenging, although even at this level, some will greatly resist and think that the expressions and values of other groups are weird and not worth trying.

It is also at this level that we often find charges of cultural appropriation. Cultural appropriation is usually the adoption of the customs of an historically oppressed group by a dominant group. The idea began by referring largely to instances where a group is relegated to inferior status but then members of the dominant group take a custom, style, or practice from that group for their own enjoyment or gain, or to ridicule the nondominant group. A classic example of that is many early rock 'n' roll artists who borrowed musical styles from black genres at the very time that black people were being systemically oppressed and denied civil rights. We might also appropriately include examples of taking something from a culture that must be earned or given. It wouldn't be appropriate for someone to wear a Native American headdress or the outfit of a tribal chieftain to a costume party. To wear something you have not earned is denigrating to the culture in many instances.

In recent years, though, some have attempted to expand the idea to include anytime someone adopts something from a culture that is not their own. This seems to thrust multiculturalism into an unrealistic model where everyone lives together and equally accepts other cultures without ever embracing or exploring aspects of the other groups. In the real world, you simply cannot adhere to this greatly expanded definition of cultural appropriation in multicultural communities without endless headaches and controversies.

Sharing, mixing with, and understanding other cultures at this visible level can be fun and a great adventure. And while the society at large does not always have even this level figured out, there are many examples of groups that have crossed over and adopted elements from other cultures, creating hybrids and new aspects of culture.

The second level of culture is the invisible or internal, and it is a far murkier world to navigate. This is the part of the culture that people rarely explore when it comes to multiculturalism. It encompasses the things below the surface such as the expectations of other individuals, situations, and groups. What do they expect to happen in this type of situation or function? What are the things this group values? What are their underlying attitudes about the various facets of life and the world? How do they understand and define concepts like authority, respect and respectfulness, modesty, fairness, and truth? What constitutes a family, and what is the proper function of such a group? What are gender roles and what is expected of a husband or wife? Who is more important: the individual or the group?

My wife and I were recently helping to counsel a young couple that was planning to get married. The groom-to-be was from an African country, while the bride-to-be was from the United States. I asked them one day if they had ever had any conversations about what the concept "family" means to them or, for that matter, what should a wife do in the marriage and how should she relate to her husband. And what is the role of the man in a marriage and what should he expect? It didn't surprise me much to hear that they had never really considered discussing these things. I warned them that they had better have those talks and do it before they got married. They were grateful that they did, and they soon discovered that they had radically different values and expectations. If they had not been able to identify and work out these differences before their wedding, they could have been in for some very bumpy roads down the line.

These internal aspects of culture run deep, and they don't change easily. When we say things like, "You can take the girl out the South but you can't take the South out of the girl," or "You can take the boy out of the Philippines but you can't take the Philippines out of the boy," this is the level of culture to which we are referring. We don't see these values and beliefs, and so we don't even think about having them or that they are merely aspects of culture that have been passed to us unaware. We no more recognize that these things are integral parts of our cultures than a fish would recognize it was wet. It just is.

The invisible level is so deep within us that we begin to assume that these are normal and right aspects of human nature and of how societies should properly operate. With these firmly embedded in our hearts, we encounter people with other assumptions that they have received from their cultural upbringing, and deep conflict ensues. "How could anyone think that or believe that way? That's clearly weird and wrong." It doesn't take much before we start thinking, "I just can't stand those type of people. There's something wrong with them."

THE POWER OF CULTURE

Culture is such a powerful concept because it involves a group of people who have found success together living this way. It works. At least, it works for them. The knowledge base around them enforces the fact that this way of acting and interacting is optimal. This perception is constantly reinforced as people in the group that act in aberrant ways find that they are outcast or ostracized by their group, thus demonstrating that their unusual cultural expression doesn't work.

Plus, the dynamics of different groups creating different cultures feeds right into the human tendency to tribalize. We will find ways to group up and divide. One of the chief characteristics that seemingly cause division in our world today is race. There is no question that the concept of race is a social construct invented by humans, but it is also true that it has had a major hand in separating humans from one another for the past several hundred years. I have written much more about this topic in *Crossing the Line: Culture, Race, and Kingdom*, but to a very real extent, race is simply a visual category that now serves to help us identify cultural groups. We don't need race to divide us. You can easily go to parts of the globe and find groups of people of the same race and ethnicity that hate each other violently. We don't like people who are different from us and we do like people who are like us.

Many of the divisions that appear to be based on race or ethnicity are either just old feuds with the original cause of the hatred buried deep in the past or long forgotten, or they are based on cultural differences.

Here's the good news. If divisions are truly based on things like skin color or ethnicity, that is difficult to overcome, because those categories are not going to change. But as stubborn and deeply rooted as culture is in us, it can change. We can adapt and learn other ways of thinking and acting and learn to accept other cultures and even participate in them. In short, the properties of human nature are biological and fixed, but culture is learned, so it can be redirected and adapted. As Christians we can learn to be all things to all people, and that brings hope.

THE DEFINITIONS OF CULTURE

Before we go any further, let's take a few moments to define a few terms so that we are sure we know exactly what we are striving for when it comes to cultural knowledge, awareness, sensitivity, and competency.

Cultural knowledge is the beginning of the journey. It means that you have some information about a cultural group's beliefs, values, behaviors, expressions, history, and preferences. Knowing about a culture is good but is a little like watching a cooking show and thinking you know how to cook. Knowing something in theory and knowing through experience are two different things.

The next level in cultural growth is **cultural awareness**. This is when you go beyond just the knowledge of other cultures and see the need to adapt to them and include their expressions and values in the life of the community.

The next stage is **cultural adaptability**. Learning about cultures and seeing your need to adapt are good. But learning sensitivity and going through the work of adapting take another level of effort. It is necessary at this point to not assign values like "right" and "wrong," "normal" and "weird," and "good" and "bad." Conflicts both external (between different groups) and internal (within our own group) are bound to occur as we embrace new practices and ideas. It will not be easy, but the conflicts can be overcome if everyone remains focused on the reasons why this process is good and necessary.

A church that is **culturally competent** has mastered the three previous stages and progressed on the journey of continual growth as an effective organization that can adapt to new cultural groups and adopt a variety of their cultural expressions. At this level, people of all cultural backgrounds feel welcomed, valued, appreciated, respected, and included. We will spend the rest of the book considering what cultural competency is and what it looks like in a faith community.

Chapter 6

The Blended Culture

You shouldn't know the name Jesus of Nazareth. The life of an obscure son of a day laborer in first-century Palestine should hardly register in the annals of history. In fact, the knowledge of a peasant from Galilee should never have lived much beyond the friends and family who knew him personally. Once he was put to death in Jerusalem for claiming to be the long-promised Messiah of the Jewish people, that should have been it. The one thing that everyone knew, including the Romans, was that if there was to be a true Jewish Messiah, the singular accomplishment of his life to prove that he was the Messiah was that he would defeat and drive out any occupying pagans from the land of Israel. Jesus' death meant none of that would happen, so he could not be the Messiah they were hoping for. You shouldn't know his name.

But less than twenty years after his death, his name had already reached the mighty city of Rome, and not just in some routine report from Judea that a pretender to the throne had been dealt with. Because of his resurrection, proving he was who he claimed to be, his name spread quickly. There were communities of people popping up around the Roman Empire and in Rome itself, worshipping Jesus not only as God's Messiah but as the embodiment of God himself. The existence of these Messiah-following communities was a source of outrage for Jewish communities around the empire. They saw the Jesus people as blasphemers who were now convincing pagan Gentiles that they were part of God's family. Can you imagine all these non-Jews from nations all around the empire who were still living in their Gentile cultures thinking that they were part of God's people? This had to be stopped.

It appears that this controversy came to a troublesome confrontation in Rome in the late AD 40s. Not all the details have survived the passage of time, but there is some evidence that a series of commotions of some sort broke out between Jews and Christians living in Rome. In the eyes of the Roman elite, this was a Jewish problem. They made little distinction at the time between Judaism and Christianity, which they saw as simply an offshoot of Judaism, if they even bothered to notice a difference at all. We do not know the scale or scope of these confrontations, but there does seem to be a record of commotions breaking out because of the "troublemaker" known as "Chrestus."[7]

Not wanting to deal with these disruptions coming out of the Jewish neighborhoods, the Emperor Claudius took the drastic step of expelling

Jews from Rome in AD 49. Just how comprehensive this expulsion was is unknown, but it does seem to have impacted most Jews, including Jewish Christians.[8]

It would appear that most or all of the Jewish Christians, including Aquila and Priscilla, left Rome during this time. For five years, the church in Rome was dominated by Gentiles, and may have been exclusively Gentile. In AD 54, the new emperor, Nero, reversed Claudius' decree and allowed the Jews to return, which again, included Jewish Christians. Suddenly a church that had been dominated by Gentile cultures for five years had a strong Jewish influence once again. This caused tensions. Even though Paul had not planted the disciple communities in Rome and had not yet been there, he decided to write them to guide them through this struggle. We can only speculate on his motives, but if we examine his letter to the Romans, it appears that perhaps because he had guided so many other churches that were a mix of cultures and nationalities, Paul believed he had the understanding to guide the Roman Christians through their crisis. He also wished to spread the gospel into Spain using the church in Rome as a base, so he needed them to be strong and capable of supporting such an undertaking.

The Gentile believers, it seems, were struggling with welcoming their Jewish brothers and sisters back fully into the community. They wanted to keep things the way they were comfortable with. They no longer wanted to make room for Jewish culture and sensitivities. And in their response, the Jewish Christians don't seem to have been any more gracious. Each side refused to accept the other's cultural approach to Christianity. They would not accept their practices or their special days, and there were a host of other issues. The text of Paul's letter even seems to indicate that some of the Gentiles were asserting that God had moved on past the Jews and that Christianity was now for the other nations, so that there was little point in proclaiming the gospel to the Jews any longer.

Paul spends the entire letter explaining to them the story of what God has been doing and promising since the beginning and why God's people must consist of all the nations. When the theology of all that has been established, in practice they must learn to accept one another's culture, which Paul directly addresses in Romans 14:1–15:7. But just before he gets to that passage, he lays out a very helpful approach when it comes to culture, beliefs, and expressions.

> Therefore I exhort you, brothers, through the mercies of God, to present your bodies *as* a living sacrifice, holy *and* pleasing to

God, *which is* your reasonable service. And do not be conformed to this age, but be transformed by the renewal of your mind, so that you may approve what *is* the good and well-pleasing and perfect will of God.

Romans 12:1–2 LEB

In this passage we find two of what I believe are three different responses to the concept of culture in God's kingdom. Do not conform, Paul says, to the present age. Rather, we are to be transformed by the renewal of our minds. So, there is a rejection and a transformation, but there is a third aspect that I think must be considered between these two. We must reject some aspects of culture and transform to a new one, but before we can work toward full transformation, we must add the heart of inclusion that Paul described when he calls believers to be all things to all people. That is not to say that this is a simple three-step process that we go through one time and then call it a day. It is an ongoing and overlapping process that must be repeated and returned to, but if we remove any of the three responses, we will wind up with something very different from a culture that can contain the gathering of the nations.

Because this is so vital, it is imperative that we look at these three general responses that will serve as principles to keep in mind and that will guide us as we continue to consider the role that culture does and should have in the church.

DO NOT CONFORM

The first is rejection or refusal to conform to ungodly practices. Paul says, "do not be conformed to this age." Some translations render this section something like, "do not be conformed to the patterns of the world." Not all aspects of every culture align with the baptized, Christlike life of a kingdom citizen. We need to carefully examine our own cultural upbringing and tacit assumptions to measure them against God's word. If we do not take this intentional step, we will be involuntarily conformed or squeezed into the cultural mode in which we were brought up. Sometimes that culture is a fine vehicle for God's kingdom; occasionally, elements of it are not.

I have visited some countries where the cultural norm is that fathers do not engage actively in the lives of their children. They work and provide for the family, but the rearing and training of the kids is considered the work of the women in the family. The fathers remain distant from their children emotionally and spiritually and do not lead them. This, of course, is contrary to the biblical model in which fathers are to connect with their children and directly train and discipline them in the way of the Lord. New disciples in those countries or cultures do not tend to immediately embrace this biblical model unless they are directly taught and challenged. The same thing is true for all of us—we simply do not grasp right away every aspect of life that is touched and changed by the gospel. It is not acceptable to assert that this distance between father and child is cultural and thus we should embrace the cultural expressions and standards in this case. When measured against God's word, this is shown to be something that needs to be rejected and relearned.

By way of another example, there are many cultures around the world that are deeply rooted in what is called honor/shame. People in these groups will avoid being shamed or intentionally shaming others at all costs. Because of this, they have in many ways developed a strong tolerance for what those in other cultural groups would consider lying. You say what you must so that others are not disrespected or caused to lose face in public. That is considered good and perfectly acceptable. But we know that falsehoods have no place on the lips of kingdom people. As deeply rooted as that instinct might be, someone from one of these groups must resolve to retrain themselves and reject this entrenched attribute of their learned behavior. They must not conform.

The materialism that characterizes the American-dream culture is another example of a cultural value that needs to truly be jettisoned when we enter the kingdom.

BE ALL THINGS TO ALL PEOPLE

Since we covered much of what it means to be all things to all people in Chapter 4, allow me to briefly discuss here what it is not. Being all things to all does not mean that we must abandon our own cultural identity and practices. Cultural flexibility does not imply that we have no culture, just as having a flexible schedule does not mean that you have no schedule. It simply means that we understand that our way of doing things is *a* way and not *the* way. It implies a willingness to learn from others and not automatically assume that our culture is the norm for Christianity or for human behavior in general.

Being all things to all people does not mean that our culture is bad and something to be shed. I want to be a servant in my marriage and meet my wife's needs as much as I am able, but that doesn't mean that my needs are wrong, inferior, or something to be ignored or rejected altogether. This is not a dismissal of what we have learned and experienced. It only becomes problematic when we are not open to the ways of others.

It does not mean that the cultures of others are better by default either. It is a common response for people who have been challenged to be more accepting of and open to other cultures, to retort that their culture is being made out to be the bad guy or inferior or is under attack, while the culture of others is being treated as pristine and perfect. Quite frankly, that is a bit of an immature response. As disciples, we must be aware that when all someone has known is domination or superiority, equality or flexibility feels like oppression.

Cultural flexibility does not mean that we won't ever get to do things in a way that is comfortable for us culturally. For example, let's say we are striving toward exploration and inclusion in a music ministry that has encompassed different genres of music but all of them fall under the broader range of so-called "white styles of music." Cultural inclusion does not mean that we would move to Sunday morning sets of only Latino, Asian, and gospel music and remove the types of music that used to dominate. All groups of people are called to be all things to one another, not just the historically dominant group. We seek inclusion of all, not exclusion of the dominant culture.

Embracing the ethos of being all things to all people does not mean that I will love your way. After over twenty years of my wife and I merging two very different cultural backgrounds into one household, we have created a new blended culture in many respects. Our sons are comfortable in three cultures now: hers, mine, and the new one we have created together. While we have learned flexibility and embraced a willingness to blend and compromise, there are still many features of her culture that I do not enjoy, and vice versa. But I do my best to participate in them and not just tolerate, although, admittedly, I still have a way to go. I am not always as flexible as I want to be. It continues to be a work in progress. To return to a musical example, if I grew up loving country music and feel that I can best express myself in worship through that style, I may never be able to worship with the same passion and authenticity through an upbeat gospel song. But that doesn't mean that I should stand there like a board and simply tolerate that cultural style of worship either. The question is: am I willing to join you in an expression that helps you and connects with you? Am I willing to step outside of my preferences and comfort zone for your benefit? When we are all willing to do that, the kingdom community can be all that it should be.

I think there is something important to mention here. Some might be tempted to reject this line of reasoning when it comes to musical styles. Music is not the only area where this conflict might occur, but it is an important and very tangible one, so we will continue to use it as a representative. Let's say that a church leadership decided that the worship music was too dominated by one cultural group and preference and wanted to diversify. Aren't we just caving in, the argument might go, to the preferences of one group or another? Isn't worship about God and not our preferences?

This line of thinking is flawed on two accounts. First, it ignores the fact that one group has already set its preferences in place as though its culture is the default. It's like walking into a room, planting yourself in the best chair, and then telling everyone else that they should just sit wherever and not worry about what chair they get. That works for you because you already took the best chair. Second, this is not about likes and preferences. We don't seek to become all things to all people because we are trying to cater to their likes. Diverse music, to use our example, is not about what I like but about how I can best express myself to God in worship. Diversity ensures that we all learn new ways of expression and worship and that we can all have times when we can freely and most naturally express ourselves to God. In the gathering of the nations, no one group will have it their way all the time, but it also shouldn't be that their style of expression is never or almost never included.

BE TRANSFORMED

According to organizational culture expert Edgar Schein, there are four possible patterns that may evolve when the cultures of different groups are combined.[9] The first is separation. This is when groups are theoretically together as one, but they remain largely segregated under the umbrella of being one community. In these scenarios there is little crossover, and although they may cooperate and align with one another, they do not truly mix in any significant way. The second is domination. This is when one culture overwhelms the others and gives them no room to have meaningful influence in the group. The third is conflict, wherein the groups vie for influence and power, each believing to some degree that their agenda is more important than the larger group mission. Finally, there is blending, when subgroups take the best of each culture and combine them to create a new, stronger culture given the mission at hand.

In many ways, being all things to all people is a blending of cultures. Paul describes this when he says that believers should be transformed by the renewing of our minds. While this principle has broad spiritual applications for the believer, it should not be missed that Paul's direct application is in the context of helping divergent cultures come together as one body. Romans 12 begins with the appeal to be living sacrifices because that is what they signed up for when they died to themselves in order to enter the life of Christ (Romans 6:1–14). The world typically divides along cultural and tribal lines, but not so with them. They must not conform to this pattern and to the pattern of their tribal conditioning. Rather, they must be transformed and come together as one. He will go on to urge them to recognize that, in fact, they belong to one another (Romans 12:5) and should do everything in their power to serve and build one another up.

As Paul moves into chapters 14 and 15, he will lay out in detail what it looks like to accept one another and even to start moving toward becoming all things to all. When we engage in this type of blending, what will inevitably result from the transformation is a new culture in many respects.

In Chapter 3, I discussed that there are at least four principles that we can glean from 1 Corinthians 9:19–23, where Paul most clearly lays out the directive to be all things to all people and become a transformed culture. First, we must become familiar with our own culture, including preferences and limitations. Second, we must be willing to give up our rights and the ease of always having a comfortable cultural climate. Third, we need to become students of other cultures and be willing to embrace and engage in their cultural expressions. This culminates in cultural flexibility, being willing to transform and create new cultural expressions and hybrids.

A NEW CULTURE

Life in the Roman church of the mid-50s AD must have been challenging. They were still relatively inexperienced in the process of bringing Jewish and Gentile cultures together as one body and one family in Christ. Being free from Jewish influence for half a decade and then suddenly confronted with it again was a unique situation even in the first-century world. From Paul's letter, we discern that this difficult situation had caused some hard feelings and threatened division in the church.

When Gentiles in the world before Christ converted to Judaism, they accepted all the cultural as well as religious practices of the Jews. They became Jews in almost every way possible. That mindset clearly continued in the first years of Christianity for many. Most Jews, especially those who lived in Jerusalem, assumed that Gentile converts would embrace not only Christianity but also the Jewish culture. A big part of that was integrating Jewish food customs based on the old covenant law and Jewish holidays.

Why would the Jewish believers assume that new Christians would embrace their culture? Didn't they know that these things were rooted in the old covenant that no longer held sway over them? They probably did at a theoretical level, even if it took them a while to work that all out. The Jewish people had been defined by these practices for centuries and in many cases had been martyred by pagans for the conviction of holding to these requirements and observances. These weren't just cultural preferences in their minds, this was their identity.

Now they found themselves in community with Gentiles whose cultural traditions were deeply offensive and often felt sinful. How could they possibly live together as one? This is exactly what Paul attempts to cover in Romans 14 and 15 with teaching that was deeply and specifically relevant to the situation in Rome at that time.

One of the important principles in the science of scriptural interpretation and application known as hermeneutics is to take a principle from the biblical text and shake it free from the situation-specific directions so that it can be applied to any similar situation in a more universal fashion. Paul was guiding the Roman believers through unique controversies that they were facing, but he gave them very helpful principles that become clear when we remove them from the specific circumstances they were wading through. Paul gave them principles to apply in their situation, but when we look at those principles by themselves, they prove useful to us today when it comes to blending different groups in an ongoing multicultural setting.

I will attempt to simplify Paul's guiding principles and show how they are the universal tenets that must give direction to our lives:

1. View your cultural expressions of worship and faith as "a way" to do things and not "the way" (14:1-3).

2. The cultural expressions of others are equally valid to your own (14:4).

3. Do not judge one another's convictions and cultural practices as sinful if they are not (14:5-12).

4. Don't force your cultural practice on others if it is something that would bother their conscience (14:13-17).

5. Choose love for your brothers and sisters over your cultural preferences (14:19-21).

6. If you don't like the cultural practices of others and they are not sinful, keep it to yourself (14:22-23).

7. Make every effort to accept the practices and expressions of one another and participate in them whenever possible (15:1-13).

Paul was steering the church toward a blended culture, which is not automatic and not easy to do. For the Gentile cultures of the first century, the primary tasks were twofold. The first was not to look down on, judge, and dismiss the practices of their Jewish brothers and sisters. The second was to not conform to worldly practices that were clearly not fitting for the kingdom of God. For example, a deep part of the Gentile culture at the time was that it was considered perfectly acceptable for a married person to have sex with a slave of any gender. That was not considered to be adultery or immoral at all. Paul makes clear in passages like 1 Thessalonians 4:3-6 that this is not an acceptable cultural practice in the kingdom. When he warns Gentiles away from sexual immorality, he is calling them to reject the acceptable culture of their time.

For the Jews, the primary tasks were also twofold. The first was the same as for the Gentiles. Don't look down on and dismiss cultural preferences and practices of your fellow disciples. Participate and accept where you can. The second was to not attempt to force the Gentiles to their cultural ways. If Jewish believers wanted to continue to observe aspects of the Jewish culture like circumcision, food restrictions, and Sabbath or holiday observances, that was fine. But when they demanded that Gentiles do so as well in order to be considered true Christians, they were then, as Paul put it so confrontationally, causing them to turn "to a different gospel" (Galatians 1:6). It is indeed a dangerous thing to marry culture to the gospel and insist that the two are inseparable.

This raises a question. Would Paul have stood against the Jews gently inviting Gentiles into aspects of their culture and teaching them to participate if they so chose, but allowing them the freedom to decide not to? I think it's clear that Paul would have celebrated that approach and enjoyed the nuances of the blended and transformed culture that this would have created.

Chapter 7

This Is Me

When I open my eyes in the morning, the first instinct that rolls through my mind is that I need to get up and get to work. Much of that has been instilled in me through my Western and familial culture. It's often been referred to as the old Puritan work ethic. If I'm awake, I should be working and getting something done.

As soon as I stand up, I make my bed unless my wife is still in the bed sleeping. Why is she in the bed with me and not in a separate bed or a different room? That's something that has been handed down to us culturally. And I make the bed because my parents instilled that cultural expectation in me since I was little. I was trained to make the bed right away and have never given it much thought.

If I don't walk down to my office and start working on something right away, I typically begin my day with a quiet time. That's a habit that I've picked up as part of my embraced spiritual culture from the church family to which I belong.

After that, I get a workout in, something that I enjoy but also value due to the culture in which I was raised. Not all cultures embrace or value exercise for the sake of exercise.

Whether I work out or not, I take a shower. I don't ever think about why, but I do it daily whether I need it or not. And if you're thinking in one direction or the other, that of course we need a shower every day or that we don't, that's likely a culturally influenced way of thinking.

After that, I get dressed in my Western clothes and head downstairs for my culturally conditioned choice of breakfast foods.

Along the way, I greet my family members or anyone else that is staying at our house, with a greeting that I picked up from within my household and regional culture.

I have a quiet time with my son, something that was again instilled in me by my spiritual culture as a good thing, and then I send out a few texts. Why do I text instead of call? Because it has become culturally acceptable in our country and it suits my personality better.

I drop my son off at school in a very systematic manner that has been determined by a number of factors including flow of traffic and the cultural belief that every student matters and should, if possible, be dropped off closest to the door that suits them.

If I stop at the store to pick something up, I go into a very American/Western-style store. I interact with others based on socially acceptable rules of culture. I get in line the way we do it in the United States, which usually means choosing the cashier line that I think will be the shortest and fastest. My culture tends to dictate that I get to choose the line I want rather than be herded into one line with everyone else and then sent to the next available register in turn. I am an individual and I get to choose. That's American culture at its core. Once given the choice, I will invariably select what I believe to be the fastest line because I'm from an impatient culture and I want to get through this and on to my next task as soon as possible. While in line, I expect that no one will stand closer than two or three feet away, respecting my God-given personal space (it is God-given, right?). I also have a reasonable expectation that no one will make direct eye contact with me unless they are speaking to me, and then they will absolutely show me respect by looking at me. I won't be surprised if someone strikes up a conversation, but it won't shock me either if people stand quietly in line with me and don't speak at all. The one thing I can count on for sure is that no one will jump my place in line, and if they do, they will be met by the ire and disdain of all who witness such an atrocity.

On the way out of the store, I smile and say "good morning" to the people I pass because my Midwestern culture has taught me that this is polite and good. In fact, it is so deeply instilled in me that if I am on a morning run, I will be sure to greet every single person I pass. To do otherwise would be downright rude. As I reach the doors, I hold them open for a woman who is exiting as well and let her out before me. I do that because my dad always taught me to.

As I'm heading out of the store, I go out the correct doors and walk on the proper side of the crosswalk to get to the cars, which are parked in a very orderly fashion, and I begin my drive home on streets with other cars that are very dutifully following the rules of the road. This is all dictated by our culture. Occasionally, someone will cut in front of my car, which greatly irritates me because I am an individual and this is a personal affront to my autonomy and to the rules of the road. These too are deeply ingrained cultural beliefs.

As I arrive back home, I warmly greet my wife, give her a kiss, see if she needs anything, and try to spend some time with her. All of this is a mix of United States, Midwestern, and spiritual culture that I have picked up over the years. Then I might go and quickly wash the morning dishes. That might seem like a countercultural thing for a man to do, but you'd be wrong. My culture has taught me that it is okay if a man wants to do the dishes and I have the personal freedom, autonomy, and rights to buck certain traditional cultural norms whenever I want.

I could go on, of course. There are a million other little things that I didn't mention. But hopefully you get the idea that nearly everything we do is culturally conditioned in one way or another. This is not a bad thing. Society could not function without culture. It is a group of people agreeing to do things in a certain way and it makes life easier for all of us because we can make assumptions of how others will act, so that our lives are not filled with constant uncertainty.

GOOD AND BAD

Culture creates what becomes normal behavior around us. We do many of the things we do because that's what everyone else around us has always done, and it impacts everything from how we interact with others to how we eat and what music we like. It even influences how we think and how we view ourselves. Culture is powerful.

Perhaps the most potent feature of it is contained in the word "normal." Our culture becomes normal to us. Normal is not a bad thing. There is a great deal of comfort in normal. I like normal. I like being normal. I like it when others around me are normal.

Uh-oh! A problem just crept in. Do you see it? Normal is good to an extent. But as soon as I begin to expect that others will embrace my concept of normal, a door has been opened. What if they don't? What if they grew up differently and have a different idea of normal? This could get stressful.

What if I come to church with the knowledge that to properly worship God, there is an opening song that's perhaps a bit upbeat followed by an energetic welcome? Then, there are a few other songs while we stand neatly in our rows of chairs, and if we are really getting into a song and want to express ourselves a bit, we might clap to the beat. But that's as far as you should go. What happens if someone comes in who grew up in West Africa and has their own version of a normal worship service. They believe that it is normal to use your whole body when worshipping God through song. When the music starts, look out.

Or what if a visitor to church hears it preached consistently that the church is a family. She has been raised to think that if we are going to be family then that means we will constantly be in one another's homes, sharing life together, and stopping by unannounced. But the culture of the church has been set along other lines because most members have backgrounds and comfort levels different than that. They prefer to be informed before having visitors, and just dropping in is considered an imposition. To show their love to visitors they offer to take them out to lunch at a nearby restaurant. This is normal for this church, and most have embraced it. But to this visitor, it is not normal. It is mildly offensive and runs counter to the message of being family. She walks away thinking that these people are hypocrites—all because they have a different sense of what normal is and did not have the training to uncover these differences.

You can see how easy it is to conclude that someone else's way of doing things is just weird, wrong, or hypocritical or to assign some other negative interpretation to it. Do you see the problem?

IDENTITY

Cultural norms provide a lot of positive dynamics in our lives. The first is that they bring identity. Our culture is more than just a series of actions or learned behaviors. It becomes as much a part of who we are as our individual personalities. As the rundown of a typical morning above demonstrates, culture becomes a part of almost everything we do. It becomes part of us as we become part of it.

Because culture is invisible and involves tacit assumptions that we make based on interactions with those around us, most of us never even think about the existence of our own culture. "Culture" is what other groups have. We tend to think that we don't have one, particularly if we are part of a dominant group. It is only when you come in contact with people from other cultures, especially when you are suddenly in the minority, that your own culture stands out to you. Only then does it become evident that it really is just learned behavior.

As we embrace the parallel cultures in which we are raised, such as our nation, our ethnic group, our geographic region, our city, and our church, the identity of who we are, how we see ourselves, and how we interact with the world starts to form. We know who we are, we know how to operate in the world around us, and that is comforting.

SECURITY

Cultural norms provide security because we know how we fit in and have a good idea of how to act and interact with those around us and what they are going to do as well. Sharing these attitudes and behaviors with others brings stability to our lives and removes a great deal of stress. We don't have to wonder why others are behaving the way they are; we already know. This is why our cultures tend to be so deeply rooted within us. We don't typically or easily give up something that brings us such a sense of normalcy and refuge.

IT WORKS

For many years I was part of a church in Milwaukee that always sang the song "Soon and Very Soon" the same way. That song was one of my favorites. When we moved to a new church less than two hours away, many of the people and most of the leaders had come from Milwaukee, and we also sang it the same way. Then we moved to Minneapolis, and I was dismayed the first time we sang it. The tune was slightly different, and when we got to the chorus, well, I couldn't believe my ears. Everything was different, and my first reaction was mild horror. I didn't know what they were doing, and I had to just stop and listen. I didn't like it at first. It was uncomfortable.

The way we sang it in Milwaukee was good and it worked for us. We all knew how we were going to belt it out and we did it in unison. The Minneapolis version just didn't work. At least not for me—not at first. But I noticed that it did work for everyone else. They knew how they sang the song and they let it rip their way.

That's another powerful aspect of culture. It works. When we all act in the same way, even if it seems inexplicable or odd to other groups, it will work for us because everyone in our group understands the actions. We are all moving in the same direction. It is easy to judge other groups for their weird behavior, but that is usually because we don't understand it. Groups have embraced the culture they have because it works in the context of their experience.

To the people of that community, their culture makes sense because it has always worked and brought order. It is unifying and useful and so they grow to value it, even if they are not always aware of it.

MINE MAKES SENSE, YOURS DOESN'T

Several years ago, I found myself with a few hours to kill in the airport in Harare, Zimbabwe. It was a late Sunday evening, and there were few other people in the airport. After an hour or so of sitting alone at a gate, nature began to call, and I needed to find a restroom. I looked around but couldn't see any telltale symbols of a man and woman, or even a sign that read "toilet" or something similar. I began to walk through the airport on a quest that was becoming more urgent by the moment. After about twenty minutes of walking up and down, I was flummoxed by the realization that apparently this airport had been constructed without any lavatory. How could this even be? The airport wasn't that large, but they had to have a bathroom somewhere, right? Finally, in a desperate move, I went down a hallway that looked like it would have some facilities. If there wasn't something down there appropriate for the job at hand, I was going to move into phase two, where you find something that works and improvise. At the end of the hallway, I saw a door that had the letters "WC" on it. I had no idea what that was, but I decided to take a chance and push the door open just enough to peek in and see. Sure enough, it was a john. I had been saved.

As I exited, some obscure thought from the dark recesses of my mind fished out the fact that in an old black-and-white movie from the 1940s or thereabouts, I had heard one of the characters refer to a washroom as a water closet. How quaint. It suddenly struck me like a bolt of lightning. "WC" was water closet. It was then that I realized that nearly every sign I observed in that airport had "WC" on it with arrows directing the way. I had been walking by these things for over twenty minutes and had neared an embarrassing tragedy all because I had no idea what "WC" meant.

As much trouble as I had just muddled through, think about this: the airport signage was entirely in English. Can you imagine the difficulty I might have had if everything was in a different language? What this illustrates, however, is the challenge of unfamiliarity. If there had been signs with "restroom," "bathroom," "lavatory," "toilet," "washroom," "john," or even "latrine," I would have immediately known that I had found the destination to my journey. Those terms are all commonplace to me and would have made sense. But "WC"? How is that a good way to label a bathroom? How does that make sense to any rational person?

The answer, of course, is that it makes perfect sense if you live in Zimbabwe. It's an old British term, and because of colonization, much of British culture has been transplanted to this beautiful Southern African country.

Language and culture are similar in many ways. Mine makes sense to me, but I have real trouble operating in yours if I don't know it. It becomes stressful and I would rather that you just utilize mine and leave yours comfortably tucked away where I don't have to encounter it or even think about it. Believe me, I've often experienced the anxiety of fumbling around in another culture or language, trying to find the right hallway to unlock what I want to communicate with others, but instead sending quite different signals.

I once stood in line at passport control in Lagos, Nigeria, dutifully waiting for my turn to step forward, hold out my little blue book, get a stamp, and move on to my boarding gate. But time and again people pushed their way past me and the agent at the gate took their passport and not mine, even though I was clearly standing there in line before them. It took me a while to realize that they were playing by cultural rules that made no sense to me. It was expected that I would push my way past people and thrust my passport forward so that I was holding it on the counter. Without doing that, I wasn't really in line in the minds of anyone around me, including the agent behind the desk. Once a brother from the church I had been visiting came up and explained that to me, I quickly received my stamp.

There is no way around the stress of not knowing. There is no escape from the fact that when interacting with people of different cultural backgrounds, we will have moments of misunderstanding, instances of high anxiety, and a general ignorance of what is expected or assumed in any given situation. This is inescapable. And for that reason alone, many people avoid intercultural interactions as much as possible. I'll save it for the family vacation to Mexico or Thailand where it is a fun adventure for a week, but I certainly don't want to have to deal with that kind of stress weekly at Sunday worship gatherings, let alone in my daily life.

This is why we tend to cluster up with people of shared culture. It is easier and more comfortable. It makes sense. I know what you mean most of the time. You know what I mean. Life works that way. When I get out of my group, it can be like navigating my way through a forest that I've never been in. I like my culture. Yours can be rather frightening.

IT ALL LEADS TO THIS

Because there are so many advantages to sharing cultural identity with others, it often leads down one road and to one conclusion: the people in my cultural group makes sense. Your culture is just weird.

My wife and I were meeting with some friends in South Africa many years ago. In fact, it was our first trip to that grand nation. As our time drew to a close, we excused ourselves to go outside and wait for another couple that had just called us to confirm that they would pick us up "just now" to have some coffee with them. Unbeknownst to us, we had mildly offended the first couple by scheduling time with someone else and cutting our time down to a specific two-hour period. They had very different assumptions about getting time together than we had.

As we stood outside, two minutes turned into ten, which turned into twenty. We were growing more irritated by the moment. It was nearly forty minutes before they finally picked us up. What had happened? Why had it taken so long to fetch us? "Sorry, we did say that it would be 'just now.'" What? How is that a good excuse? Well, as it turns out, in South Africa "just now" is a vague term that means "in a while." If they meant that they were going to be right over, they would have said "now-now."

Are you kidding me? Let's review this. First of all, who gets offended because you scheduled another appointment after a solid two-hour time period of dinner and fellowship? That's being touchy, not to mention ridiculous. And what kind of maniac culture uses the term "just now" to mean exactly the opposite of "just now"? How is that rational? How can one function in such an absurd society? It's a wonder that this whole culture hasn't devolved into violent anarchy. No one could function by such tacit assumptions like that you should never schedule something right after getting time with us because it sends the signal that you do not value the relationship and have said as much by putting a time limit on it. And certainly no one could thrive with such illogical use of phrases like "just now."

But those are all biased assumptions on my part, aren't they? These things are not weird at all if I understand the cultural context a bit. After many years of experiencing different qualities of African culture, I have grown to love the emphasis on relationship and the deemphasis of chronology. You don't constrain relationships to a time window. You leave the schedule open so that the relationship can flourish. That's beautiful, isn't it? That's why the language is a bit imprecise. It's a reminder that time is not the master of all that we do. Connection with others is what matters, not schedules.

That has taken a massive reworking of my value system and a colossal project of rewiring my brain, but it has been worth it.

THE DARK SIDE

When we get too comfortable with our own culture, we start to view others as strange. The danger in that is that it is a short leap to dislike, segregation, and division, and it only goes downhill from there.

There is much that is good about having a cultural identity. It helps societies and groups to function. It takes a series of actions and turns them into assumptions that we can all operate under without having to stop and think about every little action we take. Cultural norms are a little bit like pronouns. They are shortcuts. Can you imagine speaking and writing with only nouns, having no access to pronouns? That just sounds exhausting. Pronouns save us a lot of time and make things inexpressibly easier. And so does culture.

But there is also a dark side to that. If I value my culture so much that I become rigid and unwilling to open my mind to another way of viewing the world or operating within it, culture becomes an incredible, and sometimes insurmountable, source of division. It has proven itself to be so throughout human civilization. And if we are not willing to accept that we have been called by God to take part in the gathering of the nations, being all things to all people along the way, it will become a source of great division in the body of Christ as well.

Chapter 8

Division Subtracts

I have a clear memory as a teenager of going to the beach with my friends and a few other people I knew and was friendly with but would not have classified as friends. The entire group of us were white, middle-class, Midwestern, small-town Wisconsinites. In other words, most of our cultural layers overlapped and we had much in common. We shared mostly the same cultural assumptions and preferences. While at the beach, we were listening to music, having a good time, and going in and out of the water. Before too long, a relatively large group of black women and children came onto the beach and set up camp close by. To be honest, we didn't know much about them other than the color of their skin.

Almost immediately upon their arrival, the general volume at the beach went up seemingly tenfold. There were other moms and kids at the beach, but they had all been pretty quiet. Not this group. The kids were loud, but the women were louder. They were playing and having fun, but I'm telling you, it was noticeably loud. When they were far apart, they would shout back and forth to communicate with one another. If one of the moms wanted to redirect or discipline a child, they would do so seemingly at the top of their lungs. There was no decorum or sense of being discreet in the presence of others around them. It was so different from the atmosphere before they arrived that it was abrasive to everyone else.

For a time, we tried to ignore it, but it was hard to go on having a low-key, relaxed day at the beach with this constant cacophony raging all around. I recall it irritating me, but that was about as far as it went. But I must admit, I had grown up in a town where no one else acted like that. The contrast was sharp.

Then it happened. One of the guys in the group turned to the rest of us and said something to the effect of, "That's why I can't stand those people. They are always loud and rude. They don't care about anyone else." We all knew what he meant by "those people." He didn't mean women and children. He was classifying them by their skin color, by their race.

The tension that had been hanging in the air before that moment boiled over, and several of my acquaintances and a couple of my friends decided to leave, but in doing so, tried to send clear signals that they were leaving in disgust and protest. I'm not sure that the group they were trying to communicate with even paid attention or picked up on their silent protests and dirty looks as they left. As I look back on that day, I hope they didn't. I wish that I had been wise and strong enough to confront the frustration and attitudes of those in our group.

To many, this could look like a racial issue, and it could easily have turned into one. But the cause of the division here was not race, not really. It was cultural differences. One group tends to value discretion and keeping your interactions as private as possible, even when in a public setting. It is considered rude to raise the volume of your presence to a level where it might invade or overpower the solitude and invisible wall of privacy of others. The values of this group, my group, tend to be more focused on the individual, so boundaries are highly prized. The other group has a more collective and communal mindset, so the walls of privacy and boundaries are set in other places. It is more acceptable for everyone to be demonstrative in public. That behavior is normal and is not considered rude or invasive. You can imagine how these two sets of cultural expectations don't mix well.

That's the power of culture. It unifies those under the same cultural umbrella, but it just as quickly divides those carrying different-colored umbrellas. There are three realities when it comes to the power of culture to divide, and we must be aware of them in the body of Christ.

THREE REALITIES

The first reality is that the potential for division will always be there. In fact, the more interaction between groups of varying backgrounds, the more we will see these areas of conflict and enmity. When there is a beach full of people who share the same unwritten rules of behavior, it is peaceful and comfortable. Until a group arrives with very different unwritten rules. The fireworks can happen quickly, and it doesn't have to be the Fourth of July.

The second reality is that wishes and warm feelings do not remove the cultural misunderstandings, offenses, and conflict that will predictably happen when a diversity of people are together. My wife and have been married for over twenty years, but we come from widely differing cultural backgrounds. We love each other deeply, but that has not taken away the fact that we have cultural clashes as an almost daily occurrence. I once talked to a church leader who told me he didn't think it was necessary for a multiracial church to talk about issues of race or to learn about cultural competence, because the blood of Christ did away with those divisions. He went on to assert that once we enter the waters of baptism, prejudice, bias, and ethnocentrism go away. They only become an issue when we make it one. Prejudice, bias, and cultural preference go away at baptism? If you agree with that sentiment, let me ask a pointed question: How did that work out for your pride, lust, and critical heart? Did they just disappear at your baptism?

This is important, because bias and prejudice are sins. James describes these sins of the heart using a term in James 2:9 that is translated "favoritism" in the NIV and CSB, "partiality" in the LEB and ESV, and "treat some people better than others" in the CEV. We all have favorites, but to treat one group with advantage and another with disadvantage, and not examine our reasons for doing so? James says that those who show this kind of favoritism "sin and are convicted by the law as lawbreakers."

These potentials for division will never go away. We can learn to manage them and turn them into opportunities, but if we ignore them, they will fester under the surface for years until they eventually explode. I'm convinced that many marriages have disintegrated in a seemingly inexplicable fashion because there were deep undercurrents of culture clash at play, but the couple remained unaware of that as the cause and never addressed the true root.

That leads to the third reality. Conflicts that develop between individuals or groups will often look like they are caused by something other than culture. Most of us tend to be unaware of the dynamics and power of culture, so we rarely suspect that as the cause of the division or tension. I will give a few examples below to illustrate this.

WHO ARE YOU TALKING TO?

The following brief story is a composite of many similar instances that I have observed. Think of a diverse group of young teens arriving for church camp. Some hail from small cities that are barely diverse in any way with the one exception being the family of churches to which they belong. Others come from big cities or suburbs and have experienced a great deal of diversity in their neighborhood, school, and church. Still others were raised their entire lives in the central city and have entirely different cultural backgrounds from their friends arriving at camp on different buses.

As they arrive, the boys and girls are given their cabin assignments for the week, and the boys race off to find their cabin and their beds. A pack of about forty boys arrive at the Woodchuck cabin, and already the instructions to find a bed, neatly roll out their sleeping bags, put their belongings under the bed, and go outside to await further instruction, have long since drifted into one ear and screamed straight out the other. A white, college-age counselor comes into his cabin expecting to find order but instead is greeted with something that looks closer to a medieval battlefield scene. The boys are wrestling, screaming, chasing one another, jumping off beds onto their prey, and even throwing mattresses at one another.

This is it. This is what the counselor has been trained for. This is no drill. He has spent a day and half learning that he must be firm upfront and establish boundaries and discipline, or things will deteriorate quickly. You can always ease up later in the week, but you can't put toothpaste back in the tube. He swiftly decides to snap things back in order rapidly and without question, raising his voice to just one or two levels below maximum volume and commanding these young stallions to get their stuff and get into place by their beds immediately with no questions asked. Most of the kids instantly grab their gear and run to a bed, standing at attention in a fashion that would make any cadet in basic training proud.

A small group of black teens from the central city have a different response, though. Rather than snapping into place at his barked instructions, their instinct is to not move. One of them speaks for the group as he looks in the counselor's direction and says, "Who are you talking to?"

Facing this potential insubordination and challenge to his authority, the counselor raises his voice one level higher and shouts from about twenty feet away that they need to be respectful and follow his instructions. He punctuates his comments, with a sharp, "Now, move!" But much to his surprise, they do not bend to his clout, and the teen shoots back with, "Who do you think you're talking to?" Now the counselor knows he has a problem on his hands and will spend the rest of the week watching out for this group and taking no slack. By day three or four, it would not be entirely unreasonable for these teens to survey the situation and speculate, "This guy is always on us and I know why. He's racist."

Clearly, there is a conflict. But is the cause of this conflict a racial one? Or is it more likely that the cause has to do with differing approaches that cultural groups have toward authority? I was raised with a mindset of what is called ascribed authority. You trust authority and follow it automatically for no other reason than that the person giving you commands is in a position of authority. This is illustrated by one of my father's favorite phrases while we were growing up, "When I say jump, you say, 'When can I come down, sir?'" On the other end of the spectrum, my wife was raised in a culture of achieved authority. You must earn your influence; it is not just given. You don't trust someone or follow orders just because they have a certain role. If they disrespect you, you disrespect back, or you at least question their position over you and challenge it. Each of these approaches seems right to those raised in those contexts. They both make sense in their setting, and it works well when everyone is operating by the same rules. But when the two mix and there is a failure to recognize the conflict for what it is, sparks fly.

WE CAN'T HAVE A RELATIONSHIP

Two American disciples of Korean descent had each been Christians for more than five years and moved from different cities into the same church. We will call them Mark and David. They initially hit it off well and after a short time decided to be discipling partners together. The relationship became bumpy quickly. What neither of them recognized was that David had been raised in a culture that was very direct in its communication. It was considered respectful to speak bluntly and tell others exactly what you were thinking and what you felt. When they got together, David carried this "normal" type of communication with him and spoke very straightforwardly to Mark.

Mark, on the other hand, had been reared in a culture that was decidedly nondirect in its communication. They considered it important to not shame others when they needed to be confronted, so nothing was said directly. Hints were dropped, or things were worded in such a way that the person might be able to come to an understanding of what the other was saying without them having to say it frankly.

Mark immediately found David's style of speaking to him during their discipling times to be abrasive and aggressive. David felt that Mark rarely made sense and never spoke plainly about what was on his heart. David could live with it but didn't feel that Mark was ever going to be able to help him much. Mark, however, couldn't live with it. After a while, he concluded that David was harsh, unloving, and not very spiritual and went to his family group leader to complain that he simply could not be in a spiritual relationship with David any longer and would need to find a new discipling partner.

What might look like a spiritual issue or a certain measure of immaturity on the part of one or both men is nothing other than a cultural difference in how they communicate. Their lack of awareness of the cause of their issue has left them unable to work through it and be united.

THAT'S NOT WHAT CHURCH IS FOR

It's Monday and every news channel site has wall-to-wall coverage of a breaking tragedy coming out of a major city in the USA. You catch that something big is in the news, so you tune it to see what all the buzz on social media is about. It's yet another heartbreaking case of confrontation between a young person of color and a white police officer. The news stations breathlessly cover the situation and come to conclusions before all the facts are even in, and that causes deep divisions across the country.

For many white members of your church, Sunday cannot come fast enough. It is their refuge from all this bad news. It is the one place they can go to and not have to think about death, violence, injustice, and all the divisions throughout the land. The one thing they know is that this will not be brought up at church, certainly not in the sermon at least, because that is not what church is for.

Many disciples of color have different expectations. For many black disciples, for example, the church is the one place where these things can be talked about. It is a safe place to express grief and commiserate with others who are struggling through injustice and oppression. It is expected that they will be guided through questions about God's justice and seeming inaction in the face of evil and that members will be comforted, instructed, and organized in how to respond to the real world. For them, Sunday cannot come quickly enough. The one thing they know is that this tragedy will be talked through at church, especially in the sermon, because that is what church is for.

Do you want to be on the leadership team of that church come Sunday? The resulting conflict is inevitable. But the cause would also likely go undetected in multiracial churches, at least at first. If nothing was said, the white members would not notice anything because their expectations were met. The black disciples would quietly walk away hurt and disappointed, trying to think the best. But when it happens another time, and another, and another, avoiding negative conclusions becomes nearly impossible. Some will just grieve a bit and adjust their expectations downward for their leaders and brothers and sisters who are white. Others will grow increasingly frustrated and begin to identify the divide as a racial one. Before long, they are full-speed-ahead down the road of feeling that the leaders don't care about what their black brothers and sisters are going through, and that prejudice is alive and well in their church.

Each situation like this is different, and it may very well be the case that the leaders are insensitive or out of touch with the experiences of their fellow disciples. But in most cases, the cause of these conflicts is clearly cultural. Very few, if any, would recognize that, though, and once again, it would look like a different kind of conflict. But make no mistake, the root cause has much to do with culture.

THIS CANNOT BE IGNORED

The warm sun can melt a chocolate bar in a few minutes, or it can harden mud into a brick. The sunbeam is the same, but the composition of different substances causes them to react radically differently to the same conditions. Culture can bring great harmony and unity to one group of people if they have the same expectations and assumptions about how situations should go. But those same forces can result in deep fissures between that group and others who have been enculturated with vastly different expectations.

I don't have hard statistics to back this up, but I am convinced that about seventy-five percent of conflicts in the body of Christ have cultural dynamics at their core. The church that skirts these issues does so at their own risk.

These differences in perspective, expressions, and preferences are not something to be feared or ignored. The New Testament church didn't run from them. Rather than trying to disregard their problems or sweep them under the rug, we are told all about the ongoing conflict between Hebraic Jewish Christians and Hellenic Jewish Christians and about the deep divides between Jewish Christians and Gentile Christians; and there are even hints that varying groups of Gentile Christians found themselves divided over topics that were cultural in nature.

In Acts 6, we are told that an issue arose between the Hebraic and Hellenic Jewish Christians. This was potentially disastrous for the young church. The gathering of the nations would be in serious jeopardy if there was a split over national and cultural backgrounds when they were just barely out of the starting gate.

The Hellenic Jews felt slighted by the leaders of the church in the daily distribution of food. Rather than ignoring it or not dealing with this divide, it is acknowledged and dealt with. The apostles took the unique step of turning over control of one of the most important ministries in the church to the nondominant group.

But what if they had not? What if they had refused to legitimize this potential split and simply proclaimed that there were no divisions in the body, for we are all one in Christ? What are some of the things the Hellenic Jews might have started to ponder among one another?

- What if the kingdom isn't different after all?
- What if those leaders are showing favoritism?
- What if they are trying to neglect and marginalize us just like it

happens in the world?

- These guys don't really love us. They are bigoted.
- Hellenic widows matter.
- We can't keep being treated like this.
- They don't understand us.
- We need new leaders . . . better yet, we just need to form our own church community to take care of our needs.

A little dash of ignoring cultural divisions goes a long way. In this case, we don't know what the exact cause was. Perhaps the two groups had grown apart culturally enough that they were handling situations of this nature differently. That's very possible. But maybe it was just an instance of the Hellenic widows being overlooked for innocent reasons. Whatever the case, the leaders knew that to ignore a small irritant like this invites in the schisms and divisions of the world, and it is not long before the church mirrors those divisions. This is why the New Testament writers were so quick to bring up cultural squabbles and work the church through them directly. An educated church is a prepared church.

THE DANGER OF IGNORING IT

My grandmother on my dad's side was one of my heroes growing up. I loved all my grandparents, but I got to spend more time with her than the others, and she was special to me. She died at just fifty-six years of age, when I was thirteen. I wish that she had been here longer. I wish she could have met my wife and sons and been part of my life as I grow older, but life, as they say, happens.

Approximately seven years before she died, she went to the doctor, complaining about some problems with her health. The doctor hastily checked her over before declaring her in good health. He told her that the things she noticed were negligible and just part of aging. He also told her not to worry about it. So, she didn't. She carried on with her active lifestyle of gardening and traveling. Six years later, her health suddenly took a dramatic turn for the worse, and she once again found herself at the doctor's. This doctor saw some things that concerned him and sent her to a specialist who informed her that she was in the late stages of cancer. He also confirmed that had she caught it earlier, she would have had a good chance to fight it and survive. As it was, she would no longer be able to win this battle. And she didn't. Not even a year later, she passed away quietly in a bed at our house.

After looking at her records and getting to know the family, her specialist hinted that the actions of the original doctor were negligent and that the family might consider taking legal action. That first doctor had not done simple tests that he could have that would surely have revealed her condition. Had she known about it then, she might have lived for many more years. I wish she had. If you ignore something for too long, the consequences are often irreversible.

A danger can be lurking on the other side of this as well. It can happen that a church starts to examine issues of cultural dominance and humility and inclusion, and the response is less than exuberant from the dominant culture within the church. They may have many justifications for it, but it can come down to the simple truth that they have typically not been equipped to examine cultural issues, let alone to pull at the threads of their own comfortable position, and they do not like these topics brought up. They might very well assert their fear that it could cause strife and disunity, but that unfounded fear cannot become an obstacle to the work that must be done. When a controversial call happens in sports, I've noticed that the fans of the team who received the favorable call never want the play to be sent to a video review. They're happy with the original call even though it may not be right. But we have to be willing to examine the cultural life of our church and determine if we are truly being all things to all people as God intends.

God has called his people to be the gathering of the nations. The churches that heed that call are in for a particularly adventurous journey. Not addressing issues of culture and teaching the body of Christ how to identify them and work through them can eventually become just as dangerous as ignoring a cancer in the physical body. Don't get me wrong, even monoracial churches will have cultural issues, but the potential is there for many more conflicts for churches that are diverse. Accept that as fact. Don't run from it. And please don't think it is a distraction from the real work of the church. Teaching cultural competency is a vital function of a church growing in unity.

Chapter 9

Dominant Dynamics

Yohannes and Rachel began dating during their senior year in college. They were born and raised in different states and met during their first year at the university after both were converted to Christianity a month apart from one another. Yohannes became a disciple first and began to like Rachel almost immediately after she came up from the waters of baptism. It took Rachel a little longer to get on board. But toward the end of their junior year, a bond had clearly formed. Shortly after graduation, Yohannes asked Rachel to marry him and she readily agreed. Within a year they had become husband and wife.

For the first year of their marriage they stayed in the campus ministry that they had been part of and helped to lead some of the younger students. A new job for Yohannes was the impetus for them to move to a new city and a new church, and after a few months there, they began to help in the youth and family ministry. Another year went by, and they decided to pour their efforts into the young marrieds' ministry.

It was at this time that they entered a discipling relationship with James and Elizabeth. Having moved around a bit, they were excited to be in a relationship of true spiritual mentorship in which they could get some consistent input into their marriage and spiritual lives. From the first time they met, James and Elizabeth started to sense that something was not quite right. They couldn't put their finger on it, and it didn't seem to be anything terrible, but something was off.

Rachel was fine and thought everything was going well. Yohannes seemed a little unsettled, though. Most of the time he would say everything was good, but neither James nor Elizabeth could shake the feeling that he was quietly frustrated. As James and Yohannes were able to grow closer and trust one another, Yohannes slowly let his feelings come to the surface. It wasn't all at once and it wasn't even something that Yohannes was aware of, but it was a growing discontent.

After about two years, the four young adults were having dinner one night when Elizabeth asked Yohannes and Rachel to describe a typical week for them in their household, which now included two young children. It was then that the real issues started to come out and confirm what James and Elizabeth had both seen and suspected. Yohannes was now at the point at which he could understand and communicate what the problem was.

"She always gets her way," he blurted out, "that's what our week looks like." Then it came like a flood. "We do everything she wants. We structure the house the way she prefers; we parent our child the way she likes to do it and never the way I think things should be done. We watch the movies she wants to see. We listen to her favorite music. We go to places she chooses. You name it, she gets her way." There was much more that he could say, but the hounds had finally been released, and he felt a rush of adrenaline from getting fully in touch with his growing frustration for perhaps the first time.

Rachel was taken aback, to say the least. This was news to her, and she honestly had no idea what he was talking about. "We don't always do things my way," she confidently asserted. "All the things he talked about, we just do what makes sense and is normal."

"Wrong," Yohannes interjected, "our household looks just like her parents' house." He continued, "We grew up differently, and she doesn't like anything from my world. Everything we do is what she experienced, what she likes, and what she feels comfortable with." He then shocked everyone in the room, including himself a bit, by saying, "Sometimes I start to wonder why I'm even still here. She doesn't need me. She doesn't listen to me, doesn't value me, and doesn't want to do anything the way I'd like to do it."

IS IT HEALTHY?

So, if you were in James and Elizabeth's shoes what would you think? Is this a healthy relationship? Would you advise them that you see no problem with Rachel dominating the family life and culture? Would you support Rachel if she dismissed Yohannes' frustrations and concerns and agree with her as she asserted that her husband was just being dramatic, and, in fact, it was he who was now threatening the unity and peace in their marriage with these unfounded complaints? In her estimation, it was Yohannes who was creating conflict where there was none. She didn't get her way all the time; they just did what was best in each situation. Evidently, it was her husband who wanted to get his way. That didn't seem fair to her, since she wasn't ever asserting her will; they were just living life together, and rather peacefully, until this little outburst.

Is this a healthy marriage?

I would hope that anyone reading this would agree that this hypothetical union would not be the environment for a healthy dynamic. Rachel is decidedly out of touch. The recipe for a healthy marriage does not include one person constantly imposing their preferences with no compromise and no consideration of what the other person would like. Even though Rachel was always sweet and pleasant in doing so, Yohannes got to the point where it was clear to him that she didn't want to partner with him; she wanted him there for his presence not his partnership.

Most relationships, even the healthiest, will have one partner who tends to be dominant when it comes to the culture of the friendship. This is especially true of a relationship like a marriage, in which a household cultural life is created by the husband and wife in their new family. The degree to which one person is the dominant force can vary, with Yohannes and Rachel's example being on the extreme of one partner completely dominating every aspect of life together. On the other end would be a totally equal partnership of give and take. Most healthy marriages will find themselves more on the end toward balance, although few could ever claim complete equity. And that's okay. To have a slightly dominant force within the relationship is normal, and it can be fine if there is a willingness on the part of both spouses to recognize their dynamic and to listen to, support, and submit to one another.

Here's something to think about as you advance through this chapter: if the above example is an obviously unhealthy dynamic in a marriage, would it be just as unhealthy when it comes to a church?

UNAWARE

When multiple groups of cultures interact within one context or community, there will tend to be a dominant group. It may be that the group was first to establish the church or had some sort of advantage from the beginning that lent itself to their dominant status, or it may have emerged over time. But without fail, one group will typically have the advantage of dominance. The most common reason is that they are in the majority, although there can be notable exceptions to that. A group can be stronger in numbers, power, wealth, influence, or other factors that lead to its cultural dominance. Whatever the causes may be, there are important characteristics in the dynamics between dominant and nondominant groups.

The first is that dominant cultures tend to be unaware of their own culture. That's one of the privileges of being in the dominant group. You are usually surrounded by your own cultural group's preferences and assumptions. You do not have to learn to operate according to the unwritten rules of other groups in order to get by. Because individuals in the dominant group spend most of their lives insulated from the behavior, customs, and values of other groups, when put in a setting where they truly must understand and adapt to another group, they simply never become familiar with that culture. This lends itself to viewing other cultures' practices as odd, inappropriate, foolish, and outside of what they would consider normal human behavior. In the eyes of a member of the dominant group, they themselves have no culture as other groups do. Theirs becomes the default mode for the way that humans should act in any given situation.

I have had several experiences in which a friend has gone to an East Indian wedding, a quinceañera party, or some other kind of event rooted in something other than a white, Western, American tradition. A typical response after such beautiful events is, "I just love their culture. We don't have a culture. I wish we had a culture in the US so that we could have things like that."

The problem is that we do have a culture, a powerful one, and we should become acutely aware of it, because it tends to gobble up and dominate any other cultures into which it comes in contact. When people say they don't have a dominant culture within their group, they're wrong. They're just not aware of it.

Many sincere disciples and church leaders have told me that their church doesn't have a dominant culture. Above all, they are certain that they don't have a white culture in their church. While it's possible that they don't have a white culture, it is fantasy to think that they don't have a culture. Every group does.

In my own spiritual tradition, the overwhelming majority of our churches around the world are intentionally and beautifully diverse racially, socioeconomically, in age, and just about every other area possible. That is especially true for the churches in the United States. But it would be naïve to say that we do not have a dominant culture. The dominant culture in our family of churches tends to be white and Western within the US, with arguably a strong North American influence in other parts of the world. There are a few exceptions, but for the most part that's true. This is not necessarily wrong, but we must be aware of it so that we can become all things to all people as we are called to be. If a community refuses to recognize the dominant forces within, the customs of that community will continue to reflect the dominant culture by default, which will feel somewhere between mildly uncomfortable and downright hostile for others.

VERY AWARE

At the opposite end of the spectrum lie nondominant groups in a multicultural setting. They are usually very aware of their own cultural identity as well as that of the dominant group. They may not know all the ins and outs of the dominant group or understand every custom or motivation, but they definitely know enough to get by, because they must to be able to operate within the societal standards set and accepted by the dominant group.

A trip to my local Walmart demonstrates this clearly. Although there is a mixture ethnically of both employees and shoppers, it seems on most days that most shoppers are white, while a majority of employees are Latino and Somali. The Latino and Somali employees have learned and understand quite well certain aspects of the dominant culture. They mostly interact with people comfortably and get across what they need to without puzzling or offending the white customers.

On occasion, though, I have observed these same employees interacting with someone from their own cultural background, whether it be a coworker or a customer, and it is obvious that a whole other form of cultural expression and rules are being followed. They can then slip right back into interaction with dominant-culture folks without even thinking about it.

However, I have also seen white employees struggle with their communication or the way they come across to customers who are of a different cultural origin. This goes beyond mere language obstacles. The simple fact is that most members of the dominant group do not know how to comfortably navigate the culture of nondominant groups.

This is the reason that around the world the reputation of US travelers to other countries is that they are rude, brash, and obnoxious. It is not so much that they are, on average, more boorish than our European, African, Latino, or Asian brethren, but that most of them are of the dominant culture in our society and so have little experience or knowledge of the cultural assumptions and expectations of other groups. Dominant groups don't have to operate according to different standards much, so they don't know how.

The obvious takeaway from this is that nondominant groups more easily adjust to and adopt the dominant group norms and can more seamlessly adapt and interact with dominant groups than the other way around.

ON THE OFFENSE

When my wife and I began dating, we met one another's families and began to spend time together with each group. As we prepared to get married, we had to navigate the ritual that most young married couples do: deciding how we would split up special times like holidays between our groups of relatives.

It didn't take me long to discover that my wife was better at it than I was. She would come in, sit down, fit right in to conversations with my parents and other family members, and be at ease. That doesn't mean that she understood everything about the culture of my group. Far from it. But, since she and I are both from the USA, there was much that we all had in common. Since we were both raised in Wisconsin, that was another layer we shared. But we were from different socioeconomic groups. She cut her teeth in the inner city and lived in mostly black neighborhoods her whole life, while I come from a small, largely white city surrounded by rural living. As a member of the nondominant culture in our society, she was better at understanding the basics of my culture and certainly wasn't offended by it.

I can't say the same for myself. I was very accepting of her family and had no prominent racial prejudices that I was aware of at the time (although we all have prejudices), but I also had a very shallow knowledge of the inner workings of her cultural group. Due to my ignorance, a lot of the things her relatives considered normal drove me absolutely crazy. I was constantly upset and feeling offended by their behavior. To make matters worse, I felt endlessly awkward around them and didn't know how to engage well in the conversations they had with each other.

This is characteristic of the dominant-culture effect. Because the dominant group is less familiar with the basics of nondominant groups, they are more easily upset, offended, or threatened by the behavior and culture of the nondominant group and can act in very intolerant ways toward them.

That doesn't mean that members of the nondominant group are saintly and have no flaws. Nor does it mean that dominant group members are inherently the bad guys. Nondominant group members can be just as unaware or intolerant of other nondominant cultures. And there are always exceptions. There are dominant-group people who have become incredibly adept in other cultures, and there are nondominant-group members who could not operate in or understand the dominant group to save their life. But in general, the people in the dominant group struggle more.

Let me give an example from church life to demonstrate this. I have been to countries outside the United States that had a small group of English-speaking North Americans living there. And while they were doing their best to fit in and be part of the congregation, they were very quick to cluster up, group together, and spend much time with each other outside of church. That makes some sense. They could understand each other better and got where each other was coming from. There is an ease with those who share your culture and first language that is magnetic. Yet if we traveled back to the US and were to find a group of Spanish-speaking people grouping together apart from the others, it would not be long before someone was "concerned" about this and upset that people were banding together.

I have heard complaints from white Christians about black members grouping together, because when that happened, the white members didn't feel welcomed or comfortable. I have never heard a black disciple make that same complaint. Again, there may be exceptions to these examples, but I'm speaking in general terms here of the most likely scenario. Dominant groups tend to be more threatened by the nondominant culture.

THE QUIET KILLER

Our fictional couple, Yohannes and Rachel, were having different experiences in their marriage and the life they were creating together. Rachel didn't fully realize it, but her preferences had become the dominant culture in their household. It never occurred to her that everything went her way and that she was able to set up permanent residence in her comfort zone. For Yohannes, it was a different world. He didn't mind at first doing things differently, but that started to wear on him as time passed. When he noticed that nearly everything was dictated by Rachel's cultural preferences, the tension began to build for him exponentially. He struggled with the unfairness of the situation and grew increasingly frustrated that he was always the one who was bending, adapting, and changing. She was always in her comfort zone; he hadn't visited his for a long time. And Rachel had no idea. For her, things were great. For Yohannes, the dissatisfaction was mounting.

When different groups make up a multicultural community, it is commonplace that they differ in the way they experience the group and perceive how well things are going. That can be true with groups as small as two people. Have you ever sat down with a married couple and asked them how things are going? The husband blurts out that things "are great," and he's excited about how they are growing in their relationship. But then, before you can even fully turn to the wife and repeat the question, she bursts into tears. They are on two different rides, and each will continue to be unaware of the experience of the other without some honest and straightforward communication.

Discontent and miscommunication will happen in communities. Differences of opinion are a sure thing. Conflict will be present, count on it. Those are not signs of disaster. When we find them in a community, some work needs to be done, but we need not panic. What is a problem is the unawareness factor. When problems are known, we can work on them. When only part of the community sees the problem, but the dominant group does not, that is a recipe for bad things to happen.

Let's say you have a nondominant group in a church community that is routinely marginalized. The dominant group loves to have them present and, in theory, loves the diversity they bring. But they make no effort to understand or grow in their awareness of cultural inclusion and the self-adaptation that is necessary for true cultural diversity to exist. The nondominant group will eventually grow tired of always being the ones to adapt and sacrifice. They will take notice that the dominant group is always in their comfort zone and that the dominant group will usually throw a fit if the church does some things differently to allow for the cultural expressions of the nondominant groups.

This will consistently lead to two things. First, the nondominant group will remain silent for a time but will quietly grow in their discontent and impatience. Second, the dominant group will grow increasingly out of touch. They believe everything is fine because the community has become a haven for their cultural preferences, and they are oblivious to the fact that many members of the community are feeling disaffected. A gap is widening, and the dominant group has no idea.

IDENTIFYING THE DOMINANT CULTURE

An important starting place for churches that want to develop cultural competency is to identify clearly what the dominant culture is in their group. Simply put, a dominant culture is the group whose members are in the majority, or in some cases who hold more power or influence than the other groups present.

Because culture is a multilayered phenomenon, there can be several ways of identifying the dominant culture. It can depend on what angle you are approaching the question from, but there is typically an element that is the most influential within the society that can serve as the primary cultural focus. If you are in Israel, ethnicity and nationality might be the most powerful factors in cultural divides. Is your church culturally dominated by Palestinians, Israelis, Jewish Ukrainians, Jewish Russians, or some other group? In many places in Africa, the question might focus on tribal culture. If you are in Nigeria, is the dominant tribal culture Yoruba, Igbo, Hausa, Fulani, or something else? In the United States, race is often the most prevalent factor, although sometimes it can be ethnic or national origin. Is your church culture predominantly a white, black, Latino, Caribbean, or Asian culture?

We don't seek these answers to divide or engage in some sort of political identity game. Quite the opposite. These divisions are already there in our behavior, expressions, and preferences. If we ignore them or act like culture is not a powerful force, the divisions will be glossed over for a time, but will eventually take root and become a problem. To be all things to all people means that we must be familiar with our own culture and cognizant of how we can make others feel welcomed and included. Being all things to all means that we purposely reject the advantages of a dominant culture and embrace all expressions. This is not about equal representation by the numbers; it is about the mission to gather the nations.

What's the best way to tell what the dominant culture in your group is? I think there are four simple things we can do to help identify which one is predominant. First, ask what is the majority group in your church. Is there an easily identifiable segment of society that is represented in greater numbers than any others? Second, look at the leadership. Is there a majority of one cultural group in leadership or that dominates key leadership positions? Third, ask minority members of your community what they think the dominant culture is in your church. Fourth, compare your church with churches that are comprised of only one race, ethnicity, nationality, or culture. Is there one whose culture most clearly compares to yours? What I mean by that is, does your church life look similar to a white church, a black church, a Latino church, or some other church that has primarily or exclusively one group?

If I look at my own church through these four lenses, the answer becomes clear as to the dominant culture. The majority in our church consists of white people of US origin. Although we are striving to be more diverse in our leadership, most of the leaders are from this background. When we ask groups that are not in the majority by population, they are clear that in their experience, the predominant culture is white American. And when we look at nearby monocultural churches, culturally speaking, we look most like a white, evangelical, suburban, middle-class church, even though ethnically we are diverse.

This means that if we do nothing in the area of cultural competency and inclusion, our church will continue to be dominated by a white American culture. Without realizing it, we will be as influenced by those aspects of identity as we are the Bible in terms of our expression, our communication, our assumptions, our worship styles, and so on.

Here is where this becomes of vital importance. History shows that if multiracial churches don't pay attention to cultural competence, they will eventually devolve to being almost exclusively populated by the dominant culture. The others will grow weary and eventually leave. Thus, if we ignore the need to be all things to all people, we will cease to be what God has called us to be.

Chapter 10

Halfway There

This was going to be the best New Year's Eve party ever. I was sure of that. My wife and I were helping to shepherd a singles ministry in our church, and the ministry had decided to throw a big celebration for the coming new year. Not only would all the amazing singles ministry brothers and sisters in the church be there, but we had invited the campus ministry as well. We spent weeks planning the event, which would include music, dancing, and an amazing array of food. My wife created an incredible menu that included new food being introduced in waves, so that at the top of every hour, fresh new options would be brought out continually throughout the night. This culminated with bacon-wrapped steak bites moments before midnight, some of the best morsels of bliss I have ever tasted in my life.

The food, the decorations, and just about everything else about the party was flawless and wonderful, except for the part that I oversaw. That would be the music. We didn't need to waste money hiring a DJ, I had confidently convinced myself; we would save a ton of money if I did it. Besides, who has better musical taste than I do? At least that was my not-so-humble opinion.

I spent hours and hours preparing the playlist of all the best songs and carefully crafting the order in which they were played to elicit the maximum effect and partygoing experience. There was just one tiny flaw in my plan. Evidently, my taste in music is not as universal as I might have thought. I was in heaven. Song after song was the perfect tempo and setting, building on the previous tune. But I had forgotten that, although there were a few people there my age or older, the vast bulk of the crowd was significantly younger. When I say significantly, I mean in the range of twenty years. They didn't enjoy the finest dance and hip-hop tunes the late '80s and early '90s had to offer. Most of the night was the music I liked, not what they would have preferred to hear.

They still had fun. They danced. They ate. They partied until well after midnight. But as the evening wore on, they grew increasingly weary with my choices of music. It was fun to have a few throwbacks at the beginning, but as hour melted into hour, they realized that the music of their generation was simply not going to get much play. The requests for current songs started slowly and then snowballed as the night wore on. The problem was that I had the playlist mostly set. I wasn't a real DJ who could just open some file on my computer and access the Billboard top 40 of that year. We were mostly stuck with the playlist I had created.

I learned something that night. It's really nice to be invited to the dance. But it's much better if they play some of your songs. Everyone was very gracious about my lack of foresight, but they weren't as engaged in the dancefloor festivities as they could have been had they been able to fully express themselves through the music that spoke to them.

It was one night, though, and I think most still remember it as a great party. But imagine if the same thing occurred at the next party and the next one, and the one after that. Suppose that party after party, year after year, over ninety-five percent of the songs were the tunes I liked, and I just was not open to what they wanted, so I offered some lame excuses but just would not budge. It wouldn't be long before the attendance at these parties dwindled drastically.

When it comes to cultural inclusion, I have heard an interesting statement a couple of times: "It's nice to be invited, but it's so much better to be asked to dance."

I should have thought about this. When we go to weddings or church dances or things of that nature, I don't like a lot of the music that's played. I still try to interact and dance a little, but I'm not a huge fan of much of the music made in the last ten to fifteen years. And I'm aware that this makes me one of those old guys that I never thought I would become. But every now and then, someone will remember that I absolutely love to dance to "Apache" by the Sugar Hill Gang and they will ask the DJ to play it for me. I will enjoy the party and dance and mingle, but when they play my song, that's when I can really get into it and express myself at a whole other level.

I think there's a universal truth here: It's nice to be asked to the party. It's really nice to be asked to dance. But we really feel valued when they intentionally play our song.

This illustrates an important difference that we will examine in this chapter. A community can be multiracial, but not multicultural. Multiracial is being invited to the party; being multicultural is hearing your music played throughout the dance.

DIVERSITY

"Plantations were diverse." I remember the first time I heard that observation. A friend of mine was graciously reviewing and giving me thoughts on a manuscript for a previous book I had written. He was part of an email thread with another friend who was also reviewing my manuscript. I don't recall exactly what the larger conversation was about now, but I remember that statement clearly. It is a stark truth.

We hear so much effort being made toward diversity these days at every level of society. We want diverse neighborhoods, diverse schools, diverse workplaces, and of course, diverse churches. Well, at least the prevailing public sentiment is that most people desire diversity; there are still many folks who don't want it but keep quiet and, I suppose, some that don't want it and are vocal about it.

There are varying degrees to which my country has achieved diversity. On the surface, it might appear that the United States of America is diverse. You see it when you go to the mall or to Walmart. Diverse neighborhoods seem to be increasing. But many of America's large cities, especially in the Midwest, where I have lived my whole life, are deeply segregated. School segregation is no better today than it was in the 1960s[10] and may even be getting worse.[11]

But what about churches? In the 1960s, Dr. Martin Luther King Jr. famously quipped that Sunday at 11 am was the most segregated hour of the week. Is that still true? It may be. It is difficult to get precise numbers, but most analyses of US churches have concluded that less than five percent of evangelical churches are multiracial.[12]

That means there is a lot of work to do if we believe that integration and diversity are good things. My own family of churches has historically been diverse. From the earliest days of our movement, the brothers and sisters were intentional about reaching out to all people and being a diverse fellowship. That instinct has remained as we now have well over 600 fellowships in countries throughout the world. In virtually every location, our church is diverse in whatever ways it is possible to be in that place.

We agree that diversity is good. Most churches from any tradition of faith would affirm that, even if they themselves are not diverse. Our society has adopted the idea that diversity is a positive thing and that we should strive for it wherever possible.

My premise here is simple: diversity is good, but it is not good enough. God's church should be diverse. I have already made that case. But Christian groups that are diverse racially can become satisfied with that, as though our work here is done. But we're only halfway there at the point of diversity. Diversity by itself means little.

That was my friend's point. Slave plantations in the South before the Civil War were diverse. It is very possible for an organization or locale to have diversity, at least visually. In fact, it is common to have visual diversity without ever reaching down further than that. One group dominates the power and the cultural norms, all the while enjoying the accolades that now come with being diverse. But is that God's plan for his people?

IT WAS ENOUGH

In 1997 my young bride and I walked into the Milwaukee Church of Christ for our first visit. Being an interracial couple made it difficult for us to find a church home that felt right. In our experience, we could choose from black churches and white churches, and there wasn't much in between. To make matters worse, we had just moved to a city that regularly finds itself in the top five of most segregated cities in the United States. So, we when stepped through the doors and into the fellowship hall where the worship gathering was about to begin, we couldn't believe our eyes. There were people of all races, ages, socioeconomic classes, and just about any other category I could think of. We were blown away by the variety of people. This was the first time either of us had ever seen anything like that, and we knew that we had found our home. And we were right.

But that was then. The world has continued to progress. Diversity was a buzzword back then. It was a good idea but was still relatively novel in many areas of society. Even though it has struggled to take hold in some of the important institutions in our society, like schools, churches, and even neighborhoods, diversity has become much more common in the everyday experiences of most people, especially young people. They have grown up with diversity as a given. It is no longer impressive or novel to them. Even if most people do not have particularly diverse lives, they feel that they do.

What that means is that when young people walk into a diverse gathering of disciples, they are not blown away like we were twenty years ago. They might appreciate it, but it is no longer the wonderful shock that it was for us.

It doesn't instantly fulfill their wildest dreams. In fact, it raises expectations for many.

Diversity itself used to be enough to feel like we had accomplished something great. But not anymore. Plantations were diverse, but they certainly were not inclusive. There was a clearly dominant culture at play. This is not to compare any diverse institution today to a slave plantation, but it illustrates in the extreme the point that you can have diversity and proximity without cultural inclusion or the sharing of influence and power.

Diversity is no longer enough. I say this for two reasons. The first is that it's biblically sound. As I have mentioned already, Paul constantly taught multicultural competency and cross-cultural skills to the new Christian communities. He instinctively grasped that without a firm commitment to be all things to all people, the great diversity of the gathering of the nations would fall apart. Diverse groups can run on excitement and passion for a time, but culture is a strong undercurrent. It will rip diverse communities apart if they are not skilled in cross-cultural connections. The second is that diversity itself is no longer impressive or enough to keep young people coming into our fellowships. Twenty years ago, a lot of people saw the diversity in my family of churches and stayed, with that being a big part of the reason (in addition, of course, to the truth of the gospel that they heard). But the "wow" factor is largely gone these days. Young folks come in, see the diversity, and immediately look for signs of multicultural inclusion. If they don't see or hear that pretty quickly, they will walk, oftentimes before even hearing the fullness of the gospel.

PRESENCE WITHOUT PARTICIPATION

In 1855 a highly regarded trial lawyer by the name of Edwin Stanton was hired as co-counsel on the McCormick reaper patent case. Stanton's partner in the case was high-powered Philadelphia patent lawyer George Harding. They hired a local attorney from Illinois who was more familiar with the lay of the land than the big-city barristers. When he arrived in Cincinnati for the trial, however, he discovered that Stanton did not want the participation of one whom he considered a country bumpkin and a backwoods lawyer. Harding only wanted his presence to show the clients that they had covered all their bases, but he wanted no input from him. The Illinois lawyer was denied a role in the trial and was snubbed by the rest of the legal team, especially Stanton. When the case was over, the country lawyer was sent a check for his services, but he at first refused it because he said that he was not truly included in the case and had done no work.

If the name Edwin Stanton sounds familiar, you've probably taken an American history course at some point in your life. Four years later, the President of the United States was informed by his cabinet that the best man for the job of secretary of war was none other than Edwin Stanton, and he was hired immediately by the president, Abraham Lincoln. He knew the name Stanton, you see, because that country lawyer was Abraham Lincoln.

Lincoln's great character shone through the mistreatment that he had received years earlier as he hired Stanton because he was the most qualified man and because he felt it was the best thing for the country.

According to those around him, Lincoln never once brought up the incident surrounding the trial and eventually became friends with Stanton. But this was despite the fact that Lincoln had experienced the stark difference between presence and inclusion. He knew the pain of not being allowed to participate in something and only being there for visual effect.

Being a diverse church is good. I believe it is God's plan. But a church can be multiracial or multiethnic and not be close to being multicultural. They are completely different things.

Your church might be highly diverse. That's good. Be proud of what God has done. But that's not enough. The question is whether your church has made efforts to include everyone, to go beyond the dynamics of cultural dominance. Is your church truly multicultural or has it neglected that aspect of church life or taken it for granted?

MULTIRACIAL BUT NOT MULTICULTURAL?

How would you be able to tell if your church is multiracial but not multicultural? There is no one simple litmus test for that, but here are a few clues to look for that can serve as symptoms that your congregation may have a lot of work to do in this area. The more of these elements you see present in your community, the more likely it is that your group needs to grow in its cultural competence.

What Do the Nondominant Cultural Groups Say?

It's not divisive to ask this question. It's necessary. If your church body is diverse, it will surely have different cultural groups, and you can bet on the fact that one of them tends to be dominant. So, go and ask members of the nondominant groups if they think the community is culturally inclusive. You might be surprised at the answers. I have talked to many faithful disciples who have no plans to leave their church but still struggle with feeling culturally accepted. They have described feeling fully acknowledged as long as they act "white" (the dominant culture in their particular church). I have been told by deeply committed Christians that they have resigned themselves to the fact that they will always feel like a visitor in a cultural sense, and that it can be emotionally exhausting at times.

A word of caution here. There is no such thing as a "typical" member of any culture. You cannot ask one or two people and assume that they speak for all members of their group. Either talk to a large sample or survey an entire group or the entire church. Don't just talk to one or two members who have been around for thirty years and fool yourself into believing that you now have the pulse of the whole church. Talk to long-time disciples and newer ones. Talk to young and old, male and female. Don't just listen to those who are happy, nor just to those who are unhappy. Have as many conversations as you can. Ask the question, "Do you ever feel like an outsider here culturally?" And then just listen.

Who's in Leadership?

If a leadership group is dominated by one cultural group, that likely will have a strong impact on the cultural diversity within a church family. This symptom by itself is not proof that multiculturalism is lacking. Simply because a church does not have a diverse leadership does not mean that it automatically will not be inclusive culturally, but it is a strong indicator. It is extremely difficult for groups of people to be represented fairly within the life of the larger group if they are not physically represented in positions of influence. Multicultural communities will make a priority of having multicultural leadership to preserve the life they want to develop and maintain.

On several occasions, leaders have approached me with a conundrum. They have a diverse leadership group, but they are still regularly fielding complaints and frustrations that church life is too monocultural and not inclusive. How can this be? There are several possibilities. One is that members of the leadership group who belong to the nondominant culture have assimilated into the dominant one so much that they no longer have validity as spokespersons for an alternate perspective. A second possibility is that they are in the group but almost as a token, and their opinion is not often heeded or is regularly outvoted in some way.

The third possibility is a little more delicate, but nonetheless can be a reality. Let's say a church staff consists of a white American congregational evangelist and his British wife. The campus evangelist is an interracial American of African and European descent who was raised exclusively by his white mother. The youth and family ministry couple consist of a husband who grew up in Kenya until he was fourteen and then lived in Canada until his late twenties, when he moved to the US three years ago. His wife is of Puerto Rican and Haitian descent. Another young staff couple are both white Americans. That's a fair amount of diversity for a small staff, but they continue to have issues of cultural inclusivity with the African American population, which is nearly fifty percent of the church. How can this be with such a diverse team? While I admire the diversity of the team, and you can never have a leadership group that is perfect in its makeup, you might be able to spot the problem. Yes, three of the eight staff members would be considered "black" by the color of their skin, but culturally speaking, not a single member of the staff grew up in the African American culture. That doesn't mean that it's wrong or must be a problem, but we cannot be fooled by skin color. Skin color does not equal culture, and this staff needs to recognize that. They will need to be highly proactive about including that cultural voice into their planning and into the direction of the community life, or it will simply not be heard.

Is One Group Almost Always Comfortable?

Most athletic trainers or coaches can agree on one simple rule. If you can talk comfortably while you're working out, then you are not pushing yourself hard enough. The thought behind that is that being able to talk easily means that your breathing is comfortable, and your heart rate is in a comfortable spot for your level of fitness. To get maximum training benefit, you need to push yourself beyond the point where you can carry on a conversation. If you're out for a nice jog with friends, no problem. But if you are working out to get in better shape, you will need to ditch the riveting conversation.

Following Jesus is never once advertised as easy. Jesus describes discipleship in often stark terms of carrying your cross; in other words, to do this you will have to die to your desires, preferences, and comfort zone. Being all things to all people is all about getting outside of what is your norm and what feels right to you. It is to put the interests of others ahead of your own and the mission of the kingdom as the priority in your life.

What does this all have to do with culture? Simply this: if you come to church gatherings on Sunday and small group meetings of various kinds throughout the week, and most if not all things seem normal, not strange, and they line up quite comfortably with the way you prefer things done, then either the group you are part of is not diverse or you are part of a dominant culture that does not venture from the norm very often, if ever.

There is no way around that. If everything your community does, including the sermon styles, the music types, the communication that goes on, the expressions of worship, the activities, and just about everything else seems normal, and you participate without ever having to think about how different it is from what you grew up with or might prefer, then you are part of a dominant culture. If something never seems uncomfortable or new to you, then it is highly likely that your church is not engaging in multicultural inclusion. If you've never thought about the topics presented in this book in any way, shape, or form, then you're probably from a dominant culture.

The opposite is also true. If many things seem uncomfortable or off to you, even if you've grown accustomed to them after a time, then it is very probable that you are in a nondominant group in a church that has yet to explore true cultural diversity.

We Don't Talk about That

My older sister was an excellent piano player when we were growing up. She could play almost anything, it seemed to me, and could have easily been a concert pianist had she chosen to pursue that as a career. I was always awed by her prowess on the ivories. And despite the fact that many people told me I could be just as good as she was because I had the hands for piano playing, I could never master more than chopsticks and the theme from *Jaws*. What was the difference? She put countless hours into piano practice and developed the skill. I never took a single lesson and refused to even try. Because of that, she was the Liberace of our family and I was the one people looked at and said things like, "Don't worry, you'll find something you're good at one day."

This might seem obvious, but typically people or groups are not good at things they don't work at. If church families do not talk about or train in cultural competency, the chances are high that they will not develop that skill. And it is a skill. A talent or gift is something you are born with. A skill is something that you develop through sustained effort.

Navigating our own culture is easy. It's like your native language, in that you begin to pick it up before you're even aware that you're learning something, and it becomes second nature. It's part of who you are. But steering your way through another culture is not typically a natural talent. There are precious few who seem to be able to do it almost naturally, but they very likely picked up the skills of cultural adaptability within their own culture, in which adaptability was taught to them. Most of us do not have that talent and will not develop the skill without sustained effort.

If a church does not train its people in cross-cultural communication and effective inclusion, they will not become all things to all people. They might be a wonderfully loving group, but the chances are low of them being culturally competent.

Similarly, churches that feel they do not need to pay attention to these matters because they are doing fine and there are bigger fish to fry are most likely going to limit their potential to grow and progress beyond where they are.

What Are You Teaching?

Those who do not know history are doomed to repeat it. This, or similar statements, have become a popular sentiment. If you are not taught something, this ignorance leaves you vulnerable. We cannot apply what we do not know.

Local church bodies may not feel equipped to regularly teach or train in the area of cultural competency and cross-cultural connection, but what about special workshops or larger regional conferences? If you look at what is emphasized and taught consistently at these events, you will quickly find what a church or family of churches truly values or wants to grow in. A lack of teaching on cultural and diversity issues is an indicator that these topics are not on the radar of those in leadership positions who make the decisions of what is taught. And that is another indicator that perhaps your group, while being diverse, is not multicultural.

Who Is Participating?

Another potential symptom that your group is multiracial but not yet multicultural is the participation level. If you observe the active participants in the various ministries and leadership positions throughout the church and notice that the percentage of nondominant culture brothers and sisters among them is less than their percentage of the congregation, that may be a sign of frustration and not feeling like they do not fit in and do not have a place.

A JOURNEY, NOT A DESTINATION

To be clear, not every symptom listed above needs to be present in order to realize that there is work to do in your fellowship. Conversely, having one or two of the elements present does not automatically mean that your church is not multicultural or does not care about the issues. And please don't equate a lack of multiculturalism with callousness or racism. There is not an automatic correlation there. Multiple factors are at play in a diverse church that has yet to fully understand or embrace the need for multicultural training and development.

We also need to be aware that this is not an issue like being pregnant. You're either pregnant or not; there is no in-between. We are talking about something with varying degrees, more like a sliding scale. I don't believe that it is possible to have a diverse church that is completely monocultural, nor is it realistic to think that we could ever achieve something like complete multiculturalism. This is a journey, and we should always seek to grow and improve. The point of recognizing that we have not embraced intentional growth in cultural competency as a community is to spur us on toward increased effort and growth in this area.

DEFAULT CULTURE

If I had spent more time before that New Year's Eve party getting song suggestions from younger people and including their preferences, the party would have been far more inviting. But I didn't do that, and it froze the music choices to what I think is good music. It didn't really occur to me that I was making choices conditioned by my own experiences, age, and taste. When I was preparing the playlist, I thought I was only selecting good music that everyone would enjoy. But my horizons were limited.

A community that does not strive for awareness, education, training, and advancement in cross-cultural areas will be locked into a default culture. If we are not actively pursuing being all things to all people, and if we don't include that as a value at every level of our church's life, then we will rarely, if ever, go beyond the dominant culture.

Imagine what it might have looked like in the first century if Paul had traveled throughout the Roman Empire from one Gentile town to the next proclaiming to them the amazing truth of the gospel of Jesus Christ and then explaining in great detail how they needed to embrace every aspect of the Jewish cultural life in order to properly worship God. What would that have done to the spread of Christianity?

Can you imagine the impact of that? It creates an entirely different gospel, doesn't it? You don't need me to say that. Paul said it. He strongly rebuked the Galatians for turning to a culturally mandated gospel that tied together aspects of Jewish culture and practice with inclusion into Christ.

I am astonished that you are so quickly deserting the one who called you to live in the grace of Christ and are turning to a different gospel—which is really no gospel at all. Evidently some people are throwing you into confusion and are trying to pervert the gospel of Christ. But even if we or an angel from heaven should preach a gospel other than the one we preached to you, let them be under God's curse! As we have already said, so now I say again: If anybody is preaching to you a gospel other than what you accepted, let them be under God's curse!

Galatians 1:6–9

In response to this imposition of the dominant culture on Christianity at the time, Paul called them to be acutely aware of cultural acceptance and inclusion of others. In short, he called them to understand that to be in Christ includes the call to be all things to all people. To not become a captive of a default culture, we must pay attention to these matters and be diligent.

Chapter 11

But I Won't Do That

In 1993 singer Meat Loaf released his album *Bat Out of Hell II: Back into Hell.* The first single release from that album was the power ballad "I'd Do Anything for Love." The song, written by Jim Steinman, soared to the top of the charts in twenty-eight countries and went platinum, energized by a video with a strange mix of the contemporary and medieval beauty-and-the-beast imagery. The song tells of all the things that the singer would do for love and how he would never lie to his lover. It is punctuated by the famous chorus as he dramatically quavers, "I would do anything for love, but I won't do that."

And that starts the great mystery. What is "that," Meat Loaf? What is it that you won't do? You won't eat vegan cheese? You won't spend twenty-four hours being forced to listen to music by the Backstreet Boys or nails on a chalkboard, which are so similar that I guess it was unnecessary to put both in the same sentence. You won't watch any Adam Sandler movie made after 1998? Those are all reasonable lines in the sand. But where have you drawn your line, Meat Loaf?

Meat Loaf has evidently laid down the parameters of what he will and won't do for love, but what about us? I would venture a guess that all of us in the body of Christ want harmony. We want to see our churches continue to grow and all the members of the family remain healthy. We want newcomers to feel welcomed and for longtime members to feel valued and included.

We would do anything for unity. Or would we? Are there certain lines that we draw, even if subconsciously? Could it be said that we would do anything for unity, but we won't do that? I believe that all Christians in multiracial churches want the fruit of complete unity, but there are some hindrances that can block us from that. There are some areas people are unwilling to work on or unwilling to overcome that can keep cultural inclusion from happening.

Let's look at some of the potential obstacles that we can face as individual Christians that might hinder us in our collective goal of moving toward cultural competency.

I DON'T LIKE IT

When I began to play organized team basketball in the early 1980s, everyone wore very short game shorts. That was the normal style. Michael

Jordan changed all that. He came out flying high, tongue wagging, and with baggy shorts that went past his knees. By the time the '90s rolled around, it seemed everyone was wearing their shorts like that. It quickly became the societal norm. All our clothes became big and baggy, and we liked it. But that has started to shift. As I walk into gym after gym to watch my fifteen-year-old play in his high school games, I have noticed that the boys want to wear shorts that are increasingly tighter and as high up from the knee as possible.

What is amusing, though, is that the athletic association in our state has now created rules forbidding players from rolling their shorts up at the waist to make them a little higher off the knee. Long, baggy shorts are now considered proper fashion by the powers that be, forgetting that when our generation started wearing that style three decades ago, it was considered "thuggish," and many schools tried to block it. So, what's the problem now with shorter basketball shorts? Nothing. It appears that perhaps they just don't like the style, so they find excuses to reject it.

It is all too easy to fall into that state of mind. We can convince ourselves that we have good reasons for not wanting something around or not taking part in it, but often the reason is little more than that it is unusual for us or does not meet our preferences. It is simply a matter of taste and no more, but we delude ourselves into thinking that we have much more profound reasoning.

What would be our response if the sermon on Sunday was theologically sound but was done in the style of a spoken word poem? Millennials might love it, but how would the older generations respond? What if a special song performance was done right after communion, but it was a moving and lyrically deep rap song? Some might not like it. But why? Could it be that some have just decided they don't like that type of music, even though lyrically it has the most possibility of being prophetic and carrying deep truths? Would it cause problems for some if a new family moved into the congregation that made a habit of just dropping in unannounced for a meal or fellowship time? That might not be your norm, but it is in many cultures. Would you embrace it or come up with a litany of excuses as to why it was unacceptable?

When we allow our preferences to define standards or limits, or to create boundaries within our groups, it can become a problem, because it restricts those who feel that their opinions or cultures are unwelcome.

THAT'S UNFAMILIAR

I have an element of my personality that annoys even me. It has been with me since I can remember. I don't like to try new things. As a child, I would not play sports or games that I wasn't good at. I wouldn't try foods that I didn't already know I liked. On the one hand, I accept that instinct and don't stray from it very often, but at the same time, I recognize how limiting it can be and wish that I could rid myself of it. Some of us are adventurous and willing to boldly go into the unfamiliar, but others of us avoid it like the plague.

This revulsion toward the unfamiliar kept me from trying things like yogurt, guacamole, and Indian food for years, until my wife finally forced me to taste them. And guess what? Turns out I love all those things. I didn't want to play ultimate frisbee for years, simply because I'd never participated in it. Once I finally played, I liked it. I was even certain that I wanted no part of a collectivist culture. I like my individualist experience and would keep to that, thank you very much. But then we started to travel and interact with these types of cultures, and I instantly fell in love with that worldview and embraced many aspects of it.

The instinct to stay with the familiar things we like works well when we are in our own little world that we have created, but as soon as we start to interact with other spheres, it can quickly become a real hindrance.

This obstacle is a bit different from the previous one. We might not be open to things because we don't like them. But often what keeps us from engaging in new experiences is that we think we won't like it, or we are afraid of the unknown. Let's just stick to what we know and like. What harm can come from that philosophy? Actually, it can cause a lot of harm when it comes to creating and maintaining a multicultural community. Additionally, when we stick to our own cultural practices, we may never experience the thrill and variety of doing things in a new and fresh way.

OOPS!

A few years ago, I was at the Minnesota state fair with my son and wife. My wife was in line to get a bucket of chocolate chip cookies from Sweet Martha's, something that has become a well-known and much-loved Minnesota tradition. The lines for these cookies can get long, so while we were waiting for her, my son spotted a friend of his from school and we went over to talk to him and meet his mother. His friend's family was from Somalia and were Muslim. If you know anything about Muslim Somalis, you know that they have a very strong culture that they have continued to maintain while living here in the United States. But I wasn't thinking through any of that as we approached my son's friend and his mother.

We struck up a conversation and talked for several minutes, even though it began to seem like his mother would rather have been any-where else than in this interaction. Eventually, we wished them a good evening, and I walked away. My son talked with his friend for another minute or two before noticing that his mother had come back from her conquest with a bucket full of cookies. He quickly said his goodbyes and joined us for the feast. It wasn't until later that I realized why his friend's mother was so uncomfortable. In their culture, it is not normal for a man to talk with a woman in public like that. She had graciously endured it, but I had committed a pretty big faux pas in that situation. I should have, at most, introduced myself as my son's father and left it for the boys to converse, not directly addressing his mother. Or, I could have waited for my wife to return and engage in a conversation. According to her cultural expectations, my behavior was inappropriate. Being that they live in the United States, I'm sure she has grown accustomed to this breech of their protocol as a member of the nondominant group, but I'm positive that it still felt rude to her.

It is the fear of making mistakes like this that can keep us from inter-acting with people of other cultures and trying to learn more about their customs, or engaging in cross-cultural interactions or activities. We don't want to offend someone. We don't want to look foolish. We don't want to expose our ignorance. So, we just avoid these interactions altogether.

How do we avoid making mistakes and offending others while inter-acting on a cultural level? We don't. We will make mistakes. We will do things that seem off-putting to others, if not downright rude. That's okay. If we keep in mind that we are engaging in the difficult work of being all things to all people and never forget why we are doing it, then the risks become acceptable. I am willing to look foolish or blow it at times, be-cause the larger goals of unity and inclusion are worth it. And I am more than willing to overlook these mistakes when I know that someone is try-ing to get to know me and my culture.

We were at an American-themed restaurant in Africa enjoying the food and ambience one evening when suddenly the entire wait staff came out to entertain the patrons. They played an American song, and while donning straw cowboy hats, attempted to perform a hoedown of some sort, punctuated by an occasional outburst of "hee-haw." They got several things wrong, and it almost came across as more of a caricature than an homage, but I knew they meant it as the latter, so rather than getting nit-picky and being offended, I enjoyed it for what it attempted to be.

People may make mistakes, but we can become a gracious commu-nity that gives people the space to learn from those mistakes. 1 Peter 4:8

reminds us that love in a community will cover over a multitude of sins. It will also smooth over a gaggle of mistakes and cultural offenses.

THAT'S TOO DIFFICULT

As a young teen, I was pretty convinced that being married was easy. You met someone, fell in love, and then got married. That was all there was to it. The magical part of that formula was falling in love. It would just happen and require no work. In fact, I thought that if you had to work at a relationship, it was probably a sign that this person wasn't the right one; it wasn't meant to be. Of course, my childish perception was about as opposite as you can get from true love. It doesn't just happen. It takes work, and lots of it. That is the hard truth about love and marriage.

Most of us understand that. Yet we can easily forget that this same principle applies when it comes to being part of God's family. It doesn't just happen without effort and intention.

In opposition of that, however, I have met a number of Christians who have resisted this. They were, in fact, staunchly opposed to any conversation about cultural competency, inclusion, or effort. One person even told me, "I shouldn't have to work that hard to be part of my own church." That's one way of looking at it, I suppose. But that mindset will result in culturally homogenous communities of exclusively like-minded people. It cements the dominant culture in place and leaves no room for growth or increasing diversity.

To be all things to all people requires effort. It demands that we get out of our comfort zone and embrace new and unfamiliar ways. You should have to work at it to be part of the diverse body that God desires us to be.

THIS IS DIVISIVE

Is it divisive for a husband and wife to talk about their areas of conflict and put in effort and hard work to come together as one? Is it divisive when two people who are locked into different ways of viewing an issue seek a conflict resolution specialist to help them come to a place of mutual understanding and harmony?

As obvious as the answers to those questions seem to be, there are many who stand opposed to a community working on its cultural diversity, because they claim that it will become divisive, that it creates divisions by fostering identities centered around things other than Christ. But this is naïve. Becoming culturally competent is not about exalting our ethnic or cultural identities, it is realistically admitting the power they have to influence our behavior. It is not dangerous to become aware of the dynamics of culture that can bring us together or split us apart. It is dangerous not to become aware of these dynamics and to act as though any cultural issues will simply resolve themselves and go away because we are Christians now.

Our cultural assumptions are not more powerful than our life in Christ. But we do bring cultural preferences, assumptions, and training into the kingdom. When Paul says that his goal is to become all things to all people, he is clearly indicating that he is willing to recognize the power of culture and to work at it so that it becomes a tool to advance the gospel rather than an obstacle that could limit its spread and effectiveness.

THE PHANTOM

New Jersey high school wrestling official Alan Maloney became a temporary internet celebrity when a story about a match he officiated went viral. Moments before the match, Maloney gave high school wrestler Andrew Johnson an ultimatum. Maloney had determined that Johnson's dreadlocks were inappropriate for a wrestling match, and despite the fact that Johnson had his dreads tied up properly in the manner required for long hair, Maloney, who was accused in 2016 of hurling racial epithets toward a fellow referee, decreed that either they must be cut off on the spot or the match would be forfeited. Johnson relented and had a coach cut off his locks, but someone in the crowd recorded the event and it went viral the moment it hit the internet. Maloney has since been suspended and will no longer be used as a referee in that school district.

Dreadlocks are often a deeply cultural expression. But this case seems to go beyond a situation where someone was just unfamiliar with that hair style and unsure what to do. We can't know what is in someone's heart, but it does seem that there was a good amount of prejudice involved and that prejudice, unchecked, turned into outright discrimination.

We don't like to talk about prejudice and discrimination these days. Most of us would like to wish them out of existence. But when we don't talk about things that are real, they merely become cultural phantoms. We don't speak of them, we don't see them (because we don't want to), but they are there nonetheless.

We would especially like to presume that the demons of prejudice, bias, discrimination, and the like do not exist in the body of Christ. Oh, that these scourges did not survive the waters of baptism. But they can, and at times they do. And we must be able to admit it. We have become so opposed to prejudice and racism that it has often become counterproductive. They are considered so bad in our culture that as Christians we dare not speak of them and certainly would not feel permitted or comfortable to admit that we have biases or feelings of prejudice that surface at times. We may not always be aware of these things, but when we are, we have learned that it is best to keep it quiet. They become the unspeakable sins, which locks them in just under the surface.

There are times that some of us oppose cultural inclusion in general or certain forms of it because we are outright prejudiced against some groups or their cultural expressions. To become culturally competent communities, we must be able to confess prejudice and bias, and to do so without reprisal or being labeled and ostracized. We can only work through sins when we can admit them openly and find acceptance and love to help us conquer them.

ETHNOCENTRISM

Through our first several years of marriage, my wife and I had many conflicts that arose over cultural differences. One of the most pronounced areas of irritation for me was when we went out in public. I was raised to keep a low profile when in a public setting. If you were talking with someone, you did so as quietly as possible so as not to disturb anyone else and so they couldn't hear your conversation. You certainly didn't want to draw any unnecessary attention or impinge upon others in any way. Then I was suddenly thrust into a relationship with a person who was raised quite differently. Her culture does not individualize in the same way that mine does, so there is not an emphasis on my space versus yours. We are all in this together, and being loud and demonstrative in public is the norm.

For years I was embarrassed by this when we would go out with other people of this culture. It bugged me way more than it should have. I viewed it as rude, arrogant, and lacking class. I could not conceive of any way, shape, or form in which that could be viewed as appropriate or proper behavior. My way was better. In fact, my way was the only right way.

That kind of thinking is called ethnocentrism. It is the viewpoint that my cultural practices and values are superior to others. It is one thing to prefer my culture. It is another thing to believe that my culture is inherently better. That will leave me closed to understanding and valuing other cultural expressions. And if I am closed to them, there will be no attempts at engaging in them or including them in the life of the community.

It is natural to prefer our own primary culture, but ethnocentrism is a danger to a community. We must seek to be aware of it and confront it in ourselves when we detect it. Ethnocentrism is a form of arrogance and can be a serious threat within the walls of a multiethnic church.

THE SINGLE STORY

In 2009 author and speaker Chimamanda Ngozi Adichie delivered an address for a Ted Talk on the danger of the single story. In it, she warns about reducing people from other places and cultures to a limited perspective in which we think that everyone from that place or group is basically the same. She describes growing up in Nigeria with domestic helpers. All she ever perceived of them was that they were poor. One day she went to the house of one of the boys who worked in her home and was shown some of the beautiful artwork the boy's mother had made. She was unexpectantly surprised, because all she had ever thought or imagined about this boy was his poverty. She never dreamed of him having beauty, artwork, and passion in his world.

When Adichie grew older and went to university in the United States. she was greeted by an American roommate who was surprised that she spoke English so well, knew how to use a stove, and when asked to play some of her tribal music, instead produced her favorite Mariah Carey tape. Her roommate, Chimamanda discovered, had a well-meaning but patronizing pity for her life as an African. This girl, says Adichie, had a single story of her as an African that left no possibility for a more complex understanding of her background and culture beyond that singular stereotype. She interpreted all Africans through a lens of catastrophe, poverty, and backward civilization.

We can all fall prey to the phenomenon of the single story. Whether it be ethnicity, nationality, economic status, or religious affiliation, we can flatten everyone from a specific group into one thing, one simple commonality, one story.

Adichie wisely points out that it is impossible to properly engage with a people or a place without understanding the complexity of stories and experiences of that place or person. The single story robs people of their dignity and makes it difficult to see them as equal, multifaceted humans. The single story, Adichie says, creates stereotypes, and the problem with that is not that stereotypes are untrue but that they are incomplete. They turn one story into the only story.

POLITICS

"I almost didn't come today, but I'm glad I did." I cannot tell you how many times I have heard that sentence or one like it just after we have completed giving a *Crossing the Line: Culture, Race, and Kingdom* workshop at a church. In the past two years, my wife and I have given over fifty of these workshops in the United States and beyond, and inevitably I hear a sentiment of that nature. What usually comes next is that the person didn't want to come because they didn't want to get beat up over their political views or didn't think the church should engage in politics. They often tattle on others as well, not only informing me that they themselves were not going to attend, but telling me of others who didn't come for those same reasons.

Although I've grown accustomed to this response, it's still curious to me that so many would automatically assume that topics of culture, race, and the kingdom of God are going to be political in nature. Now, when they say "political" what they usually mean is that they assume that the workshop is going to take a decidedly liberal view of things and bash their conservative values.

Let me be clear, I am not taking political sides or denigrating one political philosophy while exalting another. I reject partisanship at all levels. I think Christians should have an approach to politics that is so novel to the categories that the world offers that it becomes nearly impossible to label us.[13]

But the hesitance that many have expressed to me reveals that for many, the topics of diversity and cultural inclusion sound like part of a worldly political agenda, so they resist it at all costs. Most are relieved when they come and hear and discover that this is nothing of the case. But that fear is real and must be addressed. Many people will hear that your church wants to become more culturally competent and inclusive and work on these issues and will automatically assume that the church has jumped the shark and allowed itself to be infiltrated by some sort of liberal agenda.

Slavery is an issue that transcends politics, but it has often become political in nature. Human trafficking is not a political issue, but it can get mired in political posturing. Inequity or abuse in the criminal justice system is not a political matter but can easily be coopted as such. Abortion should not be a political issue but has often been used as a political tool on both sides. We can make almost any issue partisan by using it as a pawn in our so-called culture wars or partisan divisions.

When that happens, as is the case with cultural diversity, we cannot just ignore it. We must make the case that being culturally competent is not a political trend; it is a biblical mandate. We must make a concerted effort to demonstrate to those who view everything as political that, while this may occasionally overlap with programs and agendas that they will see outside of the church, that does not mean that it is worldly. Becoming all things to all people is as biblical as it gets.

Several years ago, I was speaking on these topics in my home church, and I wanted to demonstrate a statistic that I had seen published by a US government task force and cited by multiple organizations as being accurate. Without thinking much about it, I found a colorful graph that demonstrated that statistic and used it in a PowerPoint slide. The graph was from what is considered to be a liberal news site, a fact of which I was unaware at the time. Needless to say, there were a couple of people for which it did not go unnoticed, and they immediately took offense at it, viewing it as a political statement. I'm glad they pointed that out to me. It was my mistake and one that I learned from.

We must stand up for what is right but also be careful that we do not set up needless obstacles by allowing cultural inclusion to be mistakenly viewed through the political lenses of the world.

PICK UP A SHOVEL

Any one of these areas can derail us from being culturally competent people or can become a point of division in a church family. We must go beyond the Meat Loaf philosophy and be willing to do whatever it takes to continue to work toward unity in the manifold body of Christ.

Chapter 12

East and West

One of my favorite movie scenes comes early in the original *Jurassic Park* where Dr. Ian Malcolm tries to explain chaos theory to Dr. Sattler as they wind their way through the park in a driverless car. Malcolm illustrates his point by dripping water on Dr. Sattler's hand twice and noting that each time, the drop of water runs down her hand on a different path. What Dr. Malcolm then explains in simple terms is the chaos theory that states that apparent randomness within systems is the result of underlying patterns that are often unseen. Tiny differences in conditions that are unnoticeable to the casual observer can result in widely different outcomes. If you've ever watched American game shows on television, think of the Plinko game on *The Price Is Right*. You can drop your chip from the same spot at the top but watch it land in different slots at the bottom. It can be the difference between winning $10,000 or nothing. While it looks like you are dropping from the same exact spot, the slightest change in hand position, angle of release, and many other factors can result in wildly different endings.

The principles of chaos theory can apply to people in many situations. Why does the same action of church discipline wind up with different results when applied to different people, for example? It might seem random, but there are many small factors that have an impact. Two young men both fall prey to sexual immorality before marriage on multiple occasions. They both fail to take advantage of the help offered them, spurn advice, and repeatedly fall into the sin. As the biblically prescribed steps of church discipline are followed, the time comes when both are removed from the community in an effort to shock them into repentance. One brother is immediately stung by the action and brought to his senses. He humbles himself to the biblical standard and works hard with the brother who is provided as spiritual support to help gently restore him to God and to the community. The other young man thinks about it for a time, and then decides he doesn't need that church anyway. He just moves on and finds another church more to his liking. The same action has been employed but with opposite results.

There are countless variables in situations like these that could lead to different results, but in these two cases, which are true stories, I have always suspected that cultural conditioning played a big part. The prescription of removing someone who refuses to be helped by the community in order to change their behavior to bring it in line with King Jesus comes from a biblical culture that was fundamentally Eastern. It was rooted in honor-and-shame, community-first cultures rather than Western cultures that operate on a guilt-and-innocence basis and foster individuality.

The brother who returned to the church community was from an African country. He had been brought up with the honor-and-shame ethic, which dictates that the primary determiner of right and wrong is in the eyes of the community. The other brother hails from the Midwest in the United States and was reared in the Western guilt-and-innocence culture, where right and wrong are established by standards and laws, and the community works to instill these sensibilities into the individual so that they are guided by those standards internally with no concern as to what others think. There are strengths and weaknesses to both cultural types.

The African brother was stung deeply by the loss of community and what he viewed as being shamed in their eyes. Since the community determines right and wrong, they spoke loudly, and he was driven to change.

The American brother was brought up in a society that didn't see sexual trysts as much of a problem. As long as there are two consenting adults, all is good. He was also taught that the individual has the right to get what they need and want, as long as it doesn't hurt anyone else. Even though he was baptized into Christ and wanted to be a disciple, he never truly challenged those core cultural beliefs. And when he was told that he was wrong for having sex outside of marriage, he never really embraced that value. When he was disciplined by the community, he didn't care that much. His internal monitor told him that his actions were okay, and his cultural training had taught him that what others thought really didn't matter. He would just go find another community with no sense of guilt following him, because in his eyes he had done nothing that was truly wrong. He had a sin issue, but his culture played into it and made the situation worse.

That's the power of culture. It can even condition us toward a standard of right and wrong. In general terms, Western cultures believe that the law or the rules determine right and wrong, and what others might think is not a major factor. Eastern cultures tend toward the community being the judge of what is shameful and what is not, and if the community does not judge the action as an offense, then there is no guilt.

Sociologists label this Western style of culture as guilt-and-innocence cultures, or what I will refer to from now on as guilt cultures. Eastern cultures are typically honor and shame based. These two broad cultures—guilt based and shame based—are both widespread, and with increased global emigration and mobility they often interact and clash with one another around the world. We will summarize the broad characteristics of these two worldviews in this chapter. It is important to understand some of the basic values and life approaches of these two cultures, because in a diverse church, it is likely that there are people bearing characteristics of each group.

There is a third cultural type, separate from Eastern and Western cultures. These groups tend to come from tribal and island locations that have been more isolated in the past. We will refer to these as fear cultures and will only briefly discuss them at the end of the chapter. You may well have members of your group with roots in one of these fear cultures, but they are far less prevalent than the two to which we will give most of our attention.

WHICH ARE YOU?

There has been so much overlap and mixing of cultures, especially in my country, the United States, that it is rare to find someone who completely meets all the norms when it comes to identifying whether you, or someone else, falls within the boundaries of a Western guilt or Eastern shame culture. For most people, it is a matter of degree, but it is also true that most people lean toward one or the other. As I look at some of the markers, it becomes clear that I have been rooted firmly in a Western cultural worldview. My wife is an interesting case. She has lived in the Western culture of America her entire life, and her family has been rooted here for centuries. Yet they have maintained many of the characteristics and values that would be more closely identified with the Eastern-style cultures of Africa from where her ancestors came long ago. She has been influenced by Western culture but still carries many Eastern features.

Here are a few questions that will help distinguish between classic Western and Eastern instincts.

1. Is the best way to train for a job to: (a) get a formal education, or (b) apprentice to and observe someone?

2. Are illnesses best initially treated by: (a) a doctor, or (b) a traditional family remedy?

3. When you do something wrong are you most bothered by: (a) your internal conscience, or (b) the disapproval of the community around you?

4. Should inappropriate behavior be remedied by: (a) formal law and punishment, or (b) informal tradition and consensus of the community?

5. Is the key to starting a new business or getting a good job to: (a) have a good business plan or strategy, or (b) know the right people and have the right contacts?

6. Should the possessions of a deceased family member be (a) distributed by a formal will, or (b) passed on by the family leader?

7. Do you think of family members over seventy as (a) an obligation, and needed care must be arranged for them, or (b) someone to be respected and revered, and caring for them when needed is an honor and sacred duty?

8. Does the definition of family include (a) parents, spouse, and children, or (b) a large network of all extended relations?

9. Should family events begin (a) on time, or (b) once the key people have arrived?

10. When you have money, should you primarily (a) save and invest it, or (b) foster relationships, help family members in need, and spend it on needs and wants while you have it?

11. Do you deeply desire (a) equality and fairness in life, or (b) to be well thought of and respected by those in your community?

12. At a meeting, should the person with the most influence be (a) the person with the best job or the best idea, or (b) the oldest or most respected person in the room?

Any "A" responses would align you with the typical values of a Western-based culture, while the "B" responses would correlate more with an Eastern approach.

As I stated, I would answer "A" for the majority of these questions and others like them, while my wife would answer "B" for many of them. Just take a moment to go back through the list and imagine how that works in a single household. You can imagine that we have had numerous misunderstandings and differences of opinion over the years. Now extrapolate those challenges to a large church body, and you can begin to imagine the chasms that can easily exist in expectations and assumptions that people bring with them into the community.

THE TALE OF THE TAPE

At their core, Western cultures are rooted in individualism. Most of their customs and values emanate from the belief that the individual is autonomous and that the freedom of the individual is the greatest value that determines most everything else. Nearly everything about Western civilization moves us toward personal autonomy and reduction in hierarchy. Eastern cultures value the collective over the individual. The greater good of the group is more important than the desires or personal freedoms of the single human. Thus, the cultural ethics of the Eastern person steer the individual toward togetherness, community good, and reduction of self, which includes valuing the perspective of the community and one's role in working toward the advancement of the group rather than personal achievements and private property.

We'll look briefly at a few other differences between the Eastern and Western perspectives here just to get a feel for the differing worldviews and potential for conflict when there is a church or other group that contains people rooted in both backgrounds, but we will return in later chapters to many of these areas and consider them in greater detail.

When it comes to relationships, the guilt cultures of the West seek equality and fairness. The shame cultures of the East see this as a disregard for the strength of the community and find the struggle for equality in relationships to be disrespectful. In their eyes, those who may be coming from a strictly Western approach don't know their place in society or have the proper deference toward earned status. They embrace hierarchy as the way to preserve the life of the group. The challenge for people from Western cultures is that they view hierarchy as oppressive and an imposition on the rights and freedoms of the individual. They see the Eastern view as dismissive of the potential of each person. The West wants a vote on everything to ensure that every voice is heard and respected. The East wants stronger leaders who are trusted to put the good of the group first.

There is a wide difference in the way Eastern and Western cultures approach how they handle time. The West values completing tasks as being of primary importance and sees time as a valuable commodity that should never be wasted. The East views relationships and events with people as the more important commodities rather than time, which is cyclical. Time, in their eyes, will always roll on, and connections with people should never be cut short nor should one be hurried because of the march of the clock. Easterners will typically see the Western method as rude, demeaning, cold, and impersonal. Westerners will view the Eastern style as inconsiderate, unorganized, and disrespectful.

What about communication of the truth? Surely there is common ground there. Of course, both sides want to ultimately know truth, but when it comes to communicating styles with others, there can be a large gap. The classic guilt cultures of the West value "getting to the point," and "shooting straight," because they prefer straightforward speech that communicates truth with no sugar coating or hedging around. To shame groups, this can be rude and cause people to lose "face," or respect, in the eyes of others. For them, it is better to avoid embarrassing someone by disagreeing with them, telling them no, or saying something negative about them directly. They value harmony, while the West places a higher worth on honesty. In their eyes, the shame cultures are willing to engage in deception, lies, and manipulation.

Because of their individualistic tendencies, Westerners approach money with the goal of being financially independent. They don't want to depend on others and expect each person to carry their own load. Charity will be given, but only to those who are truly in need at no fault of their own. This is seen as greedy, stingy, and flatly wrong to people of Eastern cultures. Wealth is to be shared with anyone in need, with little attention to the cause for the need. There is reciprocity, in which those with resources provide for those without in exchange for power, influence, and honor within the community. For Easterners, this is the way the community provides for everyone. For Westerners, it looks and feels corrupt and exploitative toward those who are expected to help someone who could earn their way but is not.

Food preferences are not exempt from the cultural divide. Westerners value efficiency. Collective cultures tend to prefer generosity and hospitality. When we are having guests over, my tendency is to make it as simple as possible. Why we are meeting is more important than the food. It can be frozen pizza or delivery from somewhere. This is horrendous to my wife. She wants each meal to be special so that the guests feel loved and honored. She thinks my way is dismissive of people and loses the sense of sharing special meals and food types with others. I am often tempted to see her preferences as over the top and taking unnecessary trouble. Our positions are indicative of the typical West-East divide.

As discussed above, Western cultures normalize behavior primarily through guilt and laws. Laws are passed and enforced, and members of society are conditioned to feel guilty for breaking rules or laws. Westerners tend not to care what others think, as long as they are technically innocent before the law. To Easterners, this comes across as being shameless. They regulate behavior primarily through the fear of being dishonored and public pressure. The relationships around you and the opinion of the community decide what is acceptable and unacceptable, right and wrong. This is viewed as corrupt and lawless by those from guilt cultures.

When we refer to Western cultures and Western civilization, this primarily refers to North America, Europe, and Australia. These cultural values, though, are constantly spread and pushed around the world. In previous centuries, that largely came through colonization and empire building. It continues in contemporary times through information colonization and the soft power of media and influence. The estimated population of the West is just over 1 billion.

Eastern cultures emanate mostly from the Middle East, Africa, and Asia. They tend to spread not through influence and power but through emigration to other parts of the world. The estimated population of the East is over 4.3 billion people.

FEAR-BASED CULTURES

The last broad culture type that we will consider briefly is fear-based cultures, which are most often identified with tribal and Caribbean groups and are estimated at about 1.4 billion globally. They are driven neither by individualistic nor collectivistic instincts. Rather, the driving force in these cultures is animism, which is the belief that supernatural powers organize, inhabit, and animate everything in the material universe. Life is about recognizing, properly fearing, and appeasing the spirits that are in everything and constantly part of life.

These cultures tend to value things like sacred knowledge that is passed along by the wisdom of elders, omens and signs, and the knowledge of where the spirits reside and how to placate them. They have a strong sense of fate, which leads them to believe that they are often little more than pawns in the hands of spiritual forces. Mystic rituals have great power and are not something to be ignored or mocked. Behavior is regulated through fear of angering the spiritual forces or opening the door to evil and negative repercussions.

There is an interesting point here that should not be missed. We can't make an argument that either Western culture, Eastern culture, or the tribal fear culture is superior or inferior inherently. There are elements of better and best in all of them, as well as there being serious flaws and negative components in each. Each one is better suited toward certain outcomes, and if we assume those outcomes are inherently superior, then we can easily assume that cultural type is superior as well. One thing we can know for sure, however, is that the predominant culture expressed in the biblical texts and worldview is that of the East. The Hebraic/Jewish culture was unmistakably honor-and-shame based and would much more closely align with the other classic characteristics of the Eastern worldview.

That doesn't mean that the Eastern culture should be considered the ideal, but it does mean that we should be firmly aware of this as we approach Scripture. We don't want to make the mistake of reading Western cultural assumptions into a world that was firmly Eastern.[14]

CONCLUSION

All these cultural types have strengths and weaknesses. They all have things that are conducive to a biblical culture and lifestyle, and they all have elements that make it challenging for disciples who have been conditioned by them to fully embrace a kingdom way of life. If you are part of a multiethnic church, then chances are almost certain that you have brothers and sisters with roots in all these groups, or at least certainly from the East and West.

That will bring challenges. We have yet to dive into specifics of how we can navigate some of these differences and turn the challenge of multiculturalism into a strength rather than a handicap, but the purpose in this chapter has been simply to help us understand these broad cultural types and be able to identify where we and others are coming from in our cultural orientation, which will help us down the road when we are considering how to bridge these gaps and come together as one community.

In the next eight chapters, we will look at some of the areas where there is a bridge to be built, and for each area we will outline a few principles that, if we can keep them in the forefront of our minds, will help us to close the gap.

Chapter 13

Family

"We're going to a funeral this weekend," my wife stated matter-of-factly. This took me a bit off guard because we had no previous plans that I knew of to go to a funeral. I answered carefully because I recognized that there were three important factors operating here. The first was that it was possible that my wife had told me of upcoming events or plans and I had forgotten all about them. I'm not fully admitting that I do things like that, but there have been accusations made. The second thing is that funerals are not something that are really planned in the long term, so they rarely come at a convenient time, nor do you get a lot of advance warning. The third factor is that we were potentially talking about family, and that can be a delicate subject and must be navigated carefully.

I responded with, "Yes, it's sad, how are you doing?" I had masterfully crafted this reply so as to tactfully elicit the information as to whose funeral we were evidently attending. It didn't work, so eventually I had to take a more direct approach and just ask who had passed away. She responded with a name I had never heard before. It didn't sound like any relative, and I was certain that this was not someone we knew from our church family. In retrospect, my next statement may not have been so wonderfully constructed.

"Um . . . why are we going to that funeral?"

"Because it's family," she retorted with a tight-lipped control that told me I was now on precarious ground. Danger, Will Robinson!

I bluntly spurted out, "I don't remember anyone by that name." This was not my best work.

"It's my granddaddy's sister's son's nephew." To be honest, I don't remember if that is the correct formula. It seems like it was even more complicated than that, but as I write this, there is no way I'm going back to my wife to confirm what the relationship actually was.

"Do we even know this person?" Those were the next words that slipped past the review board of my brain and out of my mouth.

Her terse reply ended the conversation, "It's family."

The trump card had been played, and I was out of options. This was an event that would now be irrevocably added to the Google calendar.

The problem here is that, although it has taken more than twenty years, my wife and I still need to hash out and bring together two very different cultural views of what is family and the need to connect with others.

WHAT IS A FAMILY?

The disparity between my wife's views and mine of what a family is are very real. We continue to have to navigate those waters. My definition of family is very restricted. When growing up it was my dad, mom, sister, and me. I still view that as my family, although now I would consider that my secondary family. My primary family is my wife and our boys. That's it. I understand that I have many other relatives, and I love them, but I don't feel the same connection or sense of obligation as though they are "family."

For my wife, that is completely foreign and can feel loveless to her. She grew up with a large extended network of family that included all blood relations but could include others who were brought into the clan through marriage or close relationships. Not only was her definition of family greatly increased beyond mine in sheer volume, there was also no distinction made between primary and secondary family members. Family is family. The reach of sharing resources and unquestioned help is extended to anyone included in the wide net of the family definition. To me, that feels overwhelming, it's hard to figure out, and it leads to abuse as you feel obligated to help people you barely know or haven't seen for twenty-five years simply because they are part of this massive group that has been labeled "family."

For the longest time, I failed to recognize that these differing definitions became a factor for us in our church families as well. I was much quicker to embrace the boundaries of our small group, which our community calls "family groups." That was our group. That's it. It's simple. Those are the folks that we need to connect with, help out, and build relationships with. My wife's attitude was wholly different, and to be honest, it drove me nuts for years. She would branch out constantly and stretch herself quite thin as she spent time with, counseled, and assisted people from other family groups all over the city. "Why do you keep doing that?" I would ask her. We needed to focus on our family group or our specific ministry when we went into fulltime ministry. In her mind, though, she *was* focusing on the family. In my mind, she was going outside of the family and stretching her limited personal resources to irresponsible levels. It was our divergent views of what families are that led to that dichotomy.

THIS DOESN'T FEEL LIKE FAMILY

It's not just the boundaries of who is and who is not included in a family that can be different. The concepts of what a family does and the purpose of family can be totally unlike as well.

Several years ago, a young single woman who was African American began coming to gatherings of our church. Then she began to come more regularly to events and get-togethers, and after a few months had studied the Bible with some of the sisters and was baptized into Christ. Not long after that, she shared with my wife that she had almost stopped coming to church gatherings and was still struggling a bit to feel like she belonged. When my wife asked her what was causing her to feel that way, she revealed that she had heard us many times say that church is supposed to be a family, but it didn't feel like family to her. Of course, my wife asked her what she felt was lacking in that area. Her response surprised me, but my wife understood her sentiments immediately.

Why didn't it feel like family to her? When she first started coming out to Sunday worship gatherings, nearly every week someone invited her to go to a restaurant for lunch with them. Sometimes it was a group of singles and sometimes it was a family or several families, but almost without fail someone offered to take her out to lunch.

What could be wrong with that, you might wonder? How would that make her feel like the church did not act like a family? Some of you might be confused while others of you have a good idea of what the issue was.

They took her out to eat. In her mind, family has you in their home. Going to a restaurant felt like a meeting to her. In her experience, families don't go out for a meal like that. That is formal. It sends a signal that we're not quite close enough to have you in our home. If people had brought her home with them and had a homemade meal, that would have met her expectations of family to a much greater degree than a restaurant meal and a quick hour together. Family spends the day together with no sense of "it is now time for us to go our separate ways and back to our separate spheres." For many people of a similar cultural background to hers, the lives of family members are intertwined. You are always together and do everything together. Going out to a restaurant for a meal and then parting ways feels more like a blind date or a business meeting than anything that families would do.

Does this mean that the folks who were extending lunch invitations did something wrong? No. But it does mean that they were limiting themselves to one cultural paradigm and probably not considering different perspectives.

I would venture a guess that a big part of this is convenience. I definitely tend toward the cultural perspective that would lead me to invite someone to a quick meal and then go our separate ways. It is much more time consuming and inconvenient to drive all the way back to our house, cook a meal, eat that meal, spend a lazy afternoon with the person, and then perhaps need to drive them way back across town later in the day. That's too much work. But my wife has tried her best to train me that family is inconvenient. You don't apply scales of ease and convenience to family. You sacrifice your time, your energy, or whatever else. Relationship trumps everything else.

It can be difficult and uncomfortable for a community in which people have very different expectations of family. For some, the family dynamic is expressed simply by being together. For others, it comes from sharing your homes and the mundane parts of life, not just by going out for coffee or a meal together. This is not easy to navigate, but we will discuss some strategies to help do that at the end of this chapter.

THE PURPOSE OF FAMILY

Many of the pathways of my life were seemingly already laid out for me before I was old enough to even understand them. These expectations were often subtly, and sometimes directly, communicated at various points so that I would never fail to understand. "When you go to college," was a phrase I heard often growing up. It was never "if" but always "when." I also heard at various times about "when you get married," "when you live on your own," and "when you move away." There were other messages, of course, but just from those I got a certain picture of what life would be like. I was being prepared to become adequately educated, get a career, move away, and begin a family of my own. I would, obviously, continue to love and be connected in certain ways to my parents and family of birth, but there was no question that the training I received was aimed at me becoming autonomous, separate, and having my own family one day.

My wife's rearing was different, as you may have already figured out. The expectations passed along to her had much more to do with the eternal loyalty that family members were expected to show toward another. Education, career, and living on her own were all possibilities but were not basic expectations that were assumed. Those things paled in comparison to the family connection. Always sticking together and caring for one another, no matter the need, were of a much higher order than individual goals or achievements.

In short, my upbringing was preparing me for life on my own. Much of her upbringing was preparing her for a life of interdependence and connection. These two extremes represent some of the differences that disciples can bring with them when it comes to their assumptions regarding the purpose of family. And this can color the expectations that we have for our church families. When some of us approach the concept of church family as something that should prepare us for an independent spiritual life, while others are expecting interdependence and lifelong reliance on one another, it can be difficult to meet all those needs and expectations.

DROP BY ANYTIME

Is it rude to just drop by someone's house with no prior communication and stay around for an indeterminant amount of time? It tends to feel that way to me. For my wife, not so much.

I remember that when we were in Wisconsin, my wife enjoyed the church we were with but there was something about it that didn't quite set right with her, though she could never place her finger on it. Then one afternoon, we stopped by the home of a family that had recently moved into town. The husband is Nigerian, and the wife was a black woman from Canada. I don't recall the purpose, but we were just swinging by their house that afternoon for a moment, completely unannounced. They invited us in immediately and enveloped us with love, food, and fellowship, and we wound up staying until quite late that evening. That was the first of many such unplanned days with them. But after that first time, it hit my wife what had been nagging at her. It was that informal, you-are-family feel that she got from just coming over with no plans and taking life as it comes. There were no itineraries, no schedules, and no boundaries. It was just community, family, and fellowship. Her soul had longed for that because it's what she grew up experiencing as true family.

To this day, she enjoys it if people come over unexpectedly to hang out, and she loves homes where she feels welcome to do the same. This is not a need I have to make me feel like we are family. In fact, my natural reaction can be to feel a bit unprepared and put out if people just show up. I've learned to adapt and appreciate the informality of this style of family, but I do still feel a pull to have a plan and be able to roll out the red carpet a bit when guests come over.

Here's the rub, though. That nagging feeling that my wife had was, at the time, an unexplainable sense that the church was claiming to be family but was not, not in the way that she understood and loved.

This is a form of the relationship versus task orientation in culture. I was raised in a culture that approaches interactions with other people as a series of tasks. You schedule tasks. You plan for them and make them great. And then they end, and you go on to the next task. For other cultures such as my wife's, relationships cannot be planned or scheduled;

they happen. Life together cannot be bound by clocks and calendars. For her, family is something you are, not something you do. That makes sense to me now, but it still often feels foreign in many respects.

BRIDGING THE GAP

It's one thing to recognize these potential differences that a diverse community can have as a result of divergent cultural approaches and traditions. Being aware of the differences is important, but that only goes so far. What can we do once we have discovered these differing views and approaches? This is of particular importance, I believe, when it comes to the understanding of family. Being a family is such a central aspect of the purpose and meaning of the church that it can be incredibly problematic if we cannot come to a common set of assumptions and expectations.

In the process of coming together as we include a wide array of cultural worldviews and continue to form a new culture in Christ, communication and education are a key starting point.

None of the areas of cultural impact are simple or easy to bring together, and the issue of family can be daunting because it is so foundational. The church was formed by Jesus to be a family and operate as such, but we often bring so many different expectations and expressions of what that is exactly that it can feel almost impossible to bring all these different threads together in one group.

The Biblical View

The first thing we must ask for any bridge-building effort is whether there is a clearly defined biblical view on the topic. In this our first case, Jesus made clear that his family of identity and security would be that of believers rather than the normally delineated family of blood relations (Mark 3:31–35). The early church operated much more like a family than just a religious organization, as they devoted themselves to sharing all aspects of life together, including their wealth and possessions (Acts 2:42–47). The family of God should be our priority, and there should be a high standard of sharing in common everything we have. That means that the Western tendency toward individualism will often be at odds with the more Eastern-oriented view of family that we see in the New Testament. This is not to imply that if you grew up in a Western culture that your experience of family is sinful or invalidated, but it does mean that you might be called upon more than others, in certain areas, to adjust your expectations of what family is and how it should operate.

The first obstacle, though, that must be embraced by all is that when we enter God's kingdom, the brotherhood and sisterhood of believers becomes our family of priority and identity. The challenge for first-century people was transferring their loyalty and identity from the group of their birth family to that of the family of God, and that challenge is similarly faced by those from Eastern cultures today. The obstacle for many from Western cultures is letting go of our individualism and perceived rights to join a one-another-focused group like what we find in the pages of the New Testament.

Communication and Education

When it comes to the practical solutions of coming together and joining many different views and expectations of being family, communication and learning are key. The small group setting is an ideal place to bring up and discuss these types of issues. The following questions might be helpful for learning about the assumptions and desires of each person in the group.

- How did you define the boundaries of family when you grew up?
- When it comes to the church family, does your boundary of comfortableness include the entire global church, your entire local congregation, your small group, or some other marker?
- What do you believe are the primary functions of family?
- What are the primary functions of family within the body of Christ?
- What are some of the things within church life that most feel like expressions of family to you?
- What are some things within the church life or culture that do not feel like family to you?
- What is the greatest obstacle for you in embracing the church as your family of priority and identity?
- What are one or two things that the church could start doing that for you would make it feel more like the family that we all want it to be?

As you have discussions like these, listen and look for ways for the group to embrace as many of these things as it can. There will be challenges, especially if some of the answers from some members are in direct tension with the answers from other members. Yet the largest obstacle is simply knowing what each other expects and feels, so as you have these discussions, the path toward developing a common culture of what a family is in the body of Christ will continue to develop and be embraced by all. Keep in mind, however, that a community that is growing creates a dynamic where this will need to be an ongoing process. Each new person must be listened to and heard, and this is an opportunity to change, grow, and adapt the culture of the church family.

The Dominant Group

Our marching orders as a Christian community are to be all things to all people. We must never lose sight of the truth that this in incumbent upon all disciples, regardless of our cultural background or level of influence within the group. There will, however, be a greater opportunity for adaptation and inclusion of others for those in the dominant culture. In Acts 15, a council was convened to work through the cultural clashes of the Jewish and Gentile Christians. The Gentiles were sent a letter asking them specifically to abstain from food sacrificed to idols and from blood and the meat of strangled animals, and to embrace the Jewish (and biblical) standards of sexual morality rather than those of their own culture (Acts 15:29). Within the global church at that time, the Jewish culture was the dominant one. What is often missed is that while they did make some requests of the Gentile believers, the Jewish culture was the one doing the most adapting in this situation. It is unstated in this letter, but to even write the letter they were willing to follow the biblical call to fully accept the Gentiles into the family. This meant that they were prepared to adapt many of their customs of cleanliness, association, and dietary laws within the community. These were not easy things to change, and some continued to struggle with the changes for a time, but they were huge concessions in the quest to be all things to all people.

All must adapt, but it starts with the dominant group. Who that is will vary from congregation to congregation, but in my own church context, it is the Western, American, white culture that is predominant. Readers in a different situation from my own can take the principles and apply them to their own situation.

The dominant cultural approach to family in my church context tends to view family as a smaller unit that focuses on equipping the individual to go off and be independent, not needing to rely on a larger family unit. Many others find this approach greedy and selfish and have been raised with the expectation that family is a more extended concept wherein all members of the larger group will be willing to share and sacrifice to maintain everyone in the group.

If the dominant group is to take the first steps to adjusting, then it is on them to examine their own preferences toward individualism and seek to learn about and appreciate the collectivist and inclusive culture of family.

The Restrictive View

Often in cultural situations, one group's approach is a bit freer, while another group tends toward a narrower or more restrictive stance. In Corinth, Paul guides them through different cultural stances on eating meat sacrificed to idols. One group felt that everything belonged to God and since they were not personally worshipping idols by eating meat that had been sacrificed to the so-called god, then it was fine. Others took the restrictive view. Their conscience steered them away from participating in pagan rituals. Throughout the book of Corinthians, Paul hints toward trying to get the restrictive group to see things with a bit broader view, yet he is careful to never call them out directly to make them feel that their approach is sinful or overtly wrong. He calls the group with the freer approach to make sure they don't pressure others into something that would violate their conscience, and to be willing to sacrifice their freedom out of love for others if it comes to that level.

Thus, the approach for us in these types of situations seems to be to call the restrictive group toward freedom if possible, while advocating for the laying down of rights for the freer position if to do otherwise would truly bring spiritual harm to our brothers and sisters.

In the case of approaches to family, the Western view is more restrictive, so they could go a long way toward unity by opening up to more of the Eastern approach. In my own household, this has borne much fruit. To force my tighter definition of family on my wife would cause her to act in ways that feel unloving. Her broader view has challenged me to widen my boundaries and expand my field of vision as to who is to be loved as family. It has been difficult, but I must admit, it feels closer to what God wants for his people. When it comes to interdependence versus individual responsibility, we have continued to work toward compromise between those two paradigms. If we err, we err toward her side, but we have found cases where my tendencies have helped set up healthy boundaries for someone that might be tempted to abuse the support and care from other family members.

One thing that can really help clarify this aspect is the "give or get" question. If I move toward the other group's approach or am including their culture as much as possible, will I be giving more or getting more? In this case, embracing the broader communal and supportive approach to family that seeks to share lives and resources with an expanded definition of the family group brings much more into our life than what we give up. On the other hand, if the Eastern group was asked to sacrifice their ways in favor of the Western-style approach, they would be giving up much and gaining little in return.

Heart Language

This aspect of bridging the gap won't be a factor for all topics, but it can be a huge factor for some. When it comes to some cultural areas, one or both groups will have their customs or preferences, but overall, it's not a core aspect of the cultural life of that group of people and can be adjusted or retrained without a great deal of problem. At other times, an issue is deeply central for that culture and takes on the significance of what I call a "heart language." It is something central to their identity and value system. In situations where a cultural variance is a heart language issue for one group but not for the other, the heart language group should be conceded to as much as possible.

Everyone values family in their own way, but the Western way of organizing and approaching family is not nearly as central as it is for other cultures. Westerners could easily embrace a church community that didn't even try to function as family. Easterners could not. They need a family in their life and will never be able to fully prioritize and commit to the body of Christ if it doesn't fulfill this role for them. Thus, in this area, the Eastern approach should be accommodated as much as possible.

The Compromise Position

We should, I believe, seek to emulate much of the Eastern view of family. It is the approach that is the natural assumption of the biblical texts and one that fits in more easily with biblical principles in most respects. That doesn't mean that there is no compromise necessary. While moving toward a more collective concept of family and community, we must recognize that certain elements, such as showing up unexpectedly at someone's house and planning to stay for a while, can be off-the-charts difficult for some people. A wise group will work toward these positions.

In Acts 15, the church decided that they would ask Gentile Christians to absolutely avoid blood and meat sacrificed to idols. When Paul writes to the church in Corinth about ten years later, he assumes that eating meat sacrificed to idols is something that should be considered but optional given the situation, and there is no mention of blood at all, as though that has ceased to be a concern. It seems that they were compromising but had slowly moved toward the Gentile culture.

The Grace Factor

One of the most important elements of grace is patience. This is absolutely vital in moving toward a culturally competent and transformed community. We must be willing to show grace to one another and value acceptance over comfort. When coming together as one, there will be times when the other group is insensitive or is not moving fast enough. This must be met with patience and love. Keep working toward an inclusive approach to family within your diverse church community, but never cease being patient and full of grace.

It will almost never work for one or more groups to completely abandon their cultural identity and completely embrace another. Within a diverse community, we will often find a series of compromises coupled with the tolerance for variations among members within the group.

If this aspect of life together is not given attention, it can cause many to feel that the church says they are family but doesn't live it out. All the while, others in the congregation are quite happy that the goal of family togetherness has been achieved. We recently saw a case where the mother of a dear sister in a church passed away unexpectedly. People paid their condolences, prayed for her, and offered help, but not in the way that this sister, who was from a more Eastern-leaning culture, expected. The church felt like they were treating her as family, but she didn't feel that way at all. Based on her expectations of family, she felt as though she had been mostly abandoned. In a case like this, the dominant group needs to be willing to learn, but grace would dictate that someone who may recognize the needs and expectations of the sister step forward and quickly educate the body on what they could do to make someone like her feel the love of the family.

In this area, perhaps the most important factor is simply being aware of the divergent views, assumptions, and expectations when it comes to family. Once we are aware of these differences, we can begin to communicate and work toward a church that truly feels like family for all involved. It will never be completely comfortable and perfect for every person, but remember that staying in our comfort zone is a sure sign that we have moved outside the zone of being all things to all people.

Chapter 14

Managing Resources

"You should be proud of me," my young wife of just a couple of years stated, with a corresponding countenance of satisfaction.

"I am," I responded, "but why, specifically, am I proud of you?"

"Because," she continued, "I just saved us over a hundred dollars."

"That's amazing," I replied, genuinely impressed, "How did you do that?"

It was only then that she produced a bag full of things that she had just purchased at the mall. She began to pull out her prizes as though this was a grand unveiling of the latest iPhone. I was no longer impressed. As she continued pulling out her trophies, I was perhaps not-so-subtly looking through the bag to find the receipt. Finally locating it, I blurted out, perhaps a little more exasperatedly than I should have, "This cost a hundred and twenty dollars!"

Not to be deterred, she proudly chirped, "I know, it should have cost over two hundred dollars."

"Let me get this straight," I continued, "You spent a hundred and twenty dollars."

"No," she responded in a magnificently confident fashion, "I saved us a hundred dollars."

I stared at her for a moment, trying to find some sort of logic in all this, and finally said, "How do you figure that you saved us money, when you clearly spent a hundred and twenty dollars?"

"Oh," she shot back confidently, "We were going to eventually need those things, so I got them on a really good sale and saved us a lot of money."

"No," I moaned, "you spent money that we didn't really have to spend right now." I was sure that I had finally gotten through to her and that the pain I was feeling was about to hit her. Knowing the agony she was about to feel made me regret, for just a moment, being so honest and logical with her. Yes, she had spent money that we should have been saving, but couldn't I have let her enjoy it for a few more moments before snapping her into reality? She was going to be crushed and it was my fault. But before I could wallow in regret and sympathy any longer over her impending torturous pain, her voice broke into my thoughts.

"You're welcome."

"For what?" I exclaimed.

"For saving us money," and with that she turned and strode triumphantly out of the room as I stood there in stunned silence.

How had I lost this argument? How was it that I recognized it as an argument, and she seemed oblivious to the fact that there was a problem at all. And most of all, HOW COULD SHE POSSIBLY BE CONVINCED THAT SHE SAVED US MONEY?!

RESOURCES

Once again, the cultural differences between my wife and me serve as a good window into two broad cultural categories when it comes to a view of money. I know what you're thinking, "This is the difference between how men and women view the world, not a cultural difference." Perhaps there's a little something to that, but I don't think that's really the issue. There is still something of an East and West divide here, along with the views of money that emanate from individualist and collectivist groups, but one of the key factors here is whether a person grows up in the middle class (MC) or in generational poverty (GP). Having a great deal of wealth tends to create its own cultural idiosyncrasies but is such a small population that we won't consider that group in this book.

The gap between cultures that can be created by wealth might be rather surprising to some, but it is a very real phenomenon in many parts of the world. It certainly seems to have an impact on people's views of money and financial resources. Those from the MC tend to believe that money brings stability. It is a limited resource, and as such must be managed and saved carefully. Thus, when money is encountered, the immediate instinct of the MC culture is to save as much as possible. The purpose of that money is not to spend; spending is the enemy. The purpose is to put away as much as possible for the future.

That is a big component of the MC worldview: it is typically future oriented. Decisions are made against future ramifications, and since tomorrow is a relative certainty, it must be planned for. The culture that stems from GP is different.[15] That worldview focuses on the present. Life cannot promise stability or even tomorrow, so any resources that you have should be used now.

When it comes to money, it is seen in the GP culture as a resource currently in hand and thus something to be used right now. I'd like to think that my wife and I have both grown immensely in our conversational skills and in how we each view and handle money. But when we were young marrieds, there was constant friction because I never wanted to spend any money and only wanted to save it. This would lead to moments of serious miscommunication. When she wanted to buy something, my first question would be "Can we afford that?" She would affirm that she thought we could, and I would, at times, give in and agree to the purchase. But when I said "afford," I meant did we have a healthy amount of money saved with enough in surplus to spend a little. Her cultural concept of "afford" meant, "I have the money to buy that in my pocket, so I can afford it." Eventually, my constant refusals to purchase anything led her to categorize me as "oppressively cheap." I saw it as being frugal and wise.

These opposing ways of approaching money caused many a lively discussion in our household until we figured out that because of our cultural backgrounds, we had opposing assumptions and conceptions of what was appropriate behavior.

Money is the most obvious resource to represent this cultural divide, but it can extend to almost any resource or commodity. Sociologists have determined that one of the fundamental causes of this split is that the primary resource in GP cultures is relationships, while things are considered the primary resource in MC cultures. That means that for the MC, those things are viewed as precious and should be cared for and treated with an eye on preservation. Resources are used to fit into the norms of society, gain acceptance, and create lasting stability. In the GP groups, nonhuman resources are fleeting and if available should be used immediately, often for the purpose of expressing individual personality or as a show of success, even where there is no lasting wealth.

Thus, when the typical person from a GP culture goes to church on Sunday, they may want to wear their very best outfit to stand out and impress, while the average MC person will gravitate more toward practicalities like being comfortable or wearing a style in keeping with what everyone else is wearing.

If we return to the context of a culturally diverse church, we can begin to imagine conflicts in this area, especially if we focus on money issues. Just imagine a scenario where half your church approaches their personal lives and church finances with the belief that money is to be saved and as little as possible should be spent. Savings accounts should be bursting, and corners need to be cut wherever they can be. But the other half approaches their personal lives and church finances from the opposite perspective. If we have the money, we can spend it. Let's get it now, because you never know what tomorrow will bring. After this, there might be no money to purchase what we want or need for a long time, so let's get it while the money is in hand.

It doesn't take an elaborate mental exercise to determine that this would lead to many conflicts and differences of opinion.

One thing that blended churches must be on guard against is unintentional favoritism. In James 2 we are warned in no uncertain terms about showing favoritism, especially toward those who are wealthy. It is easy for churches to slant church life and opportunities toward the middle class and those who have more economic means. The church might sell books and resources, expect everyone to come to the big regional conference and sign up for the marriage retreat, dress up for the marrieds' formal dance or the men's night out, and join everyone at a restaurant for a hangout time, all without ever considering how difficult that can be for some of the members. Or a lesson might be given on managing money and retirement that is helpful if you are middle class or higher but has no practical information for those who may not have steady income or a job with a 401k. Great thought must go into each event, lesson, and community get-together to ensure that a middle-class bias has not set in.

This is a real challenge for churches like mine that meet centrally in one location in a large metro area. That circumstance alone proves to create barriers for lower income individuals to get to Sunday worship or a midweek gathering if they don't have reliable transportation. Churches that meet in configurations like this will very quickly become middle class and wealthy if they don't take measures to strategize how they will include, value, and create options for men and women of lower income who rarely leave their neighborhood and who might otherwise be excluded if they are not thought of and a plan put in place. Neighborhood churches tend to be more convenient and realistic for this portion of the population, so if a church like the one I belong to wants to appeal to them, we must be very intentional about making that work.

TIME

Time is a resource, but there are divides in the way we approach time that go back largely to the Eastern and Western cultural approaches.

Western cultures typically are what is referred to as monochronic. "Mono" refers to "one" or "limited amount," and "chronic" refers to time. After teaching this concept, I've had many people come up to me and describe themselves as naturally preferring organizations that are "monochromatic." I often don't have the heart to tell them that "chromatic" refers to color, so ... yeah ... there's that.

Monochronic cultures view time as a linear concept. It is limited, valuable, and irreplaceable. Because of this, they tend to structure much of life around time and being on time. If you've ever said phrases like, "time is wasting," "time is money," or "if you're on time, you're late," then you might be monochronic. These cultures typically focus on one primary activity at a time and value order, believing that there is an appropriate time and place for everything. They set great store by keeping to the schedule and do not appreciate interruptions to it or last-minute changes in plans. Time commitments are prized in these groups, and to be late is considered rude and unmindful of what someone else's time is worth. These cultures tend to place high value on the individual, and thus, on private property and personal space.

On the other end of the spectrum are polychronic cultures. They view time as being cyclical and so, in a sense, virtually unlimited. This leads to an entirely different way of approaching the world. Time comes around again and again, so there's no need to be a slave to it. It is a "what goes around, comes around," method of dealing with life. People from these groups are trained not to rush and tend not to develop the internal clock and ability to estimate how long things will take that people from monochronic cultures do. The polychronic person can characteristically accomplish multiple activities at the same time and have no problem dealing with distractions, interruptions, or changes to the schedule. Plans can easily be changed and will be if need be. Time is not a dearly valued commodity, but what is highly valued are relationships. Relational time is never infringed upon for the sake of a schedule, and hurrying is considered an unnecessary overreaction to something that is largely unimportant. Being polychronic doesn't mean you're just a person who is chronically late or unorganized. It is an orientation to time. It means that your life revolves around connections and relationships rather than schedule, time of day, and the concept of being on time.

This conflict has been my life. I am extremely monochronic, while my wife is classically polychronic. As I sit here this morning and write this, these concepts are on display. Our eighteen-year-old nephew lives with us and works at a manufacturing facility. He works third shift and needs to be picked up when he gets off work. On days when I am to pick him up, I leave our house at 5:48 am, as it is an eleven-minute drive. I know that and plan accordingly. Today, my wife is picking him up. At 5:49, I started to become concerned that I hadn't yet seen her leave. At 5:53, I walked into our bedroom to ask if she wanted me to go get him. She said, "No, I'll get him." At 5:58, I left my office and returned to our room to see if she was sure she didn't want me to get him. Her response was, "No, I just need to get up and go get him." Here's the thing: at this point, I'm internally melting down. And for no other reason than that she will be late to pick him up. It feels like a major moral indecency to me. Her attitude is something more like, "He's not going anywhere. I'll be there, and he'll be fine."

She's right, of course. He is of the same orientation so it won't bother him that much, if at all. Our sons, however, have managed to contract my view of the world and are different. They are decidedly monochronic. If this situation were happening to our younger son, the most monochronic of the two of them, we would have received a text at 6:01 wondering where we were and what was going on.

Just to update you on this, she finally left the house at 6:04, I'm sure with the thought that she will get there, pick him up, and then they can stop at the store if he needs anything and be on their way with the rest of the day. Do you want to guess the foremost thought on my mind? It is simply this: she will be arriving at 6:15. That's fifteen minutes late. I would feel stressed the entire drive over there. I guarantee you that not only is my incredible wife not worrying that she is "late," but there's no way that she could tell you that it takes eleven minutes to get to his jobsite. She is focused on their relationship and his personal needs when she gets there, and the time factor isn't her major concern.

This divergence in how we interact with time is bigger than you might realize. It's not just about being on time or not. It dictates much of how we view the world and go about ordering our lives. It determines much of what feels like respectful or rude behavior. Putting monochronic and polychronic people together in the same spheres can be difficult and lead to much conflict. Let me give three examples in church life to demonstrate.

The music team ran a little long today in warming up, which pushed back a few other things and it's now 10:04, and the Sunday service that is supposed to start at 10:00 am has yet to kick off. Half the church is well aware of this and annoyed that this sloppiness has happened yet again. Who is in charge of this? It reflects badly on all of us. Meanwhile, the other half of the church has no idea we're late. They are lost in fellowship, and it wouldn't bother them one bit if we didn't start for another twenty minutes. And it wouldn't bother them if we then finished twenty minutes late. But you'd better call a fleet of ambulances, because several of the monochronic folks might go into a full-blown breakdown if we randomly run long like that with no warning.

The church staff decides that it is easier to plan and communicate churchwide events one month at a time. So at the beginning of each month, they hand out the upcoming events. Even with that, there are usually one or two events that are changed, cancelled, or added along the way during that month. For the polychronic folks, this is fine. Once again, our poor monochronic brethren are struggling. How can a group possibly function like this? How can anyone plan their lives? There's even a possibility that they start to intentionally disregard these last-minute events as unreasonable and refuse to change their schedule to adhere to such an inconsiderate lack of planning.

Two brothers set up time to grab some coffee and discipling time with one another. The monochronic brother arrives precisely at 4 pm as they planned. The polychronic brother decides that on the way he will drop off a meal that his wife made for another family that just had a baby. Once he gets there, he wants to see the baby, and then chats for a few minutes. The new dad has a few questions and needs advice on parenting, so they talk for a bit and then he gets on his way to meet the other brother. He arrives in the parking lot at 4:22, only then noticing that he has received two texts from this brother wondering if he is still coming. As he walks into the coffee shop, he expects a big hug, but instead is greeted by a halfhearted half hug. The first words out of the mouth of his friend are, "Do you understand how limited and valuable my time is?" How is that relationship going to go from there?

BRIDGING THE GAP

Is it possible to come to some sort of common ground in the areas of resources and time? I will be honest; it's not going to be easy. With over twenty years of marriage behind us, my wife and I are still learning to navigate these differences. It can be done, but it will not be quick, it will not be easy, and it most likely will take ongoing and constant attention and tweaking to keep harmony. These types of issues can rarely reach a point where they can go on cruise control and we can now assume that we have conquered them and no longer need to worry about them.

The Biblical View

There isn't much for us to go on here. We might want to make time orientation an issue of respect, and thus a moral one, but it's really not. Polychronic people are not disrespectful. They just value different things. Monochronic people are not dismissive of relationships. They have been trained to value relationships, but within the parameters of schedules and time considerations. This truly is an issue about valuing and respecting contrasting things. In neither case is it as simple as that the other group is wrong and disrespectful.

There are no scriptures that seem to directly address this issue within the body of Christ, although I could perhaps make a case that God might lean toward the polychronic view. In 2 Peter 3:8–9, we are reminded that with God, a day is like a thousand years, and vice versa. He is not slow in keeping his promise but has delayed so that more people will come to repentance. That sounds a lot like the polychronic worldview to me.

I wrote that previous paragraph with a bit of humor intended, but perhaps I shouldn't take it so lightly. Many monochronic folks can get pretty uptight and even holier-than-thou about time issues (I know I can), so we might do well to remember that God does value relationships above all else, including time.

When it comes to money and resources, the Bible is more direct. Scripture does teach clearly on the importance of being a good steward and wise with our resources, so whatever our background, we should attempt to orient ourselves toward responsibility and wisdom. That doesn't mean that the middle-class approach is completely in the right and the generational poverty group needs to do all the changing. Over the years, my wife has learned much about the value of saving and waiting to purchase things. But from her, I have learned the value of relationships, generosity, and being sacrificial.

Communication and Education

Knowing is usually half the battle. It definitely is in these areas. Understanding the differences we have in our view of resources and where those differences come from can be invaluable. Recognizing divergent orientations of time will probably not help us avoid conflict in this area, but it will assist in avoiding assumptions about the other person's motives or lack of character.

When we dig into these issues, we will probably find that those who come from generational poverty need to learn more about wisely handling their resources and that those from the middle-class background will often have the very knowledge they need. At the same time, while not always true, there is often much that the MC can learn from the GP culture about empathy, generosity, and helping others in need.

The Dominant Group

This aspect of bridging cultural gaps probably doesn't come into play as much with the topics we are considering in this chapter. When it comes to resources, who is the dominant group is irrelevant. We can learn from one another, but the path of wisdom and good stewardship is one that should always be sought. One warning here: it is important to follow the biblical wisdom and not a Western version of biblical wisdom when it comes to money. It can be harmful and misleading to buy in to the many programs created for churches that have a veneer of biblical teaching but heavily embrace the American dream as a legitimate starting point for financial wisdom and peace.

You may find that you are in a church group that is dominated by one or the other of these approaches to time. Most of the multiethnic churches that I have visited are split fairly evenly between the two. They are often dominated, however, by the more Western, monochronic approach. I'm not advocating that being all things to all people dictates that on some Sundays services begin on time, while on others they start once the fellowship begins to wind down. I have been to churches, primarily in Africa, where the entire church is polychronic and that works for the community.

Where there is a mix, though, compromise should be sought. I would advocate that corporate events still run on time, but that in all other cases we tend toward heavy communication and understanding of what the other person meant in their culture. For instance, in the above example of the brother who was late for coffee because he stopped to bring a meal to someone, according to his culture, he was not communicating disrespect or unconcern at all. If I can recognize that, I can interpret into my world what he intended in his and be flexible.

The bottom line when it comes to both resource and time issues is that they will most likely have to be communicated about and dealt with on a case-by-case basis.

The Restrictive View

In the case of resources, both money and time, the Western approach is a little more restrictive. Those of us who come from this background can ease up a little in the time department and give room to our brothers and sisters. Being overly concerned with the length of a church service and ending "on time," for example, can restrict some brothers and sisters who came from more relationally focused backgrounds and who long for the Spirit to be allowed to move during worship, even if that means we get out ten or fifteen minutes later.

Heart Language

I would make the case that the view of resources has equal importance in the competing cultural views. They are deeply embedded in both but would not reach the level of what I would qualify as a heart language.

It's different when it comes to time orientation. Monochronic cultures typically care deeply about time order and structure, often in ways they never even realize. The level of stress one can feel about being late or changing schedules repeatedly cannot be fully understood by the polychronic person. Likewise, the amount of disrespect communicated by valuing time over relationship cannot be overstated for members of the polychronic group. It's a heart language issue for both, which is why this can be such a source of irritation and conflict if not constantly attended to. The fact that it is equally central to both cultural views means that there is no clear directive in favoring one or the other, but it does highlight how vital it is to make sure that we are aware of the differing approaches and constantly seeking to communicate and educate on the issue.

The Compromise Position

With resources, there is a compromise position that can be found. As stated above, I do think the biblical guide on money tends to go with saving and spending wisely, but it also leans heavily toward generosity and helping those in need. The MC position has much that is good in the sense of following the biblical teaching on stewardship, but the GP approach often has much that is biblical in its tendency to help those in need, even to a sacrificial level. Simply spending money or using a resource because it is currently in hand is not always a wise approach, but if we're not careful, we can become oppressive or almost greedy in the drive to save and preserve.

It is important for any community to reach a position that is a wise combination of the two cultural approaches, while probably leaning toward the MC position in many respects.

When we consider personal finances, it is helpful to have knowledge of the situation and both the MC and GP perspectives. I have heard many classes or lessons on finances that were completely oblivious to the realities of those who grew up in GP and are still in financial poverty in many respects. It is also true that there are many disciples who don't make a lot of money and grew up in GP but are wise with their money and incredibly rich toward God in their sacrifice and giving. Their perspective and wisdom should be considered as well when teaching and addressing these issues rather than only hearing from those that are better off financially.

To bridge the gap between monochronic and polychronic peoples, it is all about compromise and communication. There is not a simple formula that works in every situation. At least there is not one that my wife and I have discovered yet. What we have found works is that we must clearly communicate and cannot assume anything when it comes to time and schedule. But that by itself will not do it. We have also found that we need a liberal dose of our next ingredient.

The Grace Factor

We know how sensitive a topic money and resources can be, so bringing together disparate views in these areas will be equally sensitive. The history of the world is full of division over economic issues, and the church will be no different if we don't keep the "why" of being the gathering of the nations that have been brought into God's kingdom constantly before us. It is required that we communicate and show a great deal of submission and grace toward one another. The effort to understand and respect one another's backgrounds goes a long way.

Time orientation may not seem like the most fundamental or important element, but it would be a mistake to underestimate its impact in a community. It reaches into almost every aspect of our lives, and the way we are brought up can affect our thought processes and even how our brain works. People who are truly polychronic, for example, will find it next to impossible to ever fully grasp certain aspects of time orientation, like estimating time or having an internal clock that keeps you on task.

Since there is no clear-cut approach that would lead us to prefer or submit to one outlook or the other, that means the only way forward is constant communication, negotiation, and planning. For monochronic and polychronic folks to work together, events and interactions must be thought through and discussed more than they would if everyone were the same. If my wife and I don't talk carefully through events and come to a clear understanding, complete with contingencies if we run late, then we will have conflict.

Most of all, we have learned to show patience and grace. When I, without thinking, value time over the current interaction, she reminds herself that I'm not unloving and cold. When she runs late, I remind myself that she's not irresponsible and selfish. When we remember that love covers over a multitude of differences, we do so much better. The same can be true for our churches.

Chapter 15

Me or We

I'm certainly not the first person to point this out, but the 1997 mega-hit movie, *Titanic,* is one of the clearest representations of the Western individualist worldview ever put on film. The main character, Rose, boards the massive ocean liner with her mother, Ruth, and fiancé, Cal. Ruth is overjoyed at the impending marriage between the two young people because she believes that Cal's wealth will put an end to the financial woes her family has experienced since the death of her own husband. It will also maintain their status among society's elite, something that almost seems more important to her than financial security. The film soon exposes a major problem, however. Cal is arrogant and not particularly nice.

Rose even considers suicide at an early point in the film, before meeting a broke artist named Jack Dawson who has gambled his way aboard the luxury ocean cruiser. A spark develops between Jack and Rose that quickly bursts into the flame of passionate romance and wild infatuation. And in the course of one evening, Rose falls madly in love with Jack. When the great ship hits an iceberg and it becomes clear that it will sink, Rose decides that she would rather follow her heart and be with Jack, even if it means risking her life. She chooses Jack over Cal.

Movie audiences across the United States and many parts of the world flocked to see this romance epic with its thin veneer of a disaster movie surrounding the torrid love story of two young people from opposite worlds. We cheered when Rose left Cal and ran after Jack, and our hearts sank when Jack drowned, denying their opportunity for true love to blossom forever. Despite that, Rose had followed her heart and done the right thing.

That is, she had done the right thing from a Western perspective. If we were able to watch the blockbuster movie with an audience from the Ancient Near East, the world from which all the biblical writers emerged, we might be shocked at their reactions. My suspicion is that they would view Rose as something of a monster. How could she do such a thing? The security and stability of her family was on the line, and rather than doing what was in her power to secure that safety, she followed an emotional whim, put her own desires ahead of the needs of the family, and ran off on a tryst. Yes, she had an amazing and unforgettable night with her "true love," and even though that didn't work out, she "found herself" and went on to have an amazing and self-fulfilling life. But what of her mother?

What of her family name? They both drift off into the night as questions that those of the Western mindset don't find worthy of answering or even remember being asked. Western minds see Rose as a hero. Most Eastern minds would see her as uncaring and selfish.

One of the divides between the Western and Eastern worldviews is the place and role of self. It is the difference between individualist and collectivist cultures. Individualist cultures think of the world in terms of "I" while collectivist cultures see the world in terms of "we." The sense of self in the individualist world comes from the journey of discovering oneself and maintaining a rugged individualism that is not dependent on what others think or might want for your life. For collectivists, just the opposite is true. Their identity is dependent upon their group and the society around them. Individualists find and maintain their identity through individual characteristics and personal desires, whereas collectivists find and maintain their identity through their status and standing within the community.

The individualism of the Western culture impacts how we read the Bible. Philippians 2:12 provides the text for a perfect example of this. "Continue to work out your salvation," writes Paul, "with fear and trembling." The Western mind immediately fills with trepidation as *I* shudder at the thought of all the times *I* have failed God and *I* am deeply motivated by this tacit threat that *I* had better get my junk together, as *my* life is on full display before a watching God who is worthy to be feared. But that reading comes to us courtesy of our Western-trained minds, which immediately read all instances of the word "you" to be referring to "me" rather than "us." Paul was of a collectivist culture and thought first and foremost in terms of "we." When we read this passage from that perspective, we can discern that this comes on the heels of calling the church to follow the self-sacrificial pattern of Jesus. This is a gentle challenge to the community, reminding them that this way of life is their salvation made manifest in the present and that they should work out, or live out, this life together with a great deal of gravity. It is not a thinly veiled threat to individuals to not take their status in Christ for granted. It is an appeal to the gathering of believers to live up to the calling they have in the life of Christ.

INDIVIDUAL OR COLLECTIVE

I have had the privilege of teaching at various ministry training academies both in the United States and Africa. In every location where I have taught, we have had snacks throughout the days of classes. But there is one interesting difference I have noticed. In the African academies, where they tend toward collectivist mindsets, snack time is preset, and so is the snack. At a predetermined time, members of the ministry staff come around and hand out a preselected snack or small snack basket. Everyone gets the same thing at the same time. In the American courses I have taught, our individualism is on full display. A wide potpourri of snacks is spread out on a back table, and the table is open all day. We can't be tied down to someone else's taste or schedule. We can go back and select the snack we want when we want it, according to our individual desire. That's right, even the snack table is affected by culture.

We have already touched on the individualist or collectivist instinct of different cultures, but it is worth focusing on here again because it can have such an impact in a spiritual community. Individualism in a culture is the putting of interests of the individual above the needs and interests of the group. It leads to the question, "What is best for me?" Collectivist cultures put the needs and interests of the group above the individual. Collectivism leads to the question, "What is best for my group?"

Most churches in the United States are firmly rooted in the individualist instinct. There are some positive things about that cultural bent. It calls its members to a great deal of self-responsibility and encourages unique exceptionalism as individuals nurture their own talents, desires, and passions and can often excel in life. There are also negative aspects. It can lead to an every-person-for-themself mentality and privatize faith in a way that does not seem prescribed or encouraged in the Scriptures.

Collectivist cultures think of and prioritize the group first. This leads to a wonderful sense of community, care for others, and strength in the group. But it can also discourage individual excellence and independent thought, which it often views as dangerous.

The point here is not to enter a debate concerning which cultural philosophy is superior or even more biblical, but to recognize that diverse churches will most likely have members who come from and prefer both of these very different viewpoints.

My wife will serve as a clear example of this. She became a disciple of Jesus in 1999 at the same time that I did. She loves God and loves the church family that we have been part of since our entry into Christ. She loves the idea of the church being called to be family and loves to be with other Christians. If she had her way, our house would constantly be full of guests, with brothers and sisters just dropping by to hang out. In Chapter 13, I described how the absence of this dynamic left her feeling as though the church was lacking in the department of being family.

She found echoes of it here and there, but that all changed in 2008.

That was the year we began traveling to churches in Africa to minister, teach, and learn from them. Our journey began in Port Elizabeth, South Africa, but since then we have visited many dozens of churches in all corners of Africa. It didn't take long being with brothers and sisters on the continent of Africa for my wife to fully realize what had been bothering her for a decade. She began to experience the life and fellowship of the African culture, and it immediately felt right for her. It reminded her much more of the mindset that she had grown up with in her African American family. They had the same cultural approach to the group that she so deeply desired. There, she found a strong tendency to think of the group first as one unit and to want to be together all the time. She found a safe haven of similar attitudes toward family, with valuing fellowship over schedule and so much more. That's not to say that everything in every church was completely collectivist with no trace of individualism, but it was collectivist to a much greater degree than anything she had experienced in the United States. She has continued to experience that same mindset in most African churches, and she loves every minute of it.

The divide between individualist and collectivist thinking is not an easy one to remedy. People who are rooted in individualist cultures tend to think first of their responsibility to themselves or their nuclear families. They don't feel an immediate obligation to be with or care for others in the same way that collectivists would, although that is not to imply that they are heartless or uncaring. They would tend to bristle at passages like Romans 12:5 that assert that members of the body of Christ belong to one another. They like to have their private space and private time and can feel that they need those things in order to function.

Collectivists can struggle with a church body that has such clear boundaries between church and personal life, even if the members are very active and committed. They feel more comfortable with a community that sees itself as one entity and that intertwines their lives inextricably from one another. They long for the all-for-one-and-one-for-all mentality and constant togetherness. An individualist-based church feels cold to them, and even if they love many other things about the church, they can struggle to feel like they have found their home. This can leave longtime members susceptible to the temptation of leaving and finding a new church even while they don't understand the urge and don't like the fact that that thought always seems to be lurking somewhere in the back of their mind.

There is another element to this divide that can create problems. Author Jemar Tisby, in interacting with the important work on the elements of race and culture in US churches, *Divided by Faith*, by Emerson and Smith, describes the impact that the cultural tendencies or toolkit that is typical of white churchgoers in the United States can be particularly difficult for nondominant cultures, especially when it comes to the practical ramifications of their individualist outlook.

> Accountable Individualism means that "individuals exist independent of structures and institutions, have free will, and are individually accountable for their own actions." This belief promotes skepticism toward the idea that social systems and structures profoundly shape the actions of individuals. The white evangelical understanding of individualism has this effect, and it tends to reduce the importance of communities and institutions in shaping the ways people think and behave. Another belief in the cultural toolkit is relationalism, "a strong emphasis on interpersonal relationships." According to relationalism, social problems are fundamentally due to broken personal relationships: "Thus, if race problems—poor relationships—result from sin, then race problems must largely be individually based." And antistructuralism refers to the belief that "invoking social structures shifts guilt away from its root source—the accountable individual." In other words, systems, structure and politics are not to blame for the problems in America; instead, the problems come from the harmful choices of individuals.[16]

What this means practically is that white American Christians, who tend to be very individualist in cultural background, will be blind to structural and systemic or group factors that contribute to societal issues like poverty or racism and will only listen to analyses and solutions that focus on individual behaviors and choices. Meanwhile, this will seem like coldhearted blame-gaming and even offensive to those of a collective cultural background. The divergence between these two streams will run deep underground in a church community but will have a massive impact in the inability of different groups to come together and stay unified if these differences are not recognized and addressed in a meaningful way.

PUBLIC OR PRIVATE

How would you respond if your child was acting up in a shopping mall and needed to be redirected? What would be your reaction if you saw someone you knew in an airport, but they didn't see you and they were about a hundred feet away and walking in the opposite direction? What would you do if you sat down in an airplane next to a close friend who began conversing with you at a decibel level that enabled anyone in a four- or five-row vicinity to overhear?

My response to all those questions would be "Whatever drew the least amount of attention." I would quietly attempt to discipline my child. I would never shout out to get someone's attention in a public setting. And I would ask my friend to talk quieter and then attempt to finish the conversation in tones low enough that only we could hear one another. I like to keep low profile and private. In general, I like my privacy. It is a fruit of the crop of individualism that has been planted in my life since birth.

Cultural preferences and responses are not a perfect science. We will always be able to find exceptions, and when it comes to aspects of culture like this, personality does indeed play a role. But we still find norms and tendencies within cultures.

Not all individualists prefer privacy, but most do. Not all collective cultures are more expressive publicly, but many are. For example, some Asian cultures are collectivist in nature but quiet and private in public in some respects.

The first time I visited Nigeria, I was a bit overstimulated. The people there are warm and kind, but they are also very expressive and very public. There is not a large sense of being quiet or private in a public setting. It seemed as though everyone spoke loudly and emphatically and there was little sense of having a conversation that was in public but intended to be private at the same time. That happens when your identity is rooted in the group more than in your individuality.

The tendency to express oneself publicly or to prefer a more private approach can have a major impact on our preferences in a worship community. Privacy-oriented people prefer more muted public interactions and can interpret behaviors that stray from that norm as aggressive or obnoxious. Not long ago, my wife happened to be fellowshipping after a worship gathering with four or five other women who were all African American. They were being very expressive in their communication, or as my wife would call it, they were "chopping it up." A nearby white sister misinterpreted the volume and passion of communication in a public setting and thought that there was a conflict going on. She meant well but burst into the circle and quietly asked if anything was wrong. After taking a second to process what was happening, the circle of women burst into laughter. They assured the confused sister that everything was fine.

This was a relatively innocent interaction, but it speaks to how easily these two approaches to life can clash in a church family.

There are other manifestations of this than just public displays and volume of public conversation. The privacy-oriented individual typically opts for an approach to worship that is much more subdued, introspective, private, and "between me and God." This has a huge impact on expectations and preferences during worship gatherings. Beyond that, they often prefer spiritual disciplines and practices that are experienced in solitude and see one's spiritual walk with God as a largely private endeavor.

The public-oriented member would gravitate in the other direction. They are more comfortable with a worship experience that is collectively oriented and more expressive and celebratory in nature. They might prefer public prayer and corporate expressions of their spiritual walk, as they often see it as a group effort.

BRIDGING THE GAP

In the United States, it can be difficult to find these cultural preferences along any neat lines like East and West, but if we are dealing in generalities, white American churchgoers would typically prefer the private, individualist approach, while many people of color gravitate toward the collectivist and public style.

Being that these cultural types often seem to be opposite of one another, is there a way forward in a mixed community?

There is, I believe, but it is never simple. In areas like this, there are group tendencies, but it can vary widely from person to person. This is a good reminder, because we can never assume that someone aligns with every cultural tendency from a group or category just because they belong to that set of people. At appropriate times, we should try to appeal to various cultural preferences and styles, but we must also be aware that there are so many overlapping lines of culture that there will be many exceptions. When thinking of the community as a whole, then, it is good to consider the cultural preferences and norms of the larger cultural groups, but when trying to connect with individuals, it is better not to make assumptions, but rather do your best to learn about their specific cultural tendencies.

The Biblical View

Does the Bible steer us toward individualism or collectivism? There are many passages that indicate a collectivist mindset (John 11:50; Acts 2:44–45, 4:32–35; 2 Corinthians 8:12–14; etc.). And there is little doubt that the prevailing culture in the Jewish and Ancient Near Eastern worlds was highly collective in nature. But the Scriptures place value and significance on the individual as well (Luke 19:15; Luke 15:3–10). Biblically speaking, the individual is important, but the Bible does predominantly presume the group-focused mentality. God values both the individual and the collective but calls individuals into the fold of his people to become one body.

That doesn't make individualist cultures wrong, but it does mean that there are many times when they will find it challenging to fully embrace and implement the vision of the kingdom community without curbing the individualist perspective and giving up much of it. An important note here. The Bible does give great value, dignity, and importance to each person, but do not confuse that with individualism. Valuing persons, which the Bible does in offering each person the opportunity for salvation, is not the same thing as valuing oneself above the group.

In the kingdom, those from individualist cultures will have some work to do to embrace the one-another community mindset found in relation to God's people. We belong to one another (Romans 12:5); our gifts are intended to benefit others (1 Peter 4:10); we are baptized into one body (1 Corinthians 12:13); and called to love one another (John 13:34–35) and lay down our lives for our brothers and sisters (John 15:13). We don't ever want to become imbalanced and lose sight of the importance of each soul, but there is much that those from individualist cultures can and need to learn from those who hail from a collectivist culture.

Communication and Education

Communication and learning about one another's perspectives will be uniquely important in this area because there can be so much misconception present. Many in the US were raised to exalt the idea of rugged individualism and be very suspect of any collectivist thinking, labeling it as communist or socialist. This is not what we refer to when we speak of collective cultures. Those are political and economic categories and, as such, are separate topics from valuing and identifying with the group over the individual.

For the individualist, learning the collective way of life takes time. Embracing the customs can be relatively quick and easy, but retraining the instincts can take a lifetime. To use myself as an example, retraining my individualist instincts and learning from my wife's more collective predisposition has been a slow go. I've made much progress to transition from thinking about "we" to thinking about "me" first, but with effort and the help of the Spirit, it can happen. One thing I have learned along the way that I can pass on is that I discovered that I already had a collective instinct in me; I just didn't know it. When I transitioned from being single, I moved my boundary marker from around myself to include my wife and children. In many respects, this "us" was now "me" in my individualist worldview. All I've needed to do is learn to expand the boundary around us to include those in the body of Christ. It's as simple as that. It's not easy, but it's simple.

The Dominant Group

In my context of the typical congregation in the United States, the dominant group is composed of individualists. That doesn't need to all be wiped out, but as I've said, we do need to be willing to let much of it go and embrace a more collective-focused way of life. Not only should the dominant group bend where it can in most situations, in this case, it absolutely should.

The Restrictive View

The narrower view here is clearly the individualist perspective. Once again, I will employ the give-or-get method. The individualist who chooses to embrace a more collective cultural model will have much to gain. Jesus alludes to this in Mark 10:29–31, following Peter's declaration that the apostles had given up everything to follow him. No one who was disowned by their birth family or disinherited would fail to receive a new family of a hundred homes, brothers, sisters, and mothers. He was not speaking directly about an individualist switching to a collective mindset, but his statement does confirm the collectivist mindset that was presumed in his newly formed family of believers.

Heart Language

When it comes to this divide, considering the importance level doesn't clear things up immediately. Individualism and collectivism are deeply ingrained in the life and expressions of both cultures to the point that it becomes part of who we are, how we think, how we interact with the world around us, and what we can and cannot tolerate. It is difficult for either group to change. As we've discussed above, much of the change here, though, lies with the individualist cultures if they are to fully embrace kingdom living. We will never be able to completely eradicate all aspects of individualism from our community life, and we don't need to. A church in Texas can make every effort to shed its individualistic instincts and make great progress in so doing but will never get to the level that a church in Singapore or the Democratic Republic of the Congo might naturally inhabit, and that's okay.

The Compromise Position

I don't advocate much of a compromise here per se. Yes, there will be compromises, but as I am advocating for more a movement toward the collectivist culture, the compromises will be situational and unique to each location. The best thing I can recommend is that those from individualist backgrounds take seriously the need to embrace the biblical community and to implement the principles from Romans 12:2 as we do not conform to the patterns of the world but are transformed by the renewing of our mind and learn what it means that we belong to one another (Romans 12:5). Make no mistake, it will take a significant amount of mental energy and working past comfort zones.

The Grace Factor

A great deal of patience and grace would be incumbent upon those from a collectivist culture who were members of a predominantly individualist group that was seeking change. It would be most helpful for the collectivists to learn about and understand the needs of the individualists in order to help them and to lovingly recognize areas of needed growth and change. The collectivists can be great resources in this process, but they must be aware that individualism is deeply embedded and will not transform easily. It will take great understanding, a lot of communication, and a series of compromises along the way as we seek to embrace the one-body mindset, while maintaining healthy and balanced aspects of individualism. At the same time, any change in this area will require a great deal of humility from the individualists as they learn to embrace a very foreign way of interacting with others and the world.

Chapter 16

Let's Talk About It

After an incredible week together teaching and fellowshipping with the church in Cote d'Ivoire, my wife and I and a fellow teacher and his wife were standing in line at the airport waiting to check our luggage and head home. I don't normally like to purchase anything when I'm traveling and go through the headache of bringing it back home, but this time we had two large and unusually shaped packages that we were sending through as abnormal baggage. My wife had purchased a guitarlike instrument as a gift for friends that were housesitting for us, and our traveling companions had purchased large, circular wall decorations. Both items were well wrapped and taped and ready to check as luggage.

When it was our turn to check in, the airport staff processed our regular luggage with no problem and then asked us to take the gift over to the left about ten meters and drop it off at the unusual luggage receiving area. We did this with no problem and assumed the process would be just as smooth for our friends. We thought incorrectly. As they brought their item over to drop it off, they were stopped and asked what the item was, and when the wife explained that they were simple wooden decorations, everything came to a halt. The inspector demanded to see their certificate from a museum that verified that this was not an important relic being taken out of the country. Of course, we had no such documentation and didn't even know that anything of that nature was necessary. My wife's item was wooden too, but we had been asked no such questions, and it was now long gone and on its way.

We stood in this area for around fifteen minutes as the two ladies tried to reason with this French-speaking inspector. I suspect that he could only understand about half of what they were saying. They were very direct with him and were trying to argue logically that this was a silly rule. They had no way of knowing it was necessary with an item bought from a street vendor for about $35, they had no way of complying with this rule, and this rule was not stated visibly anywhere in the airport. Rather than causing him to back down, the more they laid out logical arguments, the more he seemed resolved and unwilling to bend. He clearly was not seeking a bribe or anything underhanded. He was following the rules as he saw them, and the attempts to directly talk through this situation were not going well.

I had no certainty that I could do any better than these wonderful women were doing, and they were being very calm considering the circumstances. I took a moment to try my best to assess the situation culturally and then came to the realization that perhaps this gentleman was immersed in a more honor-shame culture, which tends to value indirect communication. It was possible that their tactic of stating what they thought was right and that they were being treated unfairly or unreasonably was threatening to shame him, implying that he was doing something wrong and dishonoring. That would not fly here. So, I stepped off to the side with him and tried a new approach.

"I wonder if you could help me," I began.

This stopped him, and he turned to me and listened intently.

"We are in trouble," I continued. "We have to go home in a few minutes, and we have apparently not followed these important rules that we didn't know about. But we have no way to follow them on a Sunday night and we have to leave your country soon."

He nodded, and I took that as a sign that I had won a hearing with him, so I continued, "We are guests here and didn't mean to cause any trouble or offend, but we are stuck and now we need help. Is there anyone that could help us in this situation? Could you help us?"

He paused, looked to the left and then the right, dropped his head slightly as if thinking, then lifted his eyes to look in my direction and said, "I will help you." That was it. We were through with all our luggage and on our way.

So, what happened there? It wasn't that I'm more charming or suave than the two ladies he had been talking to. And I'm certainly not smarter or prettier than they are. But they were speaking to him in a very direct Western style, and it wasn't working. For him to let the package through at that point would have meant for him to lose face and admit that he had somehow wronged our friend and his wife. What our conversation did, though, was to turn the tables. It was indirect. It wasn't aimed at him or the rules but at the situation. The problem was that we were travelers in need of hospitality and help. We were stuck. If he didn't act, these travelers in need would be shamed and lose face. Now, for him to capitulate was an act of kindness and hospitality rather than one of losing face. With a changed perspective, he was happy to help, as he was clearly a very nice young man.

Communication can be a tricky thing in cross-cultural settings, and if we don't have some awareness of different styles and assumptions in communication, we can set ourselves and our communities up for some real heartaches and headaches.

We will look at a few of the styles of communication that can become problem areas in cross-cultural settings.

HIGH AND LOW CONTEXT

Low-context cultures tend to be characteristic of the Western world. They rely heavily on words and explicit communication. They don't typically utilize other contextual clues such as tone of voice, body language, situations, facial expressions, or other methods of interpretation. These cultures rely on straightforward, word-based interactions and prefer facts to feelings or other data.

High-context cultures are often characteristic of the non-Western world. They rely heavily on relationship and interpersonal dynamics of the collectivist context. In these groups, implicit messages and contextual clues such as tone of voice, facial expressions, and perceived feelings are important and heavily relied upon to communicate truth.

That might all sound somewhat technical. You might even be skeptical at this point that something like this is really that important when it comes to diverse communities, but I can tell you it can be huge. I cannot tell you how many times I have said something to my wife, who is undoubtedly from a high-context cultural background, who has then read some sort of meaning into what I said and how I said it that I did not intend at all. My response is often to point out the words that I said. That's what I meant. She will dispute that and maintain that I implied other things. I will then assert that I most certainly did not say anything else. I want her to pay attention to my words. She is reading my emotion, body language, and a host of other things. It can be very frustrating, because it is literally like two people who are speaking different languages trying to carry on a conversation.

While these styles typically fall along Western and Eastern divides, they don't always. Don't assume that because someone grew up in a predominantly low-context world that they are automatically low context. The only way to tell is through communication and observation.

DIRECT AND INDIRECT

Direct communicators prefer the other person to speak clearly, concisely, and directly. If you have something to say, say it. It doesn't matter if it is controversial or could cause a bit of embarrassment. If it is true, then they would rather know what's on your mind.

Indirect communicators are different. Directly stating something seems rude to them in many situations. It's better to drop hints or talk about something in subtle, indirect ways so that the speaker can pick up on it without having a confrontation.

This area is tricky because it's not clear-cut along cultural lines. Although many would argue that Western cultures tend to be more direct and Eastern cultures tend to be indirect, that's not always accurate. I grew up in the United States but come from a more indirect home and surroundings. My wife also grew up in the US, but her cultural background was very direct. Canadians are typically of a more indirect nature, but I know a few Canadians who are extremely direct. Many African countries are stereotypically direct in their communication, but others are not. And in each of those areas, there are many exceptions.

The challenge, then, is that two people can grow up in the same area, yet one could be a direct communicator and the other very indirect. To make matters worse, this is one of the areas that is most likely to cause irritation, misunderstanding, and conflict.

My wife was raised her whole life to speak directly and ask for what you want. That feels invasive and rude to me. It irritates me, a lot. I was conditioned, without ever realizing it, to not ask for things directly. It seems like that obligates people, and I would rather have them offer things because they want to. So, I don't ask for things. That drives her nuts. It feels manipulative to her. She won't offer things, reasoning that if I want something, I will ask for it. Even though we have been together a long time and have learned that the other doesn't mean to be disrespectful, rude, or manipulative, it is still challenging. It demands constantly choosing to interpret the actions of the other by what it means to them and not what it feels like. But imagine if we didn't understand the cultural dynamics at play here. Over time, it could easily cause irreparable damage to our ability to communicate, and eventually to our entire relationship.

NONVERBAL COMMUNICATION

Is it respectful to look someone directly in the eye or is it disrespectful and aggressive? As simple as that sounds, it could be a real problem in a multiethnic community if people have different assumptions about the simple act of where to look when someone is speaking to you. It can be fraught with difficulties. Some women are raised in groups where they would not make direct eye contact with a man because it could be taken in a sexual way, but then when interacting with a male from outside that group, their manner is interpreted as not paying attention to the conversation or being aloof.

There are many forms of nonverbal communication that can be taken differently than intended by those with different cultural conditioning. North Americans, for example, use their hands quite often when they speak and would think nothing of pointing a finger at another person in conversation. Other cultures would consider that inappropriate and would gesture with an open hand and palm up but would never point their finger at someone else.

In many countries it is normal to move closer than arm's length when speaking with another person. For others, like myself, "No, thank you"—that's too close for comfort. In some cultures, men hold hands when they speak, while in many others that is deemed abnormal.

In many Western nations, hugging is the standard greeting in the context of a church gathering, but there are some cultures that perceive the hug as a sexual act. Unaware of this, churches that were planted by Westerners caused problems they never would have imagined when they assumed that new disciples and visitors wouldn't mind being hugged. What they intended felt like a very different act to their recipients.

Hand gestures can also be problematic, as quite often the meaning of a harmless hand gesture in one culture or country can be quite offensive in another.

WHEN TO SPEAK

There is a bevy of other culturally conditioned aspects of communication that could be analyzed, but I will mention just a few here. When should you speak up? When is it okay to insert your opinion in a group conversation or a meeting? Some of us would say that the time to speak is when you have something to say. To hold yourself back would be inauthentic or a sign of feeling oppressed. Be respectful but speak freely. For others, that sounds independent and rude. Their culture has taught them to wait to be asked. You don't just speak up and insert yourself in certain situations. I know this is sensitive, but to be straightforward, many people of color have inherited a cultural pressure both internally and externally to defer to white people and not speak openly to them.

The present danger in these types of cultural clashes is not only the obvious misunderstanding of the reserved group finding the free speakers to be rude and having no consideration for proper order and respect, it also comes when members of the reserved group don't have their voices heard because they are drowned out by the free speakers. They expect that they will be invited or asked to share their opinion, but when that doesn't happen, the free speakers will assume they have nothing to say, and those who are more reserved will often be hurt or offended, assuming that they were not asked because their opinion or input is not valued.

Cultural groups often have different norms about when it is okay to give feedback to those in positions of authority. The West, for example, tends to have a rather free approach to airing opinions regardless of the level of authority that a person has. Eastern-based cultures, on the other hand, trend in the opposite direction. You don't give input to authority figures and may not fully disclose your thoughts even if asked by the authority figure.

For Westerners, we have been raised that there is no hierarchy when speaking in a group. Whoever has something to say should say it. For many cultures, though, that is disrespectful. There are hierarchies, and the oldest person or the one with the most authority has the right to speak first.

What about resolving disagreements? Are those handled directly between the two people who are disagreeing or should they automatically share the problem with another party who then may choose to act as a go-between and bring resolution to the divide? For many groups, issues simply would not typically be resolved directly between the disagreeing parties. Members of the community are brought into knowledge of the situation, and they work to resolve it. For people who are not of that cultural background, though, such a sharing of information feels like a violation of trust and creates further tension.

ROUND AND ROUND

There is one other fascinating aspect of communication that I will briefly mention before moving on to solutions. Sociologists typically identify two broad approaches to communication and storytelling, and the divide often falls along upbringing in the middle class or generational poverty. Middle-class folks value logical, concise storytelling that starts at the beginning of the story and follows a clear chain of progression right up through the end. I refer to this as linear communication, although it can also be described with the more technical term, formal register. Those from generational poverty use what I call spiral communication (casual register). This is a highly interactive form of communication, in which the story can start from any point and will jump around. This type of storytelling is aimed at more interplay with the listener, who is supposed to join in and interact with the story, occasionally asking questions.

If you have ever stood confused, trying to follow what seemed like a meandering tale from your friend, only to finally grow frustrated and blurt out, "Just get to the point," this is the dynamic that might very well have been the culprit. Interestingly, experts surmise that casual-register people can much more easily learn to use linear forms of communication and that it is far more difficult for linear thinkers to learn the art of spiral communication.

BRIDGING THE GAP

I'll be up front from the beginning here. This will be one of the most difficult areas to resolve consistently in cross-cultural situations. The reason is simple. The most effective way to overcome communication gaps in culture is through healthy and vibrant communication. Do you see the problem there? I will go quickly through the categories to consider in bridging the gaps of cultural divides, but I'm warning you now, this one is going to be thin, beyond efforts to become more informed, have lots of open dialogues as we work through the many potential communication issues that can arise, and show much grace.

The Biblical View

The one clear-cut biblical directive is that we must be honest. Many cultures, especially traditional honor-and-shame cultures, accept a certain amount of lying in normal communication as a way to save face and avoid embarrassment or shame for anyone involved. While we do not want to be harsh or unnecessarily offensive, it is vital that we always pursue honesty. Most of these other aspects of communication are not directed by the biblical witness, but we must be honest.

Communication and Education

There is simply no way that we could begin to adequately cover all the issues that can arise in the area of communication across cultures. Hopefully this chapter has given you a leg up in being aware of and sensitive to some of the potential pitfalls. A general start is to learn not to take offense when someone says something or speaks at a time that feels wrong or offensive. Reserve judgment until you've had the time to think through whether there might be an unlike cultural paradigm from which they are working. Just doing that might help you discover that they were not acting inappropriately in their cultural framework, which will assist you in interpreting their communication style.

There are two primary approaches to growing in your understanding and education about cross-cultural communication. The first is to fill up your life with people from multiple cultures. Interact and learn as much as possible. Just as the best way to learn a new language is total immersion in that language, so the best way to learn cultural patterns of communication is to immerse in other groups as much as possible. There will be bumps along the way, but you will learn as long as both sides are aware and committed to being humble.

The second option is to take a course in cross-cultural communication online or through a local university or seminary. These can be helpful to an extent, but they pale in comparison to the real-world experience of getting into the trenches and intertwining your life with a diversity of people.

The Dominant Group

When it comes to communication, the dynamics of dominant groups can become a real problem if there is not awareness and sensitivity. Communication issues extend to daily interactions, crucial conversations, conflict resolution, sense of humor, public speaking, and so much more. Without recognition and openness to learning about other communication norms and corresponding work toward their inclusion, the result can be exclusion and marginalization of nondominant people in areas of impact, influence, and leadership within the community.

It is incumbent on both dominant and nondominant groups to be flexible, humble, and willing to learn and grow in this area, but there is a special level of responsibility on the dominant group to be aware of the gaps, make efforts to recognize when they affect interactions, and take steps to grow in competency.

Heart Language

Communication is a central issue to all cultural groups. I don't think a case could be made that it is more important or more of a heart language issue for any one set of people. This is of equal importance and impact to all people, but I wouldn't characterize it as a heart language for anyone, so I would refer to the discussion in the section above on "The Dominant Group" and move on to the next consideration.

The Grace Factor

Showing patience and grace to one another during miscommunication issues is huge. For example, those from a direct-communication background can quickly grow irritated with indirect speakers and be very tempted to withdraw from them and eventually break community.

At all levels, misunderstandings are constantly around the corner, and it is easy to marginalize individuals and groups of people without intending to.

Perhaps the greatest tool to aid growth in cultural communication competency is the simple question, "What did you mean by that?" We must foster an ethos in our communities where it is acceptable to ask this question and will not cause offense. We must be able to explain that a certain interaction or communication felt rude, aggressive, manipulative, or whatever the case may be. The only way for that to happen is for us to accept that we will have communication misfires. We should anticipate it as part of the daily reality for a diverse community. Miscommunication happens even in societies that are not diverse, so we should absolutely embrace it as a normal part of the everyday experience in a diverse church family.

Once we come to accept the difficulties involved in cross-cultural communication, we can go to work in our ongoing effort to be all things to all people.

Chapter 17

What Are We Here For?

Somewhere around 1993 I went with some friends to visit the Greater First Baptist Church in Bartlesville, Oklahoma. I didn't know much about the church and had decided at that point in my life that I didn't much believe in God and didn't like Christians. But a group of my friends were going for a visit, so I decided that I would join them. On my first visit, I was struck by how good their choir was. I had never heard singing like that in my life. It was incredibly entertaining, but that's not why I went back. Visiting Greater First Baptist was the first time in my life that I had been to an African American church, but that's not why I went back either.

I was a long way from home, and I had many friends at the school there, but I would still get homesick from time to time and think of leaving the school. It was, after all, in Oklahoma, and home for me was in Wisconsin, over 700 miles away. What I found at Greater First Baptist was community. It was nothing like the family or community I had experienced at home, but I loved it. They took in this white boy from Wisconsin and made me feel like part of the family for the few months that I sporadically attended.

The sense of community was amazing, and it was nothing like anything I had seen growing up going to church. My parents were committed to their church my whole life, so it was normal for me to be at church events three or four times a week or more. Their church was growing, strong, and vibrant. But it was event centered. We went there for services or for meetings or for a building and grounds cleanup day. I'm not saying that there were not relationships there; there were. But for the most part, it felt like a performing arts center. We would go when there was a show or performance, get filled up, and then go back home to our lives.

Greater First Baptist was different. It was a church building, but it was like a giant family home at the holidays where people are coming in and out from near and far to gather together after being apart for a while. Someone was always at that building. I don't think I ever remember driving by there that there weren't people coming and going. They had meals together. They constantly had Bible studies, prayer groups, tutoring groups, after-school play groups, choir practice, and just about any other kind of gathering you could think of. But it wasn't just those planned events. People would show up at the building and hang out, kids and older people alike. It seemed like this building was the heart of the entire community.

When something bad happened in the area, impromptu meetings were held there to talk about it. And whether it was these meetings or a Sunday worship gathering, they talked about the real things going on in the world and the community. They talked about hot-button issues and how Jesus was still in control despite the struggles. And they sang about those struggles too. I always got the sense that you could ask any question there, bring up any problem in your life, and lament about the evil you saw in the world. There didn't seem to be anything that was off limits.

I would go on to graduate from the university and head back home, eventually marrying and moving to Milwaukee, where my wife and I became Christians and part of the diverse family of the Milwaukee Church of Christ. Even though we loved that group and remain part of the larger fellowship of believers to which the Milwaukee Church belongs, the sense of what a church is was much different from that little building pulsating with life on the corner of W 10th St. and SW Jennings Ave.

WHAT IS THE CHURCH FOR?

Jesus said to go and make disciples of all nations, but what does that mean for the purpose and emphasis of individual church communities? Is the church to be a globally attentive missionary machine, laser focused on bringing all people into the kingdom of God? Or is it a missional community that is called to be a visible outpost of the life of the age to come, beckoning people in the local community to come join this new society, transforming the world one neighborhood at a time by serving and loving the people directly around them? In other words, are churches focused on converting scores of individuals and growing the church so that it can spread the gospel across the globe, or are they more like embassies, planted within communities and meant to be points of light of the kingdom into that area? Are they globally focused or neighborhood focused?

My point here is not to resolve that debate. It's a good discussion to have, but that's simply not my purpose. Diverse churches will often have people with both of those cultural assumptions about the purpose of the body of Christ. Are we even aware of that divide, let alone working toward bridging that gap?

Church members who have embraced the global mission mindset and culture will not necessarily feel the pull to become the type of community hub that Greater First Baptist was. That's what community centers are for, they would argue. We're in the business of saving souls. When those with that cultural mindset own a church building or rent a meeting place, the things that matter most are gathering at a central location and doing so as cheaply as possible. Churches that are dominated by this culture can meet in one location for years without the neighborhood around them being anything more than vaguely aware that they meet there. Sure, it would be great to have more people from the neighborhood come to church, and we might occasionally make efforts to invite them out, but far more important is to get out into the larger area and find people who are open to the gospel. Growth outweighs serving the community.

Those that come from the neighborhood church culture will have vastly different expectations. They will grow increasingly grieved in their spirits at the lack of being a force for change in the community. They will notice a hole in their heart, wishing that they had that neighborhood-based building that could serve as the heartbeat for the public as well as for members of the church. They will long for that feeling of being safe and being home when at the church's building and a sense that they are one community and facing life together, come good or bad.

This divergence in methods often leads to different approaches in engaging in social issues and even political topics. The global missional church will want to avoid those things. That's not what church is for. Church is about escaping from the cares and concerns of the world. We come to worship God, leave our troubles behind, and save souls. The neighborhood church must deal with those realities of life. They are deeply concerned with life issues like alcoholism and drug abuse because they affect the neighborhood. As do unjust housing policies, unfair zoning issues, corrupt police officers, activities for families and kids, safe parks, and more. Those are all pertinent issues for the community-focused church. They need to talk about those things, to imagine how the kingdom of God can restructure and reorder life for the whole surrounding area as it pulses forth from the neighborhood church.

This doesn't all line up neatly all the time. Some churches that have a neighborhood building and church community have other cultural reasons for not wanting to engage in hot-topic issues or politically charged items. Some globally focused bodies that don't own a building are still passionate about serving the needy in their own area. The point is that wherever the lines are drawn that separate the cultural expectations and assumptions about what a church is and what it does, it can leave deep divides in a diverse church and be the source of growing frustration for many of the members if not recognized and addressed.

Perhaps at this point, if you haven't already, you might be feeling a little overwhelmed. "It seems like there are a thousand things that can cause cultural frustration and angst within a community," you might exclaim. Yes, there are. Now you're getting the point. "But this is going to be a lot more work than I ever imagined." I'm glad you realize that. It does demand constant attention and work. "Will it be worth it, though?" Yes, it will.

EVACUATION OR PREPARATION?

Sometimes we have strange childhood memories imprinted indelibly in our minds, and we're never quite sure why that memory, above all others, stands out so clearly. I recall like it was yesterday repairing a rubber innertube with my dad while on vacation in Northern Wisconsin when I was about five. There was the one day when my sister and our neighbors and I all walked up to the corner store to get candy. We did that dozens of times, but for some reason a specific trip when I was about eight stands out, even though nothing significant or particularly memorable happened.

And then there was *A Thief in the Night*. This was a movie they showed our youth group at church when I was about thirteen. I will never forget that movie. It was a dystopian look at the future through the lens of a dispensational approach to the book of Revelation. It takes place moments after the "rapture" happens and all the Christians have vanished. It revels in the *Left Behind*-type approach to the "end times," complete with a tribulation for those that didn't truly believe and who must struggle through as the Antichrist, the leader of the New World Order, begins to craft the world in his image and force people to take the mark of the Beast.

I will save for another occasion my opinions of the many faults of this type of interpretation of Revelation. This movie is etched in my mind. I will never forget the scene at the end as the sound of a guillotine rips through your ears and a balloon floats past the window, cluing the audience in to the fact that another person who came to faith after the so-called rapture has been put to death for their allegiance to Christ.

That movie was representative of what I believed about Christianity growing up. The world was desperately lost, and the only hope that Christians had was to believe in Jesus so that we would be evacuated to heaven with him some day before the rapture.

This doctrine had a major impact on the church community I grew up in. It resulted in a church culture that was very evacuation focused. Our job was to save people before we were rescued by Jesus. What was going on in the world didn't matter much; that was all going to be destroyed one day anyway. We just needed to hang on until we were spirited out.

The rapture doctrine and subsequent mindsets have only been

around since the nineteenth century and didn't come to dominate Western religious thinking until the twentieth. Having been raised in the atmosphere of believing that God's primary goal is to save a few souls before evacuating them out of the world has impacted many of us and our approach to church life more than we might think.

The primary message of the gospel, however, is that Jesus is the true King, he is establishing his kingdom through his people, and he will one day return to a restored heaven and earth and rule with his people forever. The gospel is not about evacuation but about preparation for the final coming of the kingdom of God. These divergent beliefs lead down entirely different roads of culture and practice.

What is the primary task of the church? Are we a rescue team trying to get as many out of a dumpster fire as we can? If so, then atrocities and injustices in the world are hardly our main concern. Let's just stay focused on conversions; that's all that matters. But if our primary vocation is to spread the message that God's kingdom is open for business and we can become citizens under King Jesus by dying to ourselves and taking up his kingdom agenda in the world, then finding ways to address the problems and inequities of the kingdoms of the world and showing how the kingdom of God has different answers takes center stage.

The evacuationists will want to spend church resources and time preparing and equipping members to evangelize and will prize numerical growth. The kingdom citizens will tend to prioritize spiritual formation, maturation, and ongoing training for members after conversion.

One interesting component to this is that because this aspect of culture has its basis in doctrine, it is possible for one's doctrine to change but not the culture. For instance, someone like myself could grow up in an evacuation model and then eventually realize that this is not sound biblical teaching but not dig down far enough to recognize that many of my cultural tendencies in this area are rooted in a doctrine to which I no longer hold.

These are not easy positions to bring together. When we bring in unexamined our cultural assumptions about what church is for, we tend to be blind to our different approaches. We assume that those with different assumptions are not spiritual and have no idea what the kingdom of God is all about.

EVENTS OR PEOPLE

One last area of cultural life that is impacted by the assumptions we bring with us about what church is for is whether a church is events focused or people focused. That doesn't mean that events-focused individuals don't care about people, nor does it mean that people-focused persons don't give a hoot about events and programs. Rather, it has to do with what we believe a church should sink most of its resources into so as to grow and be what Jesus has called us to be.

Those with an events-focused mindset will believe that the best use of church resources is in planning events and developing programs, ministries, and classes that will train people in the work of the gospel and holy living, and in hiring as much staff as possible to keep the church running well and thriving. They will be thrilled over more church plantings, more staff hired, and more conferences scheduled. People-focused folks will believe that those things are well and fine, but that the heart of the church should be about taking care of people. The bulk of the resources are better spent on benevolence, serving the poor, programs that change the trajectory of the lives of those that are in need, counseling classes, grief recovery programs, and parenting and marriage training. They will get excited about service days, expanded benevolent ministries, and community-based connections.

I don't want to create a parody of two extreme positions here. We are talking about focus and priority in our cultural assumptions for the purpose of church. There will be many areas of overlap between these types of preferences, but the larger point stands. Our churches can be full of people with these divergent preferences as to what a church should be doing, and that can create tension if we are not aware that these differences do exist in our vision of what the church culture can or should be.

BRIDGING THE GAP

There is not a clear line that runs down these issues perfectly dividing them into two cultural camps. There are patterns that develop, though. Those with the global mission mindset tend toward being events focused and having an evacuation mentality, while those who are community focused tend toward being people centered and having a preparation-based outlook. Is there a way to bring them together in one diverse community, or would it be best to give in to these differences and create different churches that cater to the cultural assumptions and preferences of these groups? The African American church in the United States has historically been deeply rooted in the community-focused model, so it is true that a much higher percentage of African American disciples would lean toward that approach, along with many other peoples of color, in comparison to the average white North American disciple.

The Biblical View

I don't believe that a clear-cut biblical case can be made solely for either the global mission or community-based approach. Both are rooted in biblical truth. The problem, I believe, comes in when we emphasize one and virtually ignore the other. That means that this is a prime area of cultural preference in which those with varying views should come together and figure out how to include both passions within the community. The same could be said for the debate about focusing on events or people.

Whether the church should center its hope on evacuation or preparation is more clear-cut, in my opinion. We don't have time for a thorough biblical examination of this topic here, but Scripture does seem clear on it. The rapture-evacuation theory comes in large part from a misunderstanding of 1 Thessalonians 4:17. In that verse, Paul says that believers who are still alive when Christ returns will be caught up with him in the clouds to meet the Lord in the air. In English, these words can be construed to have a different meaning than what Paul was most likely communicating. When God or the Son of Man rides on the clouds in Old Testament language, it refers to him coming in judgment and renewal. The word Paul uses for "air" here means specifically the air around us that we breathe and move in, not the sky. And the term translated "meet" was a technical term that spoke of going out to meet an important person and escorting them back into your town. Paul is describing the same broad flow of events that Peter does in 2 Peter 3, and that John does in Revelation 21. One day Christ will return to our space, renewing his creation and his people and living with us forever. These passages are not about evacuation but about cleansing, restoration, and the new heavens and earth (see also Matthew 19:28; Acts 3:21). In my opinion, then, the church should work toward embracing the preparation view and ensuring that this is reflected in its culture and actions, and attempt to root out any evacuation tendencies or mindsets.

Communication and Education

Because strong biblical cases can be made for the global approach as well as the community approach, a church family would do well to study the strengths, weaknesses, and characteristics of both. They could study successful churches in each model and consider what aspects of those churches could already be found in their congregation and what elements could be added. It will take creativity to consider how to blend these two models. They are not mutually exclusive but are often approached as though they were.

The Compromise Position

As I don't believe that some of our categories like the dominant group, a restrictive view, or heart language are significant factors for this grouping of issues or tilt us toward one position or the other, we will skip right to the compromise position. Overcoming differences in these areas is going to come down almost entirely to communication, compromise, and finding balance.

The positions of global versus community focus tend to pull us in the exact opposite directions, so finding a middle ground that accommodates both views will not be easy. It will require finding advocates for each position who can clearly identify the vision for each area of concern and focus.

The next step would be to give opportunities for each side to present their standpoint. They must each be able to clearly identify specific outcomes and goals that they feel are important to their position. For example, a global advocate team might cite one of their primary goals as establishing a strong relationship with a congregation in a foreign country and partnering with that church both relationally and financially to help advance the gospel in that part of the world. Meanwhile, the community-based advocates might find it important to find a building to meet in that is in a lower-income area so that the church can integrate into that community, advocate for its needs, and begin programs to bolster and invigorate economic and educational opportunities in the neighborhood.

What might a compromise position look like in this case? It could be challenging for a local congregation to adequately support global ministries and have the means to purchase and maintain a church building in a specific neighborhood (the difficulties of that task increase exponentially if the church is a larger group split into distinct regions throughout the city that meet separately). It is possible that both could be accomplished, but very often their advocates will find themselves competing for the same limited pool of financial resources. In this situation, church leadership might propose a scenario in which the mission goals are met and accomplished, but the church would partner with a community center or school in the neighborhood to serve members of the community. They could develop a plan to use church volunteers partnering with the resources of the school or community center to accomplish the desired goals within the community without having a physical building that belongs to the church in that neighborhood. This way, the primary goals of the community-based advocacy group can be met, but through a different means that still allows the financial flexibility to also fulfill the goals of global missions. This is just one example, of course. There are countless ways that these two aims can work together to create a balanced church that takes care of both areas of focus.

The Grace Factor

Although I skipped over discussing the issue of heart language in this chapter, that does not mean people are not extremely passionate about the issues over what a church is for and what it should be accomplishing. All disciples can agree that we want to expand God's kingdom, but we can have very profoundly different opinions on how to best accomplish that goal. It can be easy to exalt our own preferences or beliefs about how to best do that and minimize the approach of others or even suppose that they don't care about the things that we are passionate about.

When we encounter deep-seated differences in what the church should be doing or focusing on, rather than jumping to negative assumptions about the position of others or an immediate advocacy for our own position, we should start with trying to understand the reasons that others have for their passions. When we understand their motivations and desires, it's much easier to patiently and graciously work together to find middle ground. How can a group focus both globally and on the community? How can a group balance people and events? Only through communication, compromise, patience, grace, and a recognition that there is value in accomplishing both sides rather than just one.

Chapter 18

Don't Stop the Music

Harmony did not come easy for my wife and me when we started dating and through the first few years of our marriage. We had a terrible problem that we just could not seem to overcome no matter how hard we tried. I hate to admit this publicly and embarrass my wife like this, but if I can help even one person with this then it is worth it. My wife has dreadful taste in music. This caused issues in our relationship for years.

Whenever we were in the car together or just felt like putting on some good music, I would want to play some '80s rock, some good '90s hip-hop, or if I really wanted to get things hopping, some good ol' Johnny Cash and Waylon Jennings. I'm certain that you're confused right now, because what normal functioning human being wouldn't absolutely love to listen to any of those at the drop of a hat?

Yet, as shocking as this might be for you, none of those genres would be her first choice. She can tolerate a few songs here and there, but as a general rule, she doesn't like them. She prefers old R & B from the '70s and '80s, and more modern singers like Norah Jones. That's right, I said Norah Jones, who in my opinion is like a rainy day, a lukewarm cup of what was once hot chocolate, and a big spoonful of sadness in musical form all rolled into one.

We simply could not agree on what to listen to when together, so we had music wars. We would try to beat one another to the control panels of whatever device we were listening to and if one left the room for even a moment, the other one would quickly change the music.

If we fast-forward to today, we still don't naturally love one another's musical taste, but we have learned to coexist. And I'm not talking about just tolerating the other's music. It has taken a long time, but we've learned to participate in one another's musical choices. We have found groups or songs that we can appreciate and enjoy together. And sometimes we do endure or tolerate song choices for the benefit of the other, but we do so without complaining or making sure that it's known that we don't care for what the other is playing. We've been able to come together and can now move back and forth between most of those genres without issue. I still enjoy my stuff better, but I've learned to embrace and appreciate much of her preferences and I love to watch her when she is really getting into one of her "jams." But not Norah Jones, that is a bridge too far. For the sake of unity, she has, for the most part, left Miss Jones in the past.

MUSIC WARS

Most of our disagreements over music throughout the years were good natured. We didn't like one another's music, but it was never to the point where we would get into a real fight over it. I wish the same were true for churches. Many of them in the United States have entered a full-out church war over musical preferences and tastes. There have been a lot of churches that have split over music wars. It sounds crazy. We sing at gatherings of the body of Christ to praise and worship God. How could something intended to honor him ever get so entangled in our preferences that we would break fellowship with other believers, or at least get angry to the point of arguing with them?

Issues over music and worship can become so embroiled in passion in part because they are often rooted in strong cultural preferences and background. They can also include dynamics of dominant and nondominant culture, and even racial and generational issues, and suddenly something that should be noncontroversial like music and worship can become a cauldron for conflict and hurt feelings. This is not to imply that music is the only or even the primary way that we worship God, but it is part of it, and because it can be one of the most culturally rooted forms, it is necessary that we spend some time considering it.

CONTEMPORARY OR TRADITIONAL

Let's look at a few of the areas that can cause conflict for a church body when it comes to worshipping God through music. Do you prefer contemporary Christian music complete with acoustic guitars for days or a more traditional style that is heavy on the hymns and acapella singing?

This has become such a divide that some churches have responded to the issue by having separate worship services. The traditional service begins at 8 am; contemporary at 9:30 am; choose your preference and you don't have to be bothered with that other style. It's the difference between "Oceans," "Deeper," and "Shout to the Lord" and "Amazing Grace," "When the Roll Is Called up Yonder," and "The Old Rugged Cross."

Much of the divide between these styles of music splits along generations. The older set tends to prefer the traditional hymns and gospel music they grew up with, which often lends itself to acapella singing or perhaps a subtle piano accompaniment. On the other end is the younger set that favors the songs they would tend to hear on Christian radio. These songs are usually more individual focused, less theologically informed, instrument heavy, and concert ready.

This gap also often includes pointed disagreements over volume.

Contemporary styles often thrive on the louder concert feel. But this can easily anger and even hurt the eardrums of older disciples (but not always just older Christians), who prefer the softer hymn style that isn't blasting in their ears.

The styles are so diverse in instrumental accompaniment, pace, feel, lyrics, depth, and just about every way that it is almost impossible to blend them together in a hybrid style. You either have one style or the other. But this can get divisive quickly because people who strongly desire one type over the other will allow themselves to feel as though they can't properly worship God through a style of music they can't stand.

IT'S SNOWING IN HERE

I was at one worship gathering some years ago where a church was working at integrating both contemporary and traditional music together in the same service. They worked hard toward this diversity, having different song-leading teams rotate in and out as they switched back and forth between styles. While I appreciated their efforts, I almost broke down in laughter when a friend walked over to me and whispered, "It's snowing in here." Confused, I looked at him with a quizzical expression. He leaned over and said, "We're really nailing diverse worship. We've got old white people music and young white people music." It was a bit sarcastic, but I understood his point.

In fact, it highlights something important. I was at a major evangelical conference last year that was focused on discipleship. Despite a disturbing lack of human diversity at the event, the organizer kept saying that he wanted this annual conference to be ethnically diverse, although he couldn't seem to understand why it wasn't. I suppose the reasons are as complex as the history of American Christianity, but I could have pointed out a major contributing factor right away. Every song at the conference was very loud, rock music oriented, contemporary Christian, and dare I say, white music. The music reflected the preferences of who was there. That will never be the way to diversity. If the perfect picture of God's gathered people is persons from every tribe, language, people group, and nation, then what message does it send if they are singing the music from only one group of people? Shouldn't the culture and music of our church reflect the gathering of the nations as much as possible?

Music choices send a strong message about who is valued and included in the community. We can say that we want to be diverse, but if the music doesn't reflect that, it will be the most obvious and visible way for visitors (or even members) to discern that perhaps their presence is wanted but not their influence, and that they aren't truly valued.

Diverse churches simply must reflect that diversity in their song choices, musical styles, and even languages. And let me be clear, it's not just about the songs. There can be great divides in the style and approach to singing. Traditional culturally white styles of worship are very ordered. You sing four songs with the accompanying PowerPoint slides or hymnbook and then move on to the sermon, getting in all four songs in a cool fourteen minutes. In traditional African American or Latino worship, for example, one song might go fourteen minutes if people are feeling the Spirit move.

There is also a difference in the type of lyrics. Traditional Western-style songs are lyric based and carry deep theological significance. That is not as true for many contemporary songs that often make it difficult to tell whether you're singing about God or your girlfriend. But that aside, I always preferred the Western songs with many words to the traditional songs of other cultural styles such as African, Latino, or African American. That is, until I had a conversation with a wise older African brother one day. Looking back on it, my question was a bit arrogant, but many African songs have a few lyrics that are sung over and over and over again, so I asked him if he preferred those songs or would rather sing songs that had deeper lyrics. He paused and then looked up at me and said, "My brother, what is deeper, to sing many words without the time to think on them, or to repeat a few truths about God over and over again so that you can meditate on them until they become part of your soul." That shut me up good and made me realize that different approaches to worship all have their value.

We have come to cherish our time in the churches in Africa, and most of them do an amazing job of integrating styles of music from different cultures, ethnic groups, and tribes into their worship. One thing that most Africans have in common, continent-wide, is the expression of using their entire body during song worship in a way that is foreign to most Americans, especially non–African American disciples, and from my own experience and upbringing, especially Midwestern white disciples. After spending extended time on the African continent, there have been times when we have come back and desired to teach our brothers and sisters in the Midwest to engage in some of the songs and physical freedom of the African style. We have found that many of our African American brothers and sisters long for this type of expression but quickly grow disappointed. Certainly not all, but from our experience, it is fair to say that a majority of white Midwestern Christians are uncomfortable with dancing or moving expressively while singing. Their responses tend toward sentiments like, "I'm not comfortable with this. Why do we have to do this weird style of song that I don't like, and I can't dance. Why are they trying to make us do this?" What they may have never stopped to think about is that they have brothers and sisters in their congregation whose souls have been yearning to worship in this manner, and it is very probable that they have been making those folks do it their way for years. So they stand there stiffly and refuse to truly enter the worship experience fully through the interactive nature of that style of song.

But we can't make people like music they don't like, right? Shouldn't it be enough for them to tolerate it, and if they just stand there quietly, then what's the issue? The problem is that this is a worldly approach. It is toleration. The New Testament calls us beyond that to participation—to becoming all things to all people.

One other objection might arise here. Isn't this making worship preference focused? Isn't calling for diverse styles of music that make all people feel included just catering to people and their desires and taking the focus off God? In a word, no. This is about inviting all people to worship God and creating space where they can do that in the most complete manner possible. If we stick with just one style, we are creating an environment where only one group of people can fully express themselves in worship to God. Everybody worships God in different ways, and a strong community will share in those ways and explore one another's expressions rather than just sticking to their own.

Playing into this dynamic is the fact that many of us have been conditioned by Western individualism more than we realize or care to admit. Because of this, we often reduce worship of God to an individual activity, even though it is often done in a group setting. We close our eyes, get lost in our favorite song and imagine that it is just me singing to God. This is my time to worship. This is not what corporate worship was ever intended to be. It is an act of us coming together, with all the compromise and accommodation that this implies, and worshipping God together as an act of submission to God and to one another.

The need to reflect the gathering of the nations is true for every congregation, regardless of the dominant ethnic group. I have an African friend who is the lead evangelist in a diverse but predominantly African American church in the South. I was telling him that our congregation in the North was working hard on diversifying our music selections to include other styles of music. At that point, we were specifically adding more African American influence from our African American brothers and sisters. His response cracked me up. "I understand," he said. "I keep telling our guys that they have to include some country music for the white people." Gatherings of the nations should reflect the music of the nations.

EVERY LANGUAGE

We can sometimes limit the discussion of diverse music to the preferred styles of the dominant group in a community. Hopefully we move beyond that and engage in diversity at the cultural, ethnic, and national level. But there is another area that is often overlooked: language diversity.

I have learned quite a few songs in various African languages. Some of them have become beloved favorites of mine such as "Avulekile Amasango" and "Jonana Jo." I love to sing the Spanish "La Montaña," and I read Spanish pretty well, so I understand the lyrics as I sing. However, I still most connect in worship when I sing in English. That's my first tongue and the language of my heart. I have been in churches where I am the only native English speaker, yet they sang a song or two in English. It provided a space for me to fully worship God, but it also made me feel incredibly valued.

Once again, looking to the picture of God's people in Revelation 5:9 is instructive. It includes every language. I'm not advocating here for a church to randomly select languages that have no connection to its congregation, but I do believe it is important to make efforts to sing in more than one language. Not only does it make speakers of that language feel valued in the community, but it also sends a clear signal to anyone present that we take God's gathering of the nations seriously. There is a reason we sing in other languages. It creates a constant opportunity to brag about what God is doing in bringing together the nations once again. This is about our mission and intentional worship rather than our own comfort zones.

BRIDGING THE GAP

Music is an important facet of the human experience. It connects with us in ways that we often don't fully understand. It can affect our mood, set the tone for an event, or get us out of our seat when we didn't think we felt like dancing. Music is one of the oldest forms of spiritual expression and is an integral part of corporate worship. Virtually all cultures appreciate and enjoy music to some extent. For some, however, music is central to nearly every aspect of life.

For many people, music is like the language of their culture. It is how they best communicate, and it is the way to speak to them, include them, and show them they are appreciated. To ignore the importance of music in a diverse community, or to be satisfied with uniform worship, is a sure-fire way to sap a multiethnic community of a huge opportunity to learn to come together and be all things to one another.

The Biblical View

We are directed throughout Scripture to worship God. That starts with a life wholly and completely given to him (Romans 12:1–2). More tangible aspects of worship, such as corporate gatherings and singing, should be reflections of a life devoted in every respect to the worship of the almighty God. Otherwise, it is empty ritual and not worship at all, like a cheating husband expecting to avert an impending divorce because he takes his wife out for a special anniversary dinner. Speak to one another, directs Paul, "with psalms, hymns, and songs from the Spirit. Sing and make music from your heart to the Lord" (Ephesians 5:19).

Beyond the call to sing, there is not much in the way of biblical instruction. Paul and Silas were praying and singing during a night they spent in prison (Acts 16:25). Paul says that he will sing the praises of God (Romans 15:9), doing so with his spirit and emotion, but also with his mind and understanding (1 Corinthians 14:15), which would seem to indicate that there was some thought and intention behind what he was singing. He offers encouragement to those in Colossae that they should sing to God with gratitude in their hearts (Colossians 3:16). James instructs anyone who is in trouble to pray, and those who are happy to sing songs of praise (James 5:13). And, of course, we see the multitude of every tribe, nation, people group, and language singing a new song of praise to the lamb of God (Revelation 5:9).

So, we should sing praises to God as the gathered people from all nations. That doesn't give us a lot of direction, but from the outset it might give us pause as to how many of our songs are more about us and our feelings than about God.

We are called to sing together, that much is clear. And Revelation emphasizes that people of all cultures are coming together to sing and praise God. While it isn't stated directly, given the diverse nature of the New Testament churches and the picture of worship in Revelation, it would seem plausible and likely that music should include the gifts and cultural styles of all, exclude no one in the body, and remain focused on being the fulfillment of the diverse people of God pictured in Revelation

5:9. Just as our churches should include all types of people, so our times of singing should include a diversity in music. That can challenge many churches that often limit themselves to their traditional song lineup or to the ability of those that lead singing. While the latter may sound like a valid excuse, how long would we put up with a preacher who asserted that putting together an interesting and coherent sermon was not in his skill set. Make an effort. Be creative. Challenge yourselves. Figure it out. But don't settle for less just because it's difficult.

The Dominant Group

I'm going to step out of the pattern that I've been following and put the issue of the dominant group before communication and education. I will try to keep this brief and straightforward. A huge portion of responsibility in being diverse in music and worship styles is on the dominant group. I believe they must work hard to include others, to step outside of comfort zones, to learn new things, and to get creative when they must.

There are a few qualifiers here. The best way to be diverse in music is to have a diverse worship ministry. That means that people in nondominant groups need to be willing to participate. Maybe you have wounds from failed past attempts, but I plead with you to work to get past them. The body of Christ needs you.

Additionally, the dominant culture does need to be careful. I recall once being at a worship gathering where an entirely white worship team led the song "Shut de Do'" complete with Jamaican music and accents. The accents were not good. Diversity and a willingness to honor others by sharing in their culture is good. Patronizing or offensive attempts at doing so is bad. Where is that line? All I can say is that it takes discernment in each situation. But the ideal will be a panoply of sharing our styles, genres, and preferences rather than just "performing" someone else's music styles.

Communication and Education

What is the line between honoring and inclusion and mimicry? This is where communication comes in. Ask those questions. Talk to members of ethnic groups and include them in the process. Inclusion is often the line between diversity and appropriation.

This time I placed the section on the dominant group first because I wanted to establish where I think most of the work needs to be done on this topic. In most cases, although not all, the responsibility lies with the dominant group. Where there is no intention or learning, there will most likely not be diversity. You may not be able to sing like Aretha Franklin, Donnie McClurkin, or Diane Williams or have a band that can cut loose with "La Montaña" like Salvador can, but that doesn't mean that your worship team cannot learn to step outside of its box and learn new styles. I'll be honest here. I'm not a musician. I don't have a musical bone in my body, so I can't give many specifics on going about learning and expanding your repertoire, but like Nike's famous tagline, just do it.

The Restrictive View

The call to Christianity is a call to diversity. Becoming all things to all people is a push out of our places of comfort and safety. Music is a place where a community can be adventurous and explore all the cultures that belong to God's kingdom. The music ministry is often the first and loudest declaration of the true commitment to multiculturalism.

We cannot afford to take attitudes like "This is not our music" or "Why do we have to appeal to 'other' people?" or even "I don't like that kind of music." Simply put, those sentiments run counter to the vision of God's gathering of the nations. If you have this type of self-focused feelings, I urge you to aim higher. Let's become a people that are ever seeking to expand our horizons.

Heart Language

Quite a few years ago, at a university just outside of Port Elizabeth, South Africa, my wife addressed a class of nursing students that was almost entirely composed of young men and women from the Xhosa tribe of Southern Africa. When she finished her talk, the class spontaneously broke into a song of thanks that everyone obviously knew well. It was authentic and touching, and we had never seen anything like it. Since then we have learned just how central music is to the everyday life of many of the tribes and people groups across the vast continent of Africa. Music is not just for entertainment in these cultures. It is part of the central nervous system and comes into virtually every detail of life. People sing together. They dance together. They have tribal songs for many common occasions in life. When they worship, they sing. When they celebrate, they sing. When they mourn, they sing. When they protest, they sing. It is as beautiful to my ears as it is foreign to my natural sensibilities.

I enjoy that side of life in Africa. My wife loves it. It speaks to her. She did not grow up in Africa, but it is thought provoking how many of these ingredients of African culture have endured the long and violent journey the African American culture has been on to arrive where it is today. Music was a far more important aspect of my wife's life than mine. And that carries over into our worship experience. I have preferences and styles of music that I like and don't like, just as anyone else does. But the state of the music ministry in my church won't have that great an impact on me. If we don't sing the types of songs that really allow me to fully engage in a deep worship experience, I won't lose any sleep. To my wife and many other African Americans, and other cultures as well, it runs much deeper. Music is their heart language. Without being able to express themselves in a way that feels authentic and touches their soul, they will always feel that a piece of them is missing. They can worship God with all their heart, soul, mind, and strength, and still walk away feeling a bit empty and longing for music that touches their soul.

That speaks to a rather large divide in the way some cultures approach music and worship. For cultures like my own, singing is something we tend to do without thinking too deeply about it. It facilitates a mood of worship, and we know that God is pleased when we sing, so we sing. But for other cultures, like my wife's, singing has a more profound meaning and connection for people. It is how they express their hurts, fears, passions, struggles, and pain. It is every bit as much an avenue to speak to God as prayer is, and through singing with others, they are brought together as a unified group, hearing God singing back to them. It is a soul language. It is a heart language.

It's true that music is not as important to some cultures as it is to others. That said, there is no question that love of music can vary from individual to individual from any culture. There are always exceptions, but as always, it can be helpful to consider the tendencies of a group while still giving room for individual exceptions and preferences.

This area of cultural expression, though, is one of the clearest cut when it comes to this category of heart language. Cultures that do not tend to hold singing and dance as a central heart language of their group should recognize how deeply embedded these can be in the hearts of others. When my wife and I plan to go out to eat, I usually let her choose the place, because I know that she cares about where she eats much more than I do. I gladly let her choose, even if it means eating at a place I don't love, because it means more to her. It would go a long way toward making people feel valued and welcomed into the community if they saw their brothers and sisters from other cultures going out of their way to recognize their love for music and being willing to adapt and embrace types of music, singing, and other related expressions that speak to their hearts.

The Compromise Position

I'll admit this is a tough one. Of course, there needs to be dialogue and compromise, but it will look so different in each church community that there is not much more that I can say other than seek compromise. Go after it. I'm not advocating that a dominant culture simply turn all aspects of the music and song selection over to the nondominant groups. But I do believe that every gathering of the body should be an intentional effort to demonstrate the amazing diversity of God's family.

The Grace Factor

Showing grace could not be more important than when it comes to this aspect of church life. So many people love and feel so strongly about music, even those not from a culture where it is a heart language, that disputes and differences over preferences can get ugly fast. Those in the dominant culture need to value their brothers and sisters and act in their benefit, adapting themselves wherever they can to be inclusive.

But those in the nondominant groups must show grace and patience as well. No one will ever fully have their way in a diverse group, nor should they. Yes, you could find a monocultural group that hits your musical tastes better, so your "why" must continue to be bigger than your "what."

Not all communities need major changes. I have visited many multiethnic churches that are amazing in their broad appeal and varied approach. But many churches do need to grow. That will not happen overnight. It will probably go slower than you would like. It takes time for people to train, learn, and master songs and be ready to perform them in a worship setting. Enjoy the journey of growth. Be gracious with the occasional setback. And never forget to be grateful for the effort that others are making rather than just fixating on the results you want.

THEY'RE NOT SINGING TO YOU

There is an old joke that a young man once remarked to the preacher after a worship service that he didn't like the songs that day. "It's a good thing," replied the old preacher, "that we weren't singing to you." We often make singing together in worship of God much more about us than we realize. Our goal should be to be churches that offer opportunities for everyone to worship in a style that most connects them to God, but that will mean that we all will have times when we don't care for a certain style. There are still many reasons to sing to God wholeheartedly when we don't like a song or style of music:

1. We may not care for it, but some of our brothers and sisters do, and they can most easily connect to God through that type of music. Celebrate that just as they will hopefully celebrate with you during styles that most help you connect in worship.

2. We are singing to God, and he likes all types and styles of singing. In fact, he's more concerned with our hearts being willing to give than with whether we like that song or not.

3. Not singing or fully participating, especially from members of the dominant group, can feel very dismissive and unwelcoming to others.

4. What are you modeling by not fully participating with others? Are you modeling putting the interests of others first or something else?

5. Singing and celebrating with the rest of the body, despite your preferences, promotes and demonstrates unity.

6. Fully engaging in all types of songs and worship styles encourages those around you.

7. Just because you don't like the tune or the style of music doesn't mean that the lyrics are not biblical and worshipful.

When you fully engage in the styles that other brothers and sisters connect with, you might just find that over time you can learn to appreciate that style and find a new way to connect with God.

Chapter 19

Tell Me a Story

I hate to use big words or technical jargon in a book of this nature, and I have made a concerted effort to this point to avoid doing so wherever possible. So, I must apologize, but I need to use one right now. I'll do my best to make it the last. The word is metanarrative. A metanarrative is a grand or overarching story that provides a pattern, structure, framework, or origin for the beliefs and behavior patterns of a group. We all have them whether we realize it or not. These stories are passed down from generation to generation, as are the values or morals behind them, although at times, the values are still shared with the next generation even though the story itself may fade away. These stories are usually rooted in truth, although there are times when they take on the patina of legend and drift more into the realm of myth than fact. For the most part, though, they are real, and they have a major impact on the identity and self-perception of the group.

A BIBLICAL METANARRATIVE

One example of a powerful metanarrative comes from the biblical text. Each generation of Israelite children heard and read the incredible story of the Passover. They thrilled as their parents and grandparents recounted the events that led their ancestors to the revelation that they were God's special people. They marveled at all that God had done as he led them out from under the enslaving hand of Pharaoh. And this set their self-identity in stone. They were God's people and would never again be slaves to anyone, regardless of circumstances that might seem to temporarily point to a different conclusion.

In John 8:32 Jesus challenges the identity created by the Passover metanarrative. He implies that the children of Abraham need to be set free, which elicits passionate protests and a deeply emotional response. That response was, "We are Abraham's descendants and have never been slaves of anyone" (John 8:33). Any other group of people would likely not have taken such offense at the implication of being enslaved, especially when Jesus explains that he is speaking of the universal slavery to sin (John 8:34). But metanarratives and their ensuing identities are powerful. These identities become deeply held, and we cherish them, typically without fully realizing how important they are to us. The Passover metanarrative had cemented in the nation of Israel's mind that they were God's children.

No matter what tough temporary circumstances they might face, like the occupation of their homeland by the Roman Empire, they were still God's family and would never be slaves. Jesus challenged both of those dearly held foundational identifiers. The pushback and vitriol were palpable.

CLASHING METANARRATIVES

When I went off to college, I carried with me the grand story of my country as the land of the free and the home of the brave. From the Pilgrims to the settlers who went West, to the Founding Fathers and beyond, we were a Christian country and the best nation that had ever existed. Then I met a friend from the First Nations. She had a very different metanarrative. I won't go into all the details here, but suffice it to say, the United States of America was not the good guy in her story. For a while, this caused considerable conflict in our friendship, and eventually it just became something we didn't talk about.

Whenever two people are involved relationally to any significant degree, conflict is virtually inevitable. In this context, conflict is simply the incompatibility between two or more perspectives. Conflict itself is not necessarily sinful. You can have conflict without overt sin. Conflict will happen. The difference is in how we handle that conflict. The danger, of course, is that most human conflict does lead to sin.

This is true for a diverse family as well. The more diverse a group is socially, historically, and culturally, the more opportunities there will be for conflict. There will be different perspectives, experiences, cultural expectations, history, preferences, and so on. This will be a constant challenge to unity, especially when difficult subjects such as nations, race, and culture are being discussed.

Yes, conflict will happen. But when that conflict involves pushing up against one or more metanarratives, we can become passionate, and negatively so, rather quickly. That's when conversations and even relationships can start to break down.

HEALTHY FAMILIES TALK

By way of example, let's say that a Bible talk group sits down to discuss an incident that has been in the news involving a white police officer and a young man of color, resulting in the tragic death of the young man. As the group begins their conversation, conflict quickly erupts. Some in the group identify with the police officers and are prone to trust them and take their side without much in the way of questions. Others may or may not realize it, but somewhere deep down, they don't trust police forces inherently. Even though we have a room full of disciples of Jesus Christ, tensions rise, and before you know it there is a heated debate. Within twenty minutes, factions have formed, divisions have arisen, and hard feelings have developed. What's even more pronounced and problematic is that these divisions are often (though not always) along racial or ethnic lines.

In situations like this, what often happens is that an awkward fear develops in one or both groups and they determine that the best solution is simply never to talk about these matters again within the body. This is deeply problematic. Healthy families talk. In fact, healthy families can talk about virtually anything. The degree to which there are off-limits or taboo subjects is the degree to which a dysfunction is bound to develop in that family.

GOING BELOW THE SURFACE

Here's the real problem. In many situations, the disparate metanarratives that we have lead to sharp disagreements. But we tend not to recognize that it is these underlying identity-forming stories that have led to our very different perspectives and resulted in severe conflict. Because of that, we stay at the surface level of the conflict and never get to the root of it.

Let's go back to the Bible talk group and see how this plays out. Some probably grew up in a middle-class, predominantly white environment like mine, where the police force was always presented as a positive entity. Every year "Officer Friendly" came to our school and spent time connecting with the students. We looked forward to seeing police officers in town, because they would hand out baseball cards to the kids. We were always told that they were the good guys; they would save us and help us if we ever needed it. This is why so many defend and support police officers before they even know the specifics of a case. They just trust them naturally. That was my metanarrative, and many of you may identify with it. It formed a specific aspect of my worldview and identity in relation to those who are given the responsibility "to protect and serve."

My wife, being African American, grew up with a different community metanarrative. The roots of many police forces, especially in the deep South where her family lived before migrating north, were slave patrols. After slavery, those forces morphed into police forces, but they often had the objective of keeping black community members "in their place." The lines of justice were frequently blurred, and they often intimidated, brutalized, and terrorized the black communities. So, the metanarrative formed that police officers were not a group that could be automatically trusted. They were to be rightly feared. Metanarratives like this are powerful and do not easily go away. They are passed down as wisdom from generation to generation. Even if a group is removed from the original context, the story and worldview often remain in place. And events that might seem like unfortunate, isolated incidents to those from one metanarrative serve as powerful reinforcements of the negative image for those from a different metanarrative.

It can be incredibly destructive if we are unable to get down to that level of understanding one another in our church life. When we stay at the surface level of conflict, we simply argue. We waste our breath trying to convince one another but will very rarely succeed. It is like two people staring at a white wall, one with rose-colored glasses on and the other wearing blue glasses, who insist on arguing about what color the wall is. They will never get anywhere if they focus on the wall and fail to recognize that they have on different-colored glasses.

As I've said already, metanarratives are an incredibly powerful cultural force. We embrace the truths of these stories before we are old enough to examine them or the impact they have on our outlook of the world. We safely tuck these truths away in the vaults of our hearts and will defend them vigorously, often without even knowing why. When we encounter someone with a different take on things, we usually don't stop to consider that perhaps they have a different story than the one we have always operated under. They have a different idea of what is true. What we must do, and so often don't, is recognize that often the realities formed by our metanarratives are just a portion of the truth, or one angle of it. The Jewish people confronting Jesus in John 8 were right. They were Abraham's descendants; that was their identity. But Jesus' truth was also right. His metanarrative would amend and redefine theirs but not completely invalidate it. They needed to put the stories together to get the fuller picture. It can be painful and disorienting, but if we develop the ability to hear other stories and put them together with ours, oftentimes a bigger picture and a greater truth appears.

BRIDGING THE GAP

The world's response to the dynamics of metanarratives has been varied. The worldview of modernism largely denied or ignored the metanarratives of others, often playing a game of "big bank take little bank," meaning the most powerful group set up their metanarrative as truth. This mindset was helpful in fueling things such as colonialism. Postmodernity is a broad philosophical worldview that has taken hold in the latter half of the twentieth century and continued to gain momentum in the twenty-first. In the postmodern worldview, every metanarrative is respected and should be held as true, which has led to the mistaken charge that they have rejected absolute truth. Postmodernity does not reject truth and claim that there is none; rather it embraces moral pluralism (where there are many truths that are equal in value).[17]

The postmodern approach to these identity-forming stories is to encourage respect for and acceptance of the varying metanarratives we might encounter. But there is a big problem with that. Our culture is increasingly losing the ability to communicate and meaningfully interact with counter points of view. Everything about our world now is customized. We see the advertisements that we want to see. Our feeds and devices only give us the news from the perspective we want to hear. We are becoming increasingly isolated in our worldviews. We are losing the ability to appreciate and legitimize other perspectives, all the while being told that we must accept these other views of the world and their underlying metanarratives. We are being called to do something that we do not as a society have the skills to accomplish. This has led to an alarming division among groups in the world, even though one of the most touted virtues has been embracing diversity. It seems that the more the world embraces diversity, the more it devolves into division.

The church must do better, and it can.

Communication and Education

We will skip right to the heart of bridging the gap between cultural metanarratives. It means listening to one another and learning.

The Bible offers us incredibly effective advice on fruitful communication. Poor communication can put stains in the carpet that won't come out for a long time, so we must beware. The tongue can be a fire that sets situations aflame if we're not careful (James 3:3–8). The proverbs caution us of the danger of reckless communication, reminding that a godless man can destroy his neighbor with his mouth (Proverbs 11:9), but also encourage us that good communication is like apples of gold (Proverbs 25:11 NASB) and a honeycomb to the soul (Proverbs 16:24). Truly reckless words cut like a sword, but a wise communicator brings healing (Proverbs 12:18).

There is much more that we could mine from the proverbs regarding healthy communication practices, but let's home in on a simple verse from the New Testament that is packed with wisdom. In James 1:19, it says that "everyone should be quick to listen, slow to speak, and slow to become angry." These are three solid-gold principles that we can use in any communication efforts, especially with difficult and emotional topics.

First, be quick to listen. When it comes to colliding metanarratives, we get riled up, and our first instinct is to assert our position. We just know the other person is wrong and can't wait to tell them. This is certainly how the Jews responded to Jesus in John 8. Take the time to hear another person's story and where they are coming from. You just might learn something.

Second, be slow to speak. This flows out of the first. If you are taking the time to listen, you are delaying what you have to say. Listen wholeheartedly without immediately trying to form a response or rebuttal. Even if you disagree with something that someone else is saying, that doesn't mean you have to shut them down. Let them speak, then you can speak.

Third, be slow to anger. This is particularly important when it comes to clashing metanarratives. Oftentimes our differing stories cut across one another's. My childhood metanarrative concerning police certainly intersected with my wife's and could easily cause conflict. Don't give in to anger. Hear what people have been through and the stories that have been passed down to them by those who have gone before them, and how they feel about things just might make sense.

We must go beyond the conflicts and seek to understand each other. Ask deep questions. Try to comprehend not just what a person believes or what they perceive, but why. They may not even fully grasp their own metanarrative at first. There are many members of my wife's family who were raised with an inherent mistrust of authority figures like the police but have little idea of why or where that fear comes from.

This is not taking sides on an issue or any specific incident involving police. If you're focused on that, you've missed the point of what I'm saying. That was simply a relevant illustration to help us understand the powerful forces at work that can weave conflict into our relationships. The next time you find yourself in conflict with a brother or sister over a serious matter of this nature, don't stay at the surface level of the conflict. Go deeper. Ask questions. Hear one another. Find out what some of their identity-forming metanarratives are (and we all have many). We may not ever fully agree on everything, but we can at least start to understand the different perspectives that others hold, and we may learn a lot more about ourselves. When we understand one another's metanarratives, their perspectives make a lot more sense, and we often feel empathy and a desire to reconcile rather than pull away or continue the conflict.

Practical Steps Forward in Communication

Here are some practical steps to help us discover and navigate the waters of the metanarratives of others. First I have a solemn warning, though. Don't attempt to do this with others until you have examined your own metanarratives and presumptions. Only then can you have a reasonable chance of understanding and empathizing with others.

1. When a conflict occurs, don't focus on the "what"; become curious about the "why."

2. Ask as many questions as you can to respectfully pull out someone's background and story, where they might be coming from, and why they see the world the way they do. Some sample questions from the above example involving responses to the police might be:

   a. Do you think you tend to automatically give the benefit of the doubt to police or official government versions of events? Why do you think that is?

   b. Do you think you tend to automatically mistrust police and people in authority? Why do you think that is?

   c. What have been the experiences that you or previous generations of your family or ethnic group have had with police officers?

   d. Do you think you have had any preconceived notions or beliefs about those in power or the underdogs in society that might influence your thinking?

3. Everyone's worldview makes sense to them given their metanarratives, so seek to understand as much as you can about a person's views from the perspective of their metanarratives rather than your own.

4. Listen to another's story without comment, objection, or rebuttal. You are trying to learn and understand, not educate at this moment.

5. Try to avoid the "whats" in a conflict until you have a really solid grasp of the other person's "whys."

6. Together you can examine, not the metanarratives themselves, but the identities and presumptions that have resulted from

them. Are they in sync with a kingdom worldview, a godly perspective of others, and a biblical response?

7. Together, do either of you see that perhaps some of your identities formed by your metanarratives need to change in light of the gospel? How do you go about that?

8. You may have to agree to disagree at times, but at least you now hopefully can better understand the perspective of your brother or sister and respect and understand their views rather than thinking that they are just "out of their mind."

The Grace Factor

Proverbs 20:5 says that "the purposes of a person's heart are deep waters, but one who has insight draws them out." Our metanarratives are certainly deep waters, and when we take the time to learn our own and draw out those of others, we move one step closer to the kind of unity in Christ that God desires for his people. A willingness to examine your own metanarratives and identities and those of others won't solve every problem, but it is a healthy step in the right direction. Because these overarching stories are so deeply rooted in our identity and view of the world, it can cause great emotion when we start examining them. But when we take the time to lovingly draw out the hearts of others, miracles can happen.

Chapter 20

Feeding the Sheep

If you were ever to come visit our house, you might not notice at first, but our front door is not fully operational. It's been like that since we moved here almost three years ago. In fact, the handle doesn't really work. It's supposed to have a little lever that you push down with your thumb which unlatches it and then you can push the door open, but that lever has never worked. And because that lever doesn't work, neither does the lock on the front door. There is a deadbolt lock above the handle, and we have just taken to using that to lock the door when need be, but the proper lock on the handle hasn't worked since we've been here.

I should fix it, but I'm not the handiest of guys, and it's never popped up high enough on the radar to get it taken care of. We had a handyman at the house a few months ago working on something else, and I did mention the door. He looked at it and didn't think he knew how to fix it, so that was that, in my mind. We don't address the issue; we have just learned to work around it. It's to the point now that we don't even think about it. We have adjusted and moved on, even though it is a less-than-ideal situation.

The truth about our door is simple. It was broken before we got here, but it's not going to fix itself. If we don't take intentional action, it will remain in its broken state.

REFLECTING THE WORLD

What is true of our front door is also true when it comes to problems in life. Most of them won't fix themselves, and without action they will stay at the status quo or get worse.

The history of the United States is a mixed bag. There accomplishments to be admired and much good that has happened. But there is unquestionably a dark side. My country has a troubling history with its treatment of nondominant cultures, particularly people of color. This is true from the treatment of indigenous peoples of the First Nations, to the mass enslavement of Africans, to segregation and Jim Crow, to Japanese internment camps during WWII, and a disturbing number of other injustices in between and throughout those tragedies. Access to economic opportunities, education, and advancement have been systematically denied people of color consistently throughout US history. This has led to wide gaps between white Americans and many other cultural groups, with African American and Latino folks typically being hit the hardest.

This raises a specific problem for many diverse churches. They often have an imbalance in leadership. To put it bluntly, many, although not all, diverse churches in the United States have a higher percentage of white leadership than the white population of those churches would call for.

I don't think the reasons for that are all that difficult to discern. Primarily, they are historical and cultural. We will discuss the cultural factors below, but first let's consider the history. Whites have had more access to opportunity and higher education, and that reflects into who is considered ready to step into roles of higher leadership, where education and training are usually valued. In my own diverse family of churches, a lack of elders, evangelists, and teachers who are not white is a consistent problem. It reflects the sins of segregation and denial of opportunity that have faced so many groups throughout American history. This is a big part of what people speak of when they talk about one group having advantages or privileges over another group. It doesn't mean that members of the dominant group haven't had a challenging life at times. It means that their culture or skin color have not been one of the factors making it more difficult.

To make matters more complex, some members of the dominant group are so unaccustomed to being led by nondominant-group individuals that they buck against it when confronted by it. However, they will almost always find other reasons to justify their discomfort.

What is the church to do? Does it keep reflecting the sins of the society that have resulted in inequities due to its historical denial of groups of people to equal access of opportunities? If the church does decide to address these issues within the church community, how does it go about it? Would that create more injustice and unfairness?

THE CULTURAL FACTOR IN LEADERSHIP

Does culture play a factor in church leadership issues? By this point in the book, you should be clued in to the fact that it absolutely does.

What makes a good leader? What are the characteristics to look for? There are certain virtues that would surely be considered universal when it comes to selecting leaders within a community or group. But there are also other characteristics that vary widely between cultural pockets of people.

Take a moment to consider the many cultural differences we have talked about up to this point that can cause different assumptions and preferences, and other differences in groups of people. Doesn't it seem logical that between those groups there would potentially be wide gaps in evaluating potential leaders?

In a diverse community, the dominant group will most typically have a dominant role in leadership as well. The dynamics of dominant culture then come into play in a huge way. It makes sense that if they are not actively thinking about their community in a deliberately different direction, people will gravitate toward being led by those who share their values, practices, and customs. Leaders who are looking to identify and develop future leaders will discriminate culturally without ever intending anything like discrimination, because they will consider those who share their own cultural traits (even if they are from a different ethnic or cultural group) to have more acceptable qualities than those from different groups that display cultural characteristics that they do not fully understand.

Let's say that a church of five hundred people is fifty percent white, thirty percent black, fifteen percent Latino, and five percent Asian and other groups. It has a staff and eldership group of sixteen, fourteen of whom are white. The church also has fifty small group leaders, forty-four of whom are white. When asked about the disparity in small group leadership, the honest answer of the existing church leadership group is that when they look at leadership qualities, those that most exhibit such qualities are those that are chosen. They will contend adamantly that there is no bias or discrimination. And I believe that in most of these situations there is no intentional bias.

Is it possible, though, that at least a few people have been disqualified in the minds of the dominant leadership group from being considered a leader because they were evaluating potential leaders through their own cultural lens? What appears to be leadership to one group of people may not seem like valuable leadership traits to another cultural group. Thus, unintentional bias creeps into and remains in the group until deliberate action is taken. This is not true in all diverse churches, but surely it is a possible factor in some.

ABILITY TO CONNECT

I met with one young African American couple in a multiethnic church community a few years ago. They were attending the church, but that's about all that could be said for their participation. There were aspects of this diverse community that they understood and appreciated, and aspects that they did not care for. Ultimately, they stayed because they believed that the truth of the gospel was being preached, but they could not be said to have been fully connected into the community. What is interesting is that several other African Americans in the church identified that couple as having the potential to be wonderful leaders, while no one in the existing leadership of the church, none of whom were African American, had recognized that same potential. One of the white leaders had even made numerous attempts to reach out to this couple and get them more involved in the community and family life of the church, but to no avail. In fact, his attempts seemed to have more of an effect of pushing them further toward the margins than toward the middle. Despite his best efforts, he could not build a connection.

Although the church leaders loved the couple and wanted them to be more active in the community, no one in leadership had considered them as future leaders. They could be jarringly blunt and direct in conversations with others. They also could be quite loud and animated, which had the tendency to occasionally intimidate some within the dominant group. The couple was also often frustrated with what they felt was good teaching on the church being a family, but it was teaching that wasn't often backed up with corresponding action, in their opinion. As they voiced complaints about this, it left the existing leaders puzzled and with few other options in their minds than to conclude that the couple was negative and critical.

Eventually the church hired a staff couple of mixed cultural heritage, but neither was white. Shortly after arriving, they began to build a friendship with this couple. They were able to connect easily with them and saw their potential, so they began to give them responsibilities and roles in the community. On the surface, others had failed to see them as potential leaders because they didn't comport themselves the way that a typical leader might. But they excelled, especially in connecting with younger people, and particularly with younger folks in the nondominant groups of the church. This new staff couple was able to turn around these amazing disciples and help them become leaders in the community simply because they were able to understand and connect with them culturally and employ their strengths in a culturally competent way within the church. What a loss that might have been had the church not had the foresight to continue to work toward a more diverse staff.

WHAT DOES A LEADER DO?

A fellow minister and I once attended the funeral of the mother of a member of our church family. She was African American, and the funeral was held in the mother's African American church. At the beginning of the service, the pastor asked for any attending clergymen to come sit on stage during the service and then preside in prayer at the end. We both sat frozen in our seats, unsure of what to do. Both of us were white and spent all our adult Christian lives in the same faith tradition. This was uncharted territory for us, and we both felt uncomfortable with being treated like a visiting dignitary of some kind. So we stayed right where we sat throughout the service. Afterward, the member of our church introduced us to the pastor who served as officiant of the funeral. She had known him since she was a little girl and was excited for him to meet us, and vice versa. On hearing that we were ministers, he was visibly disturbed. Why, he wondered, had we not come on stage? He was gracious, but it was obvious that we had offended him. The member of our church was understanding and forgiving, but she easily could have been upset with our violation of this protocol that was so obvious to everyone else there.

In retrospect, we should have complied with the cultural expectations and gone up front. It was the expectation of that cultural setting that one of the roles of ministers is as visible community leader. Pastors should always be visible leaders that set the pace and stand out from others so that they know who to look up to and imitate. That is not my cultural vision of church leadership, but it is for many folks who come into our fellowship.

I can think of another occasion while leading a church in Wisconsin. Two young single men had recently been baptized into our community. They had been nominal Roman Catholics their whole lives. I tried for months to build a friendship with them, but there always seemed to be a barrier that I could not explain. It took quite a while to get to the bottom of it and realize that they were uncomfortable with the idea of being friends with me and treating me like a regular person. They had brought with them expectations of leadership they had learned from their parish priests growing up, and they felt that as the minister, I should have a certain amount of separation from the congregation and be viewed as spiritually above those that I served. Again, I did not share that assumption.

Some folks come from the spiritual background of a priest or minister that presides over the congregation and remains somewhat aloof. Some come from a tradition where the pastor serves as a father figure for every person in the body. Is the pastor dad, general, role model, inspirer, motivator, coach, facilitator, or something else? Some expect leaders to be vulnerable, while others dislike when leaders show weakness or display too much emotion. Some think leaders should lead by example and get their hands dirty, but some perceive this to be poor leadership and think that leaders need to stay out of the fray so that they can more efficiently direct affairs. Some think that the pastor should visit every sick person in the congregation, but many do not have that expectation. I could go on, but I think you get the point.

I am not suggesting that leaders can be all things to all people in all these situations and meet the expectations of each member of the church. The important element here is to be aware of these things and talk about them as a community. A culturally competent church will regularly talk about the roles and expectations of the leaders and seek to be sensitive to times when a conflict arises that could be caused by differing cultural preferences or assumptions about what leaders should do in general or in specific situations.

BRIDGING THE GAP

Cultural misunderstandings between church members can cause rifts and hard feelings, but divides between leaders and members can exponentially increase the likelihood of people feeling disaffected from a church community and even members leaving the church. A lack of cultural competency can be dangerous to a community, but when these same types of disparities involve leaders, it can become far more serious far more quickly.

The Biblical View

Should churches be intentional about having diverse leadership, or should they just let it happen naturally? That's really what much of this comes down to. In my opinion, the answer to that is clear. If God's family is not intentional about displaying the gathering of the nations at every opportunity, especially in leadership, then it is doomed to reflect the past sins of the society around us. The divisions, the segregation, the denial of equal opportunity, and the imbalance of power that are built into the kingdoms of the world will be baptized into the kingdom and locked in place. The church will be no different from the world. That is simply not good enough.

It is important to note that the first time we see cultural and ethnic tension in the church, in Acts 6, is also the first time we see an intentional transfer of power away from the dominant group. In fact, a case could be made that at almost every opportunity, the church displayed something of an inversion of power from the world surrounding it. As the church was formed in Jerusalem, it was disregarded Galileans rather than impressive Judean leaders who led the way. In Acts 6, important leadership power was transferred from Hebraic Jews to the often-marginalized Hellenic Jews. As the gospel spread into the powerful Roman Empire, it was despised Jews who held most of the important leadership roles in a world dominated by Greek and Roman culture. But as the church was established and Jewish leaders were dominating the power grid within the body of Christ, there seems to have been a concerted effort to transfer leadership and influence to Gentiles and include them whenever possible.

Whether it is Jesus' diverse group of Jews among the twelve to the multiethnic leadership in Antioch, wherever leadership groups are mentioned in the New Testament church, we see diversity. That cannot have just happened without forethought.

The kingdom of God should and must lead the way in this. We need to be on the cutting edge of overcoming the past mistakes and inequities of whatever society we are living in and of developing not just multicultural communities but diverse and culturally competent leaders to serve in them.

Communication and Education

Every church should go through the New Testament Scriptures together and study the cultural training that Paul and the other authors gave to the followers of Christ. It was a major component of education and community life in the first century, and it should be in churches in the twenty-first century.

Cultural competency classes should be a regular feature for diverse churches. This is not something that can be taught one time at a workshop and then forgotten, with the assumption that we now know what we're doing. As new disciples are added to the kingdom, they must be taught how to operate in a multicultural body, but older disciples will need teaching and training at least once a year. Additionally, sermons should consistently include the topics of gathering the nations and being all things to all people. I'm not saying that these things need to be talked about every week and in every lesson, but not too many weeks or months should go by without a refresher. Without that, it will be easy to slip back into worldly patterns and ways of thinking.

I believe that if a church is going to achieve and maintain a certain level of success in cultural competency, it will need to require that any leaders, including small group leaders, ministry organizers, ministry staff, deacons, and shepherding and eldership groups, take a course on cultural training and diversity or intercultural communication. There are many options available for this. Many universities offer such courses, as do local community organizations from time to time. There are also online options. And, of course, I am writing this book with the hopes that it will meet some of the needs of many multicultural churches who can use it as a resource for training leaders and members.

The Dominant Group

We would all like to think that every disciple in a diverse church wants diverse leadership. While that is largely true, sadly, it is not an entirely valid statement. Many real-life situations I have observed demonstrate that dominant groups are not always any good at being led by nondominant people. They might be fine initially with individual leaders of a different race or ethnic group, but if things start to change or diversify culturally, many members of the dominant cultural group start to howl or find reasons to leave the church.

When all you've ever known is superiority, equality feels like oppression. Because the dominant group is usually unaware that they have a culture that is squeezing everyone else into its mold, without education on the topic, they may view any cultural change as an attack on their group. "Why are we suddenly bringing worldliness into the church and attacking my culture?" they will argue, completely blind to the reality that the church has always operated through cultural expressions. They just didn't notice, because the default culture was theirs.

Striving toward inclusive leadership and cultural practices is a must for a diverse community. *The New York Times* recently published an article detailing what they termed "a quiet exodus" of black worshippers from white and multiracial churches.[18] I believe that the primary reasons are cultural incompetence and the lack of a solid base of diverse leadership at all levels (not just symbolic levels) that can influence the life, practices, values, beliefs, and actions of the entire church community.

The Compromise Position

We will come to the table with differing expectations of leaders, how they should function, and what kind of authority they should have. We will also have very different backgrounds in how we relate to authority and whether authority figures should be respected simply because they hold a position of leadership (ascribed authority) or because they have earned the right to lead and have shown respect to others (achieved authority). This will vary from church to church, so there is no simple formula here. Churches will do well to consider carefully what their leadership and structural models are and make opportunities for people to share honest and respectful questions about the leadership or how it operates. Transparency and communication are vital in working toward a common understanding of leadership in a multicultural community.

When it comes to having diverse leadership, I don't see much room for compromise as to whether that should be a goal. The only area of compromise is in how long it will take to achieve it. Some churches are already there, and that is wonderful. Many have a long way to go. Understand that this is typically not a quick fix. Simply going out and hiring a couple that adds diversity to your staff or leadership group does not usually solve the problem. Churches that have a diversity deficit need to be willing to take an honest look at why that is.

Are they reflecting and perpetuating the historic inequities of the society around them?

Has it not been a priority and so there has been no growth?

Is the church located in an area where it is difficult to maintain diversity?

Are there things about the church culture that discourage or dissuade non-dominant members from stepping into leadership?

These questions and more like them need to be asked and discussed thoroughly to better understand how to move forward.

The Grace Factor

The goal here is to develop racially, ethnically, and culturally diverse leadership groups at every level of church life. If that is a consistent value and central vision for a church body, it will happen. We are not talking about putting people into leadership positions for external qualities or to satisfy some quota. We are talking about valuing diversity and spiritual maturity in leadership without ever compromising or giving up on either area.

The goal for the body of Christ should be to have culturally competent leaders. What does that look like? There are at least five important characteristics that leaders should possess in a diverse and competent community.

Cultural sensitivity is a must. To be a culturally sensitive community requires culturally competent leaders who understand the basic dynamics of cross-cultural life and communication. They will not necessarily have a thorough knowledge of every culture that might be part of their church, but they will be willing to learn and able to recognize cultural differences and potential culture clashes. And they will keep an open eye for such issues without being consumed by them. They will value and be able to encourage diversity of all types in all aspects of their ministry and all areas of church life for which they are responsible.

Racial sensitivity is a must. The concept of race is an unbiblical social construct that often serves to divide humans into tribalism. That's true. But the concept of race has existed in our culture for hundreds of years and has become something that we cannot simply ignore or pretend does not impact our congregations. Culturally competent leaders will not simply brush off different racial perspectives or experiences that members of the church family have. They will seek to hear and understand all the different viewpoints, pain, and perspectives present in the church. They will also work to learn about and grasp these issues so that they can educate and occasionally challenge the body when they need to grow in their knowledge or sensitivity to others.

Historical knowledge is a must. When Paul ministered to Jews, he understood their history and where they were coming from. That was easy; he was Jewish, after all. But when he ministered to Gentiles, he also understood their history and what they believed and had been through. We cannot simply say that the only job of Christian leaders is to study and interpret the Bible. We must also study and interpret the people and cultures to whom we minister. Competent leaders will not limit themselves to one perspective. They will push beyond their boundaries and listen to history from multiple perspectives, which will enable them to understand where people have come from, why they are where they are, and how the gospel calls them forward from where they are. I have seen many well-meaning leaders who don't have a clue about how certain events or trends in history have had an impact on situations today and have done real damage to their credibility and the credibility of the gospel they were preaching because of their unwillingness to learn and hear from differing perspectives.

Socioeconomic sensitivity is a must. In 1 Corinthians 11, Paul chides some of the presumably wealthier members of the congregation for their approach to the Lord's Supper. What it appears was happening was that wealthier members were bringing their own food and drink to the communion meal. Because they had more leisure time, they were arriving early and getting full and even drunk before the hard-working laborers and slaves that were disciples could arrive. Some of these, it seems, did not have the means to bring much food, if any at all. The wealthier members were not being sensitive to the varying economic situations in the body, and Paul told them that when they acted the way they did, they were eating and drinking judgment on themselves. This is serious. We should never show favoritism toward the wealthy (James 2:1–12), but leaders must also understand the perspective of those with lesser financial means. Do we plan expensive events and retreats and then scold members who cannot come? Do we have leadership groups that also reflect the socioeconomic diversity in our communities, or do they only include the middle class and up?

Leaders must set the pace in learning and humility. Paul instructed Timothy to strive after growth and progress to a degree that everyone in the community could see it (1 Timothy 4:15). Culturally competent communities have culturally competent leaders. In fact, I've never once seen a culturally competent church that had leaders who were impassionate or unconcerned about these issues. But overconfident or disinterested leaders will often think they are fine although they have a frustrated and culturally needy congregation behind them. Leaders must show the way forward in their willingness to listen, learn, take classes, and explore other points of view. They need to have vision for their church family and encourage others to have vision as well. I will say this without hesitation: every single time that I have seen a church grow and make strides in their cultural diversity and competency it started with a humble leadership group. Every time.

Chapter 21

World War Z

"Why is Mom so furious?" This question was posed to me, stardate 96641.56, or for you younger folks, January 2019. It came from my twenty-three-year-old and fifteen-year-old sons. They were serious, too. They felt like their mom was angry with them and they couldn't figure out why. She was at work at the time, but earlier in the day my older son had texted her and asked her to do something for him the next day. Her response was a simple "K."

Do you see it? Do you see why they were so convinced that she was enraged? I certainly didn't at first, although I suspected there was some sort of generation gap at play here. That shouldn't come as a huge surprise, since I just made a stardate joke, which may have tipped you off to my general age (although I will point out that I watched *Star Trek* in reruns as a kid and not the original airings). But I did not see what they were seeing in that simple one-letter text. The original conversation was between my older son and my wife, but the younger boy was in the room, and he quickly agreed with his brother without any explanation needed. Mom was seriously upset.

When they finally explained their reasoning to me, all I could do was laugh. It seems that replying with just one letter, "K" as an affirmation rather than "OK" or "okay," is acceptable but may indicate annoyance in their modern vernacular. But putting a period at the end of such a short reply signifies that you are angry and done with the conversation. But there's more. Apparently, the fact that the "K" was capitalized bears significance. Capital letters imply that a person is yelling. She intended to respond with a simple "okay," but my son perceived an enraged mother screaming, "This conversation is over because you have made me really angry!!" Communication can be a funny thing. And gaps between generations are a real thing. This gap might be the one we think about the least when it comes to culture, but it can be one of the most profound in many respects.

A word of warning before reading this chapter. Each country and region of the world will vary in the experiences and characteristics of their generations, although there are growing similarities and commonalities throughout the world as a result of the internet. There are still significant differences, however, and in this chapter, I will focus on the context within my own country, as that is the one that I know best. Readers in other parts of the world will have to use this as a paradigm to analyze their own cultural context and apply the principles suggested here to navigate that context.

THE GENERATIONS

Most discussions of the different US generations these days start with the Silent or Greatest generation, those born before 1945. They lived through the Great Depression and World War II and built the United States into a superpower in the world. They moved into the suburbs in droves, cementing geographic segregation; they built up the nation's economic prosperity and laid a comfortable foundation for future generations. They valued loyalty, which was reflected in their adherence to church denominations, and they supported overseas missions around the world.

The next group that sociologists usually identify is the Baby Boomers. Phase 1 of the Baby Boomers were born in the years immediately following WWII, usually demarcated as 1946 to 1955. Phase 2, sometimes referred to as the Late Boomers, were born between 1956 and 1964. The Boomers were the rock 'n' roll pioneering generation. They were also the first to experience two-income households, television in the home, divorce as an acceptable option, and the beginnings of the tolerance movement. The Boomers are known for their passion, self-indulgence, and willingness to fight for what they believe in. They built countercultural movements that broadly ranged from everything to antiwar protests to the Jesus freak movement, but by the 1990s and 2000s they largely settled into a stable existence, living comfortably off the post-WWII economic boom that they grew up in and enjoyed. They rejected much of the institutional reliability of their parents' traditional mainline churches and opted for a more intense evangelical approach, creating many new denominations and increasing evangelism in the United States and around the world with a newer version of Christianity that was a mixture of American exceptionalism and prosperity and religious fervor.

Then came Generation X, who were born between 1965 and 1980. They grew up with career-driven parents and became the generation of latchkey kids. They were deeply committed to entrepreneurship, and most went through school without using a computer for anything serious. They are the first MTV generation and are highly susceptible to brand names, instant gratification, advertising, and going into debt to get what they want now. Gen Xers were typically more focused on experiencing life and self-actualization than settling down as previous generations did in their early twenties for long-term career and family. Compared to previous generations, they were late to marry and quick to divorce. These nomads average more relocations and career changes than any previous generation. Their "what's in it for me" attitude gave birth to the seeker-sensitive megachurches that appealed to felt needs and aimed to guide them on their way through their personal struggles, although those churches also appealed to the passion of the Boomers as well. After becoming disillusioned with the megachurch approach, Gen Xers turned in large numbers to independent and nondenominational churches that fostered unique spiritual expressions but were not beholden to a particular set of creeds or doctrines.

After Gen X come the Millennials. Although the dates for the Millennial generation vary a bit, we can generally identify them as being born between 1981 and 1996 (some analysts go up to 2001). The Millennials have been often criticized and demonized over a generalized tendency to delay steps of typical adulthood such as living apart from their parents, a career, and marriage. They grew up with technological change as the norm, encroaching globalization, and an up-and-down economy.

They have often been identified as the first generation of digital natives and show a much greater affinity for sharing lifestyles, community, and even socialism than previous American generations. They are more conscious of environmental issues and value personal health and an active lifestyle more than their forerunners. Millennials have strong views and have often been perceived as aggressive. They are decidedly less brand loyal, which has carried over into their spirituality as well. They have walked away from Christianity in droves and started a growing trend toward identifying themselves as atheist, agnostic, or vaguely spiritual. Millennials have a deep passion for justice at any level and are deeply suspicious of entrenched or traditional power.

Generation Z are those born between 1997 and 2009. After that comes what some are now calling Generation Alpha, but we will only go as far as Generation Z for our purposes. They have never known anything but advanced technology and a world at their fingertips. Digital information is more accessible and often more authoritative to them than more traditional formats such as books. They are comfortable with technology in every aspect of their lives, integrated with technology to the point of dependence in many instances. They are globally aware but have short attention spans; socially defined yet often isolated and awkward with extended social interaction; educationally savvy yet easily fooled by a digital world with unvetted resources. They have grown up with easy access to pornography and gender fluidity and are much more comfortable with those things as a normal part of life. This group is more ethnically diverse than older generations. They are very aware of a troubled planet and are extremely justice minded. They are also the first generation to be born into a largely post-Christian worldview as the norm. In the United States, only about 40% of Generation Z attends a religious service weekly, although 78% of older Zs say they believe in God, according to one study.[19]

WHAT WORKED THEN MIGHT NOT WORK NOW

We live in a unique time of change. In many respects the world shared a common approach to life and knowledge from times of prehistory right up until the 1650s. During that time, knowledge and truth were revealed from authoritative sources such as divine beings, sacred texts, or elders and ancestors.

In the mid-seventeenth century, the world underwent a massive shift as it moved into what is now called modernism. Now scientific discovery, reason, and logic became the basis of truth and knowledge, and universities and other institutions of higher learning became the primary sources of authority.

Since the latter half of the twentieth century, the world has been in the throes of another cataclysmic shift, to what has been dubbed postmodernism. It has rejected the idea of one approach to knowing or authority and has opted for the concept of plural truths. There are many ways, according to this worldview, to discover knowledge and truth, including revelation, experience, science, reason, intuition, relationally, spiritually, and others. Postmodernism seeks to deconstruct any previous source of authority and power, striving for a less hierarchical approach to those dynamics.

What all this means is that you're not crazy. If you're over thirty-five or forty and feel like you live in a different world than the one in which you grew up, you're not wrong. We are in the midst of changes that have only happened a couple of times in known human history. The world today is literally a different place than it was the 1970s, '80s, and even '90s. These have not been just subtle differences in the experiences or goals of the generational groups described above. The foundations of what is considered truth, knowledge, and authority have seismically shifted. And this has created a problem that the church has been slow to respond to or even become aware of.

In 1991 my parents gave me their old computer that they had purchased around 1986. I was so excited because now I was going to have my own computer in my dorm room for the first time. I even had a printer, so that meant I could work on papers without going to the computer lab. This was life changing for me. I remember that computer well. It was a Tandy, which will sound completely foreign to you if you're not at least forty. I have no idea what the computing capabilities of that thing were, but it was probably one step above a brick. There was no internet to think about, and the graphics were laughable, so even the most rudimentary PowerPoint slideshow would have been far beyond its capabilities. Microsoft Windows was out, but nobody had really heard of it yet, which means we were rolling in DOS on this high-powered piece of technology. It got the job done for producing papers and that was about it.

I can't fathom using that dinosaur today. It was big, bulky, limited, and slow. I would be in trouble if that was my computer today. I could save work on the gigantic floppy disks, but they wouldn't be compatible with anything. I couldn't get on the internet. It wouldn't run any programs, and there was no Bluetooth, so it couldn't communicate with my printer. Looking back, I loved that computer, and I still think about it fondly, to be honest. But I wouldn't want to go back to it. It couldn't operate in the world today.

The world has shifted at least as much culturally as it has technologically since the 1980s and early '90s. Think about that. I was talking recently with several young ministers in their twenties about their persistent discouragement in the ministry. They are faithful but feeling pretty defeated in many ways. One of the things they mentioned that caused them to doubt themselves was the frequent stories they hear from older ministers. These tales from the 1970s and '80s are packed with action and excitement as dozens, and hundreds, and sometimes even more people streamed into churches and were baptized during those years. Growth was explosive and evangelism was aggressive. The implication that these young ministers feel, often just below the surface, is that maybe they don't know what they're doing because they aren't seeing the kind of growth and effectiveness that ministers did in the previous generation. The message being sent is often that these young guys should sit and listen and learn about the techniques that worked so well thirty years ago.

"These older guys are great ministers, but the problem with that," I responded to these young men, "is that even if those guys were in their early twenties today, what they did and the way they did it wouldn't work like it did back then." I'm not saying that no one would come into the kingdom of God, but not in the droves that they did back in the day. The world has changed.

Before I get accused of being faithless or humanistic, I believe that God does the primary work of converting the heart through the Holy Spirit, but he does use human agents. I don't think there's any question about that. He used Paul to great effect in the Gentile world, because he utilized Paul's unique abilities and talents to adapt to the Gentiles that he encountered while still being able to root the faith in the context of the Jewish story better than anyone else. God partners with us, so what we do does have impact in the mission.

And I'm afraid that in many respects, the church is trying to connect to Wi-Fi with a 1986 Tandy. It is trying to operate in today's cultural questions with yesteryear's approach.

A STEP BACK IN TIME

Perhaps a step back into the first century will help clarify what I am saying. Corinth was a Greek city known for its pagan idolatry and massive prostitution rings related largely to temple worship. So much was that so that a form of the word "Corinthian" became synonymous with a person who indulged in sex. But Corinth was destroyed by Rome in the middle of the second century BC and lay dormant for a century before being rebuilt as a Roman city in 44 BC as a provincial capital of Greece under the rule of the Roman Empire. It became a center for trade, burgeoning wealth, entertainment, pagan temples, and a rejuvenated sex trade. It was a pulsating center of life that has led one commentator to refer to it as "at once the New York, Los Angeles, and Las Vegas of the ancient world."[20]

When Paul arrived in Corinth, he didn't find a city deeply impressed with Christianity and bursting with a profound respect for ministers of the gospel. It was quite the opposite. He reminds the young Corinthian church that in the world's eyes they are foolish, weak, lowly, despised, and amount to nothing (1 Corinthians 1:26–28). "We are brutally treated," Paul proclaimed without shame. "When cursed, we bless; when we are persecuted, we endure it"; and in case you haven't gotten the idea yet, he says, "We have become the scum the of the earth, the garbage of the world—right up to this moment" (1 Corinthians 4:11–13). Paul and the early Christians proclaimed the gospel in a world that saw them as weak, foolish, and immoral. They looked down upon the Christians and certainly didn't have any initial respect for them. The believers needed to embrace that. They could not be effective until they did. They were nothing in the world's eyes, so they shouldn't expect warm treatment, fairness, or honor. They would have to humbly proclaim that their king was a crucified man who had resurrected from the dead, something that Greeks and Romans didn't believe was remotely possible.

How would they do it, then? How could they spread the gospel in such a hostile environment? Their two primary weapons were in living as a family that put the interests of one another first, and love, which is really just two different ways of saying the same thing. By being the gathering of the nations and living differently, they would show the world that this was something they had never seen before. They had seen plenty of religions, but never this. Simply going out and inviting people to come to a weekly meeting was not going to do it. No one would have any reason to go. The life of the community had to stand out as something unique. That's why Paul is so insistent in 1 Corinthians 6 that believers should not sue one another in Roman courts. In that culture, it was looked down upon for family members to sue one another, which means that when Christians did so they were sending a message to those around them that they were not truly family.

THE CHALLENGE AHEAD

Here's where this parallels our situation: in previous generations you could divide most of the society around us into two groups—Christians and pagans. The mission was to go to the pagans and invite them to become Christians. Most of the time, even if someone wasn't interested, they knew that Christians were the moral people. They might not want that kind of moral life or might think they were not good enough to try, but most people respected Christians. When you asked someone to church or challenged them on their sin, there was often a guilt that came over them, and they knew at some level that they needed to pay attention to God at some point in their lives. They may not do it right away, but most would indicate that they knew they needed it. So, blitz-invitation evangelism could be effective. Get out there and pound the pavement, and people would come.

I'm not saying that we should not evangelize anymore, but things have shifted dramatically. The world is no longer split between Christians and pagans. There is a new group that has developed: the post-Christian culture. In fact, for those under the age of thirty-five, this might be the fastest growing spiritual group in the Western world. They grew up around Christianity, or at least their parents were culturally Christian. But they no longer have an interest. In fact, in the postmodern fashion, much of their worldview is constructed as a response against Christianity.

They love many of the values of the church, though, and have embraced kindness, justice for the oppressed, passion for the marginalized and poor, caring for the sick, and so on. But they have no time for Jesus as King.

But it gets even more difficult. In the eyes of this post-Christian culture, those who claim Christianity no longer have the moral high ground. They see themselves as more moral than the church. They mix together all versions of Christianity as one, without distinction, and they see "the church's" stance on sexuality, women's rights, gender equality, homosexual and transgender rights, the predatory prosperity gospel, militarism, nationalism, sexual abuse scandals, environmental indifference, etc., and they view themselves as superior in morality to these scumbag Christians. We have become the problem. Not only do they no longer think they might need to listen to us one day, they have no intention of ever doing so.

And there is one other looming danger in this new world in which we find ourselves, a world that is more like the one Paul faced in Corinth than the one we remember from the 1980s. When the categories are mostly just Christian and pagan, the danger is that Christianity will blend too much with the culture of the disciples spreading it, and they will colonize the places where they take the gospel with their own culture as much as the gospel itself. The task with a pagan culture is to become all things to those people and learn to adapt the gospel to that culture. We have been talking about that throughout this book.

And that is still true on a personal level and within the community. But there is an impending threat when advancing the gospel into a post-Christian culture. Because they see Christianity as an immoral threat, if Christians try to identify at a macro level with the culture and "fit in," we will be colonized by them. Paul constantly warned the first-century believers of that, and it is a similar point of peril for us. It is no longer just that they are not yet Christian; they have intentionally rejected that as an option and will do everything they can to oppose it and make Christianity accept their superior values.

Starting with Millennials and Generation Z, the Western world has become increasingly post-Christian, and that likely is not going to slow down with the Alphas. The world we are looking at down the road is one where Christian culture is not the norm and will not be respected as a source of morality or wisdom. What happens when you employ methods of the past, such as an assumption of Christian morality and mass invitations, to spread the gospel? Not much. One need only look at Europe (where more than half of people under thirty never attend religious services) to see where this is headed for the United States.

We are approaching church life and evangelism meant for a world that is pagan but that is quickly giving way to a post-Christian world. If we do not adapt, we will become obsolete.

HOW DO I USE THIS STUPID THING?

About ten years ago, I got my first smartphone. It was all the rage, and I figured it was about time I gave in and got one. A year or two later, I got a new one and was trying to set it up the way I wanted. The problem was that I could not figure out how to find some of the functions I needed. I was expressing my frustration at not being able to figure out how to get this phone to bend to my will when my then six-year-old son huffed, walked over to me, grabbed the phone, and said, "I'm only going to show you this one more time and then you're on your own. You have to learn to do this for yourself." The kicker is, he immediately did what I could not and handed the phone back with this smug little look on his face. Mind you, he had never owned a smartphone before, and to my knowledge had barely used one at the time. But he has never known anything but advanced technology. It is his native language. To this day, when I can't figure something out about a device, he can decipher it effortlessly. It's his world. For me, it's a second language at best.

Churches need older, wiser Christians to guide them, share their knowledge and wisdom, and keep them from mistakes. Because of this, churches are usually led by older disciples. They develop the vision, wield the influence, and hold the institutional power. And they employ methods that are tried and true and have worked in the past.

But we are living in unusual times of rapid change. The methods of the past will continue to fade into obsolescence. This is a culture clash of monumental proportions. So, what is the solution? Well, here's the bad news: I don't have the answers. I can point out the disconnect and the problems we face, but just like with my smartphone, I don't know how to solve the issue. I do my best to analyze the post-Christian culture and understand it as best I can, but it's not my native tongue. I will never fully comprehend it.

Just as I turn to my son for technological help, I believe we need to turn to the younger generation for the way forward in reaching out to the advancing post-Christian world. We need to invest in Christian thinkers and leaders who are under thirty-five, and especially under twenty-five, and we need to trust them to lead. The older generations should guide them and offer insight where possible, but also be humble and willing to turn over influence and power to these young people. It's easy to say that they're not ready, or not as wise, or not as successful in ministry (whatever that means) as we were, but we are fast-forwarding into their world; ours is vanishing.

Paul was willing to adapt his methods when he needed to. Have you ever noticed that much of the language that permeates the Gospels, terms like kingdom, disciples, and Son of Man, all but disappear from the letters of the New Testament? Paul and the other kingdom missionaries understood that as they pushed farther into the Gentile world, the language, methods, and approaches that worked so well in Judea would be misunderstood, misconstrued, or ineffective, so they found new ways to express the same truths. It is also clear from Paul's letters that he entrusted this ever-changing mission to young men like Timothy who understood the times.

We need to adapt. The older generations don't become irrelevant; we still serve an important function, but we need to trust that the Spirit will use these young folks to use new methods, create new visions of what it looks like to be the body in the world today, and to lead boldly into the future where Christianity will once again flourish if we allow it to. Let me be clear, this doesn't mean just adding on more young ministry interns to train with our tried-and-true methods. It means taking risks and putting these Millennials and Gen Zs in positions where they can lead the way and we can follow. Let them develop new ideas and learn from them. Demonstrate humility. If we were planting churches in a new country that had only a few disciples, wouldn't it make sense to include people from that culture who could help us to be most effective in that new context? This change in generational cultures is big. This might be the biggest cultural challenge I have described in this whole book, and it might be one of the most important for the future of the kingdom in the United States and the entire Western world.

Chapter 22

Catching Our Breath

My regular physical activity of choice is running. I find it relaxing and therapeutic and over the years I suppose I've built up pretty good "wind," meaning I don't easily get out of breath. But about a year ago I began to mix in two to three days a week of cross-training and cut my running down to three or four days a week. It has helped balance my fitness and saves some long-term wear and tear on my knees and ankles. The high-intensity cross-training that I've taken to challenges my body and breathing in a whole different way than distance running does. The other day I was well into a very intense workout that was all body-weight focused. After about forty minutes I seriously felt like I was about done for. I had another twenty minutes or so left to complete the exercises that I had scheduled for the day, but I didn't think I could muster one more rep. I have never quit a workout early, but this one was intense, and the app that I use had thrown so much at me that I was sure there was no way I could go on. My muscles were burning, and I was huffing and puffing harder than I remember doing in a long time. So I stopped. I stood there bent over just trying to catch my breath for a few seconds. Finally, I stood up, put my arms above my head and took in three or four deep breaths.

Suddenly, I felt like a whole new person. I had caught my breath, so to speak. My body, which had felt like it was about to quit on me, came to life again and I felt ready to go. I didn't need to give up. I just needed those moments to catch my breath, and then on I went and was able to complete the workout.

We've covered a lot of ground in this book so far, and it can feel overwhelming. There's so much to know, so much to be aware of; there are so many potential misunderstandings and miscommunications. It can seem like too much. If you're feeling that way, let's stop and catch our breaths. Let's recap and restate some things just to make sure that we've caught the main ideas before moving on to what comes next.

WHAT IS CULTURE?

To put it in the simplest form I can, culture is the accepted way of life of a group of people that they pass on from one generation to the next through the means of daily actions and thought patterns. Most of what people do is based on their culture. That doesn't mean that every single person from any one group acts the same. There is room for individual personality, of course, and each person has many different microcultures they were brought up in that have an impact on their personal beliefs and behaviors. So, while people from the same country will share much in the way of cultural assumptions, they may have differences as well based on their geography, religion, ethnicity, race, and many other factors.

To what degree we share in culture with or differ in culture from those around us often depends on which streams of culture are the most primary as influences. Some people are heavily influenced by their racial group, while others have never embraced that, or have even intentionally rejected it to some degree. Some people are deeply influenced by their religion growing up, and that trumps other cultural streams that might otherwise be more influential. Others can be very influenced in their cultural beliefs and assumptions by a political ideology, yet still share much in common socially with someone who grew up in the same area but has become quite different in their cultural worldview because they have a different ideology.

Complicating the concept of culture is that we cannot simply assume that because someone appears to be of a specific culture, especially racially or ethnically, that they are. Just because someone appears to be Chinese does not mean they know anything about that culture if they were not raised in it or by Chinese people, for example. While it does help at times to understand general truths about certain cultures, we must not peg any individual into a stereotype and need to give them room to express their own cultural preferences, as surprising as those may sometimes be.

Additionally, the predominant culture for a person can change over time. Culture can be pliable to different situations and changes in life. Many of the practices and beliefs that impact both my wife's culture and mine have transformed after becoming followers of Christ. At the same time, there are many aspects of culture that are remarkably resilient and remain despite massive life changes or relocations. Having become familiar with the culture of my wife, her family, and the African American community in which she was raised, I marvel at how many elements have been retained from West African culture. Even though they do have many differences from Africans today, there is an amazing staying power to many cultural aspects despite having been separated from the African culture by an ocean, many unique experiences, and being surrounded by Western culture for hundreds of years.

AN AREA OF FOCUS IN THE CHURCH

Culture pervades every element of our lives, so for a church community to not pay careful attention to it is to risk great peril. For many churches, though, it will not seem like a natural fit with traditional topics of a spiritual community. For starters, because culture is passed on without typically being aware of it, it is just the normal things that everyone around you does, so most people are blind to many of the dynamics of culture. And if you're part of the dominant group, you're much more likely to be almost entirely unaware that the things you do and think are culturally conditioned. What is a dominant culture? It is the group whose behavior and thought patterns are either in the majority or hold the most power and influence within the reach of a specific society that has more than one cultural group present.

The second reason that many churches will not see culture as a necessary topic is that it has been incredibly neglected in church teaching and training. And that makes a certain amount of sense. When churches drop the good news of the gathering of the nations off the menu and embrace homogenous congregations and communities, then both the clash of cultures and the need to bring them together into a new transformed community diminish exponentially. You don't need to focus that much on cultural competency when everyone in your body shares similar primary cultural influences. But when the whole gospel is proclaimed, including the gathering of the nations, then the need to train people to become all things and understand the dynamics of culture becomes much more pronounced. If this side of biblical training is ignored, most multiracial, multiethnic, or multicultural groups will cease to be so in a few decades.

The third reason that so many churches neglect or reject cultural competency training is that to many, it seems like it is paying too much attention to worldly things and amending the gospel to appeal to current trends. It smacks of humanism to many. But the idea that cultural training is some modern, progressive idea that is being smuggled into the Bible is to ignore the context of much of the New Testament, especially Paul's letters, which consistently walked diverse Christian families of believers through their very different cross-cultural experiences and problems.

TROUBLE COME MY WAY

The old hymn "Trouble in My Way" ends each verse with the simple chorus,

> *Jesus, he will fix it.*
> *Jesus, he will fix it.*
> *Jesus, he will fix it.*
> *After a while.*

When it comes to the topic of culture, there are many opportunities for clashes and divisions and numerous obstacles that can make it difficult for a diverse community to maintain its unity. Being a multicultural community is challenging. There is no easy way out. And, unfortunately, I don't think Jesus is going to come and just fix it after a while. No, he expects us to do the work. Becoming all things to all people is our task in the great mission of gathering the nations.

If two or more people are in proximity, conflict will happen. That's inescapable. And if two or more cultures are mixed together in one group, then it is a sure bet that misunderstandings and divisions will develop.

We must keep on guard, because many of our cultural assumptions and preferences are below the surface, and that means they have become ingrained into who we are as part of our identity, which in turn means that when our cultural norms are violated or infringed upon by someone acting differently than we would, it can be an emotional issue. In other words, we can get pretty worked up by clashes of culture.

Divisions are most likely to come when one of five things happens. The first is that we are simply unaware of the power and pervasiveness of cultural dynamics, so we misinterpret clashes as having a different cause than the real one, which leaves us unable to truly deal with them due to misdiagnosis. The second is that when we encounter a conflict that is caused by culture, we interpret the other person's actions by what it would mean if we took that action. A guest might come into the house of an Asian person and leave their shoes on, causing the host to assume that they are being thoughtless and rude, because that's what it would mean if they themselves were to leave their shoes on in someone else's house. But that may not be the case at all, and the guest may just not have thought about it because it is not done at their house. The third is when we give in to ethnocentrism and presume that our way of doing things is superior. The fourth is when we reject humility and compromise. We may not think our way is superior, but we just like it better and will make no effort to bend or try new things. The fifth is when we refuse to exert ourselves to become all things to all people. For many, cultural flexibility seems like too much work, and they are unwilling to make that kind of effort.

Similarly, once divisions have occurred, there are a number of obstacles that can stand in the way of reconciliation and cultural unity. The first is that we don't like someone else or their culture and are unwilling to work toward unity. Second, we are unwilling to venture into practices or ways of thinking that are unfamiliar. Third, we don't want to make mistakes, so we avoid attempts at cultural understanding. Fourth, we would rather live with or ignore the division than put in the work it takes to reconcile. Fifth, we claim that to give attention to cultural differences or divides is divisive in itself, so we avoid the whole concept. Sixth, prejudice and bias are hidden or not dealt with. Seventh, ethnocentrism does not just cause division, it can also serve as an obstacle to reconciliation because we look down upon other cultures and won't take their opinion or perspective as valid. Eighth, we can reduce people to a single story, which keeps us from understanding the totality of their cultural expressions. Ninth, political divides serve as a major obstacle to unity when we allow them to dictate cultural norms and worldviews over and above the kingdom of God.

FEELING CONFIDENT?

We've made it this far in our analysis of culture and cultural competency and have just a short section yet to go, about where to go from here. Maybe by this point you're starting to feel confident about your understanding of the culture of others and your ability to navigate any situation that might arise. Allow me to share three short stories that may erode that confidence a bit.

Story 1

We were having a small group meeting at our house recently, and just before we were to begin, my wife asked me to run to the store to pick up a few things we needed for refreshments. As I arrived back from the store and pulled up to our house, I noticed that several people had already arrived and parked their cars. But as I came past the large evergreen tree that blocks the view of the driveway until you pull up perpendicular to it, I saw that someone had pulled up in the driveway and parked in front of the garage door. I parked on the street and brought the groceries in, but I must admit, I was annoyed. I mean, really annoyed. As I walked into the kitchen, I think my wife sensed that something was bugging me and asked me, so I told her, venting a bit about the moral crime that had just been committed. She looked at me bemused, and then said something to the effect that she would have parked in someone's driveway too. She didn't see the problem. They had no way of knowing that I was at the store or that our car was not in the garage. Then it hit me why I was so irritated. A cultural norm had been violated. In the world I grew up in, you just didn't park in someone else's driveway. No one ever said that, of course, but it was an unwritten rule that I must have picked up over the years. Driveway parking was by invitation only or for close family who had a standing invitation. Otherwise, you parked that car in the street.

There was nothing wrong with our friends parking in our driveway, but it caused me to be upset for a moment until I was able to understand why. This was not a major issue, and I wouldn't have started the meeting with a screaming rebuke of driveway violators, but these types of little cultural clashes can build up over time or get blown out of proportion if not understood and dealt with.

Story 2

My wife and I have an ongoing feud in our house over phone charging cords. I am fairly particular about my cords. I like to put them in strategic spots where I use them regularly and leave them there so that I can plug in quickly whenever I need to. I have one by the bed, one by my desk, one in the car; you get the idea. Every so often, though, I will sit down mindlessly, grab for the cord while focusing on something else and be unable to find it. When I look closer, I discover that my cord is gone. Not again—you're kidding me! So, I hunt her down and inquire as to the whereabouts of my missing cord.

Her response is usually something like, "I don't know, I needed a cord and I think I grabbed that one, it might be . . . ."

To which I respond, "This is why you have your own cords. I don't understand why you need mine."

Exchanges like this happened for years in my household. I could not figure out why she kept taking my cords, and she couldn't fathom why it mattered so much to me. So, why did it matter? You may have guessed. It's cultural, but it took me a long time to realize that. In short, I'm deeply individualistic in my thinking. My worldview is that everyone has their own stuff. You take care of it and you use it, and if someone else, even a family member, wants it, they have to ask for it. My wife is from a collectivist background and family where everything was communal property and open to being used. Anything that anyone has is everyone's, and no one feels entitled to it or sees it as being just theirs. This is why she could not comprehend why it drove me nuts when she would take my cords, and I couldn't believe that she had violated my space again. I even put pieces of tape with my name on them on the cords to deter any future theft. And you know what? She didn't even notice. We had a clear cultural divide that was a source of conflict and annoyance for years, and only after understanding the dynamic were we able to find a solution.

Story 3

A minister was recently messaging back and forth with a brother in

Christ from another country. He had been asked by this African friend to get some paperwork together for him. The minister responded and let him know that it would take some time and that he was quite busy, but he would send it on as soon as possible. Two days later, he started to receive messages at least daily reminding him about the paperwork and prompting him to get it to him quickly, even though it was not needed for several weeks. A couple of times, the brother mentioned that he was still waiting for the papers "that you promised you would send but haven't." This bothered the minister. He felt badgered, and to him, appealing to a promise was implying that he was being negligent and dishonorable. It felt manipulative. I have seen this kind of interaction and language with wonderful people from that part of the world before, and I'll admit I don't completely understand it. It seems very rude to me, but I know that this is not how they intend it. But how could they possibly know that language that seems normal to them comes across badly to their brothers and sisters across the ocean?

How could we possibly know all the potential cultural differences and clashes that we may encounter in a diverse community? If you were feeling confident before, has that eroded some when you think about the potential task ahead to become culturally competent? There are so many areas of culture, both those above the surface and those below.

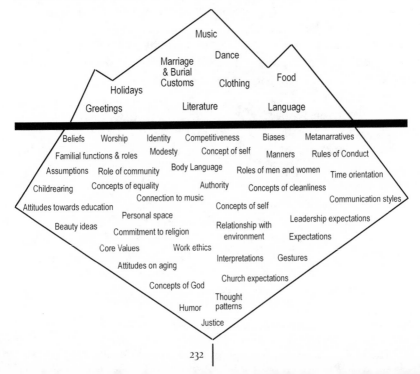

COMPETENCE, NOT PERFECTION

Now consider that all those areas of cultural thought and expression are individualized for each person in each culture. Multiply that by the large number of cultures you may interact with on a regular basis, and it can seem overwhelming. Why even try? It seems like it's too much to ever be able to navigate.

And it is. That's my point. We are not advocating for anyone to be a cultural expert in every culture and every conceivable situation. How could our friends know that it would clash with my cultural upbringing to park in my driveway? How would you be able to decipher that a disagreement over a phone charging cord was rooted in cultural differences? How can you know that language that is completely normal to you is offensive to someone from another group?

You can't. That's not what cultural competency is about. Knowing that I spend a lot of time thinking, learning, and teaching about culture, people occasionally come to me and express that they are taking a trip to Korea and want to know if I could quickly fill them in on the Korean culture. No, I can't. I've never been there. I wouldn't have the first clue beyond some broad basics about Eastern cultures. I am not an expert in every culture and I never could be.

Think of the difference between a tour guide and a negotiator. Tour guides know the site where they work like the back of their hand. They know every stop on the tour and all the information about each spot. There are few surprises, and they know exactly what they will say at each place. Negotiators, however, have a certain competency. They know the principles of their trade and they have picked up a great deal of understanding of how to read people and how to get the best out of a negotiation. But each situation is different. They don't know every single deal, and they don't have intimate knowledge of each person they will interact with. They have a base of knowledge that provides them a certain ease and capability in negotiating situations.

It is this comfortableness and capability that we seek when we speak of cultural competency, not perfection. What does cultural competency look like? That's what we will spend the remaining chapters considering.

Chapter 23

The Culturally Competent Person

Paul grew up loving his own culture and people; there's little question about that. As he wrote a letter to the people of Philippi, he called them to imitate Christ rather than the culture around them. Yes, all they saw around them were people striving for social mobility, praise from others, and doing whatever they could to advance themselves and get ahead. And yes, in Roman eyes, humility was considered a weakness, while being self-determinant was considered the greatest freedom. But Paul called them to lay that down and follow Christ, which meant giving up selfish ambition, embracing humility, and acting in the interest of others in all situations. As Paul is laying out the challenge of this call and reminding them of men whose lives exemplified that very way of living, he turns his attention to what they will have to give.

In so doing, we get a small glimpse into the cultural world that Paul was raised in. As a Jew who grew up as part of the diaspora, meaning his family had been scattered outside Palestine, he was still steeped in Jewish culture. He was born into the right tribe and trained in all things Jewish. His family followed customs to the letter, and he embraced it all. After moving to Jerusalem, he continued not only following God but learning and excelling in every aspect of Jewish cultural life. He was a "Hebrew of Hebrews" (Philippians 3:5). And when it came to the connection the Gentile nations had with the one true creator God, Paul didn't have a high opinion of non-Jewish peoples.

So, when he was confronted by the resurrected Christ and had a hole blown in his worldview, we might be more than a little surprised at his response. When Paul suddenly realized that Jesus was the long-promised King of Israel, and of the world, he dedicated his life to proclaiming that to whomever would hear the message. He was willing to take that message around the world and declare it to Jew and Gentile alike.

Based on his upbringing, though, if anyone would have connected the gospel to the Jewish culture, we might have suspected Paul to be at the top of the list. Yet he was just the opposite. The Judaizers were the group that could not separate the gospel of Jesus from their own cultural preferences and background. In their failure to do so, they created what Paul called a different gospel, one in which following the law and the customs of the Jewish people became required for the Christ follower. Marrying the good news of Jesus to any cultural practices or preferences is to create a different gospel. We must rely on Christ alone. But there is a second danger in conflating Christ and any specific culture. When we do that, the mission to gather the nations becomes endangered. It means that embracing the gospel suddenly becomes as much about being willing to cast off your cultural beliefs and perspectives and embracing a new default culture as it is about entering God's kingdom.

God's kingdom is pliable to any culture; it does not have a default human culture, not even Jewish. It will welcome and adapt to any culture but will also challenge any person to both bring their culture into the kingdom and to adapt parts of it to the standards of kingdom living.

For Paul, the gospel allowed for and even demanded cultural flexibility. Disciples would lay down their lives for the benefit of others and would be willing to become all things to all people (1 Corinthians 9:22). We see Paul's heart for that clearly when he ambled into Athens, the center of Greek culture, to proclaim that Jesus was King and that there was a new way to live in response to that (Acts 17:16–34).

Paul earned the ear of many who were present that day because he was not a cultural elitist. He was troubled at their idolatry, but he still respected these people. There is not a hint of disdain for them or their culture. In fact, he had paid close attention to their culture. He knew how to operate in it. He didn't assume negative intent in their actions but praised the intent of having an altar to an unknown god, as misguided as he thought that was. He knew something about their customs and their values, and was able to quote some of their poetry. Paul was a student of culture, and because he was, he was able to transcend the culture and become like these Greeks to a degree to help win some to the gospel. He didn't teach them a mixture of Christianity with a heavy dose of Jewish culture. He declared to them that Jesus was King in a way that they could understand and live out in their own context. Would they have to change aspects of their lives to follow him? Of course; we all do. But they didn't have to become Jewish. Paul was unquestionably a culturally competent person.

GETTING STARTED

Back in the days before GPS navigation, when we used MapQuest to get around, I printed out directions for returning home from the house of an out-of-state friend I was visiting. Shortly after leaving, though, I had a problem. I couldn't figure out the directions, nor could I find the highway I needed to take. I wandered around a bit and realized that now not only did I not know where I was going, I wasn't sure I could find my way back to my friend's house. It turns out I had the wrong starting address, so the directions were never going to help me.

Having the right starting point is essential because everything else we do will flow from there. If we want to become culturally competent disciples, where do we start? What is the first step in becoming all things to all people? Paul says, "Though I am free and belong to no one, I have made myself a slave to everyone . . . I have become all things to all people so that by all possible means I might save some" (1 Corinthians 9:19, 22). Paul understood that he was free and not under compulsion to adapt and modify his own cultural practices and preferences for the benefit of others. He then set about intentionally doing so. He was able to make that observation and begin to adapt himself because he was aware of his own cultural tendencies and how they differed from others. Paul's first step was to be aware of and know his own cultural boundaries.

If we are going to be culturally adaptive persons who are on the mission of the gospel, then our first step is self-awareness and self-analysis. This is not for the sake of identity politics, whereby we section off by groups and then stay as separate as possible while at the same time calling for tolerance between groups even as we constantly accentuate the differences. That is how the world has largely responded to the issues brought about by diversity. We identify our differences so that we can overcome them using Jesus' method of bending and sacrificing ourselves. This is not limited to one group within the body of Christ; we must all be willing to embrace this.[21]

Here are some areas in which we can start the self-assessment. For each topic, ask yourself how this aspect of your identity has helped to shape your cultural beliefs and practices. What are some specific cultural elements that have been grafted into your life as a result of these forces?

- Nationality
- Region where you grew up
- Town or city
- Race/Ethnicity
- Gender
- Socioeconomic status/Class
- Religion
- Family

These certainly are not all the categories that have an impact on your culture, but being aware of how these things affect you is a huge start.

Refer to the diagram in Chapter 22 and start thinking through the many different areas of culture depicted there and how the topics above will affect each of those areas. Don't feel that you need to rush this process. Take your time at self-analysis.

CALIBRATE YOUR THINKING

It is vitally important that we not get off track in how we mentally approach this task. In no way is anyone implying that culture is bad or inferior. Sometimes when people are asked to be flexible, they overreact and argue that they feel as though their culture is being diminished or demonized. No one is saying that. But your culture is not superior either, and that is an important takeaway.

The process of becoming all things to all people is not a compulsory one. We are not called to this process because our culture is more flawed than others and it needs to be phased out. This is not about the worth or lack of worth of any individual culture. This is about the gospel and what we have been called to do in order keep God's mission pressing into a world that desperately needs it.

A church community that does not have people willing to be pliable and culturally competent is a church that is doomed to never grow past a dominant culture. It will be the least likely group to have a truly transformed gospel culture that embraces all people, because it will never escape the clutches of the default culture of that society. In order to grow, the dominant group must be willing to adjust itself and include and value other ways of doing things. In order to thrive, every group must be willing to engage in this process.

WILLING TO LEARN

Once we have taken the steps to identify our own culture and understand the power it has in our life, our emotions, and our interactions with others, we can start to grow in our cultural competence. It doesn't matter how little or how much we have paid attention to this area of the gospel in the past, we can all grow from whatever our starting point is. I believe the gospel-focused person will pursue six areas in their heart.

The first is a willingness to be actively aware of the culture of others, the dynamics of interplay between theirs and ours, and potential sources of conflict. We won't be able to foresee every conflict or difference before it happens, but sensitivity to these issues will help us more quickly identify and work through our differences.

The second is a willingness to learn. Being aware is a good start, but we need to go beyond that and put in the effort to learn the expressions and attitudes of others. This will range from everything to spending time with people of other cultures and truly inviting them into our lives and entering theirs, to taking a class on cross-cultural communication. Not everyone will need to take a special course, but everyone can intertwine their lives with brothers and sisters of different cultural groups, with a willing heart to learn.

The rest of the list must all be present to truly engage in the first two. As Paul teaches the church about the importance of unity in the gathering of the nations in his letter known as Ephesians, he urges that they "be completely humble and gentle; be patient, bearing with one another in love" (Ephesians 4:2). To be culturally proficient toward others requires:

1. Humility
2. Gentleness
3. Patience
4. Love

Someone who is pursuing these four virtues in their life will find that they slot in quite naturally to becoming all things to all people. These attributes will orient our hearts toward awareness and willingness to learn. For the remainder of this chapter, we will be more specific and move on to principles for the person striving to grow in their cultural flexibility and adaptability.

PRINCIPLES FOR PERSONAL CULTURAL COMPETENCY

What's the difference between rules and principles? Rules can be followed with little to no heart, thought, or effort put into it. We can go through the motions and check off the boxes. Applying principles asks more of us. It demands that we engage our heart and mind and discern how to be guided by these precepts as we react to situations that arise. Following principles is more difficult than keeping rules. When it comes to cultural competency, I will suggest eleven principles that will help us to navigate the choppy waters of the diverse community.

Be Curious and Ask Questions

In an English play from 1598, we find the first recorded used of the proverb, "Care killed the cat," by which was meant "anxiety." That saying remained in use until 1898, when the first known recorded instance of the now more well known "Curiosity killed the cat" appeared in a Galveston newspaper. Curiosity has not exactly been thought of as a virtue over the centuries, going back as far as the theologian Augustine, who wrote in 397 that God "fashioned hell for the inquisitive."

I am going to propose that sometimes curiosity can be a good thing rather than just a ticket to the inferno. When we are not curious, we don't learn and won't grow. Be curious. Become a student of other cultures, especially as it relates to life within the body of Christ. Curiosity leads to the second principle, which I have included in this section: ask lots of questions. Ask questions and then listen with the sole intent of learning. Spend time thinking about ways to include other cultural expressions into the body of Christ as we throw off the shackles of a default dominant culture and strive toward the kingdom culture of all things.

As with anything, being curious and asking questions can be done in an annoying or negative fashion. We obviously don't want to annoy people, so make sure the person you are talking with doesn't mind being interrogated a bit and take care to ask questions in a respectful way. If direct questioning is not appropriate to the situation, then just observe and learn as much as you can.

Don't Judge Others

There is an old saying, which I will not repeat here, about what happens when we assume things. Suffice it to say that human beings get ourselves into a great deal of mess when we jump to conclusions. This is nowhere truer than in cross-cultural contexts. When we encounter an unfamiliar cultural value or approach to a situation, it will often elicit a negative reaction on our part because that's not how we would do it. Their approach often makes no sense to us. But people rarely do things that make no sense to themselves. Withholding judgment is a vital skill for the culturally competent individual. I will not try to sugarcoat this: it is not easy to do. We can jump to conclusions effortlessly. It takes a tremendous amount of self-discipline no to. Just think, though, how many avoidable conflicts in your life have taken place because someone leaped to an assumption that turned out to be incorrect.

There is a monumental difference between observing and attempting to decipher the actions of others, and judging them. Judging includes observation but then jumps forward to assigning value as well.

Give the Benefit of the Doubt

For the longest time, it drove me nuts when my wife would take trivial things like a pen or phone charging cord (I described that struggle earlier) that I viewed as mine. I didn't mind her using things, but she would use them and move them, and then I couldn't find them. I assigned the worst possible motive: selfishness. But as I have detailed above, as I began to pursue cultural understanding, it dawned on me that this tendency came from her collectivist cultural background. Rather than selfishness, it was a signal of love, acceptance, and inner-group identification. In the world from which she came, it was a way of saying, "We are one people."

I missed that message for a long time, however, because I jumped to conclusions and did not give the benefit of the doubt. I often wondered, how could there be a positive motivation behind taking someone else's stuff? Well, I found the answer. One of the best skills I have learned is that when I'm annoyed by someone's behavior, to find the best possibility behind the action. Someone cut me off in traffic? Maybe they just found out their child is sick and are trying to rush home to tend to them. Someone speaks rudely to me? Perhaps they just found out their spouse has cancer and they are overwhelmed. Someone walks by me on the street and doesn't offer a greeting? That feels rude, but maybe in their culture it is considered invasive to greet strangers and, in their mind, they were simply being respectful of my privacy. I am imperfect in applying this skill, of course, but it saves me a lot of grief and conflict when I do.

Translate Actions

Once we have taken the initiative to avoid assumptions, the next step is to translate the actions of others. I've already alluded to this principle at various points in this book, but it deserves its own space and explanation. When people from another cultural background do things that feel inappropriate or rude, we do well to not jump to judging them negatively but instead assume the best. But we can take it one step further if we do the work of interpreting their actions.

Linguists will tell you that there is a big difference between translation and transliteration. Take the word "baptize," for example. Traditionally, there was no word "baptize" in the English language. In the New Testament we find the Greek term *baptizo* sprinkled throughout the texts. That word means to dip or immerse. But most English translations of the New Testament opted to transliterate the word rather than translate it. That is, they just transferred the Greek word into English and invented a new word, "baptize." Over time, many faith traditions have slowly changed the meaning of that word to mean sprinkling. They can get away with doing that with the word "baptize" because it doesn't have a meaning in English. It is a word used nowhere outside the Bible to give it context. Had the English Bibles translated it "immerse," it would be nearly impossible to justify forms of baptism that didn't involve full immersion. The term "immerse" has its own meaning in English and cannot be changed quite so easily.

We make a huge mistake when we transliterate actions of others. In other words, we take their action and simply transport it into our cultural framework and what it would mean if we did the same thing. Thus, if my wife takes a pen from my desk, well, I would never do that. And if I did, it would mean that I didn't care about that person's things or was flat out stealing from them. Do you see the conflict that could cause? If I translate it, though, I come up with something far different. In translating, you change the word in the original language to a word that means the same in the second language. If I translate her action rather than transliterate it, I realize that she is doing something that was respectful in her culture. It may not feel right to me, but at least I know that the intention was not nefarious on her part. We cannot control how interactions with others will feel, but we do have power over whether we transliterate or translate their actions.

Reject Ethnocentrism

Ethnocentrism is feeling that your culture is superior to that of others. This goes beyond simply preferring what you know and looks down on the practices of others as substandard. This form of pride is a surefire community killer. You can appreciate your own culture, but check your heart for ethnocentrism on a regular basis. Once it gets a foothold, it is difficult to root out.

Allow Each Other to Make Mistakes

The pressure to be perfect is an unbearable load for any of us. Even in the Sermon on the Mount when Jesus urges, "Be perfect, therefore, as your heavenly Father is perfect" (Matthew 5:48), he is not speaking of mistake-free living. He uses the term to mean "complete" as he speaks of the Father's love for all, including enemies. There is no person or group that falls outside God's love. He is complete in that, and that is the target for which we aim.

We will make mistakes. We will be insensitive or rude in the eyes of another. We will respond badly to their culture and make premature judgments. We will misinterpret actions. It will happen; count on it. I will blow it and so will you. This is where grace comes in. This is where mercy triumphs over judgment.

I've watched my sons play basketball throughout their lives. My older son once had a coach who demanded perfection. He would yell at the players and immediately take them out of the game for the smallest errors. The result was players who were nervous, jumpy, and could never get the most out of themselves or overcome the fear of messing up. My younger son recently had a coach who was just the opposite. He did not yell at them for mistakes or take them out of the game. He would just clap his hands in a show of positive encouragement and then later, when they came to the bench, would calmly explain what they could do to improve next time. His players flourished because they weren't afraid to make mistakes. They were willing to take risks, and they developed as young men and as players because of the environment he created.

We want to create church families that encourage us to reach out to one another, to learn, and to grow, but we can't set up a punitive atmosphere that reflects our world's outrage culture and jumps to conclusions, publicly chastising people for mistakes or insensitivities. Do we call out sin? Yes, lovingly and patiently. But we also understand that all mistakes aren't sins, that we all make them, and that we can overlook, forgive, and love. Because "love covers over a multitude of sins" (1 Peter 4:8).

Be Sensitive; Don't Be So Sensitive

Down the road from where I live stands a bright new Super Target. It has a pod of doors at the entrance point marked "enter" on one side. On the other side is another pod of doors marked "exit." A remarkable amount of foot traffic constantly flows in and out of those doors. When people follow the directions and enter and exit through the correct spots, it works well. If people ignore that two-way flow, things can get mucked up quickly.

When it comes to cultural interactions, a two-way flow is invaluable. Be sensitive to others and their needs but try not to be so sensitive concerning your own. This doesn't mean jettison your own cultural preferences and always defer to others. This is about level of sensitivity. When everyone in a community strives toward this dual flow of sensitivity to others and a bit of steel with their own feelings, amazing things start to happen in the community. This is particularly important in an age when so many are so easily offended. As Christians, we must not be influenced by this oversensitivity. Let the sensitivity flow to others but not into your own life. When only some are doing this, that's better than nothing, but it will eventually wear on those who are trying.

Be Proactive

I have a good friend who is suffering through some significant back problems. In response, he is working with physical therapists, stretching daily, following a moderate exercise routine, and doing everything he can to care for his back. That's all good. But do you know what is even better? To care for your back before a problem appears. Strengthen your core and lower back. Stretch every day. Do the things that experts agree will help keep that important part of your body healthy. But most importantly, do it now before problems develop.

My wife and I have been invited into many churches that have begun to experience problems, some small and some big, in the areas of race and culture. It's good to address problems when they appear. But my recommendation is to be proactive. If you think your church is fine, start educating and training in these areas now. Take the initiative to become cross-culturally competent before you have a conflict. Commence talking with others in your group about culture and potential conflicts before they become actual events. There is no time like the present.

Get Out of Your Comfort Zone

The safest place to be is your comfort zone. It's also the place that will afford the fewest opportunities to grow. Becoming all things to all people, by definition, will call us out of our comfort zones. Jesus' initial call to disciples was to lay down our lives and follow him. If you want to be comfortable, you have chosen the wrong religion. Cross-cultural competency is not about comfort, it is about growth and loving others. Please, take the risk. It will be worth it. You may experience some bumps and very awkward moments, but it will be worth it in the long run.

Relax

Cross-cultural interactions can be anxiety inducing by themselves. Add to that the hypersensitive, outrage culture we live in, and many of us would rather just not even try for fear of making a mistake and being called out. But just listen to Frankie. Those who grew up listening to '80s pop music know what I'm talking about. Just relax. Don't relax to the point of insensitivity to others, but don't be so afraid of making a mistake that you become paralyzed. Surround yourself with some brave comrades who are willing to wade into cross-cultural exploration with you and agree that you will have fun with this and treat it like an adventure. My wife and I still bump about cultural issues almost daily, but we have fun with it. We laugh at ourselves and the power that culture has over us.

When we take a step back and relax, we are much more likely to learn, to love, and to grow.

Chapter 24
Culturally Competent Leadership

The church had hit a snag. In one sense, this was nothing new. It was a group forged through controversy. The apostles had followed Jesus, watching him engage with detractor after detractor. He was eventually tortured and executed in the most humiliating manner available in the first century, Roman crucifixion. After his incredible resurrection, they began to proclaim the good news that Jesus really was the long-promised King of all, and his resurrection and ascension proved it. But it wasn't smooth sailing. They were threatened with violence or imprisonment from the Jewish leaders, threats that they could only take all too seriously. Then they had to deal with an internal issue, as a well-known married couple in the church pretended to fully identify with this new family forming around the Messiah, but they were lying, and the Holy Spirit took swift action. That sent fear and shock waves throughout the body. After that, there was another wave of persecution for the apostles. Yet the church overcame each one of those obstacles and continued to thrive.

Then came another snag, but this one seems potentially different. This was the first time their unity was threatened. That's a significant problem for a group whose primary message is that God is reconciling the nations with each other as his family. Demonstrating disunity with a message like that is problematical, to say the least.

They were certainly acting like an extended family. They spent the bulk of their resources in those early days ensuring that there was no surplus or lack in the church. Those in need, especially the vulnerable widows, were given daily portions of food. But the old cultural and historical tensions quickly arose. The Hellenic Jews believed that their widows were getting short shrift, implying that the Hebraic widows were getting the better of it. We don't know all the details, but we do know that the leadership of the church at this time was likely dominated by Hebraic Jews. This looks like a case of a nondominant group feeling neglected by a dominant group. The church was in peril. Was the gathering of the nations at risk before it even got out of Palestine?

How would the leadership respond to this impending crisis? We are not given a great deal of information, but what we are shown reveals to us a culturally competent and spiritually wise group. We see a team that was quick to listen and validate the concerns of the nondominant group. They showed compassion and understanding. They were quick to act but without overreacting. They displayed respect without ever patronizing the Hellenic believers. They implemented a spiritual solution and took a countercultural approach: they surrendered power and influence to the nondominant group.

The spirituality and skill of these culturally competent leaders staved off what could have been a disaster. And it raises the question, what will a culturally competent leadership in the twenty-first century church look like?

Most people don't do so well under leaders who are controlling, co-ercive, unwilling to listen, fearful, and prone to keeping power in their own hands. Conversely, humans flourish when they have leaders that are humble, sacrificial, willing to admit mistakes, trusting, and inclusive. Given the choice of those two extremes, I think we all know what kind of leadership we would choose.

There are churches that truly have diverse leadership and diverse in-fluence at all levels, but most multicultural churches that I have seen still have a leadership team that primarily represents the dominant cultural group. This means that most leadership teams in multicultural churches have some room for growth toward cultural inclusion and competency. For the rest of this chapter, we will look at the characteristics of compe-tent leadership in dealing with others, particularly nondominant cultural groups, in terms of the groups themselves, their approach to the church, and their vision for the future.

LEADERSHIP AND NONDOMINANT GROUPS

The first characteristic that leadership groups must have is the will-ingness to listen. This does not mean that they merely have an open ear if, and when, approached. They must seek out the opinions and stories of others. They will ensure that they are hearing from groups that are di-verse in their authority and power, influence, age, ethnicity, background, gender, etc.

I have seen four types of leadership groups when it comes to issues of multiculturalism and inclusion: 1) the kind that is oblivious to these issues and doesn't see it as a need to listen to people's concerns, 2) the kind that thinks they have a handle on this issue but doesn't have their ear to the ground (or has an incomplete team that they hear from) and are often disconnected from what some segments of their population are feeling, 3) the kind that knows there are issues and is willing to hear from people but does not seek out opinions or pursue learning and growth for themselves, and 4) the kind that knows they need growth and is not just willing to listen, but actively tracks down the thoughts, opinions, and input of others.

The second characteristic is to believe the frustrations of the nondominant group. That doesn't mean we should overreact to every individual opinion or complaint, but there is a very real dynamic where nondominant group members often feel marginalized. They feel that their observations are dismissed because they are not noticed by those in leadership. When people say they have experienced something, especially when it is more than one person saying it, pay attention. Believe them.

In my context, in the United States, leaders who are white often have very little concept of how damaging and even traumatic it is for people of color and nondominant groups to muster the courage to point out an area where they feel they are being marginalized in some way, only to be met with defensiveness or being told that they did not perceive things correctly. Leaders that are of the dominant cultural group must understand that it is very possible that, while they did not intend something, the impact it has may be quite different than the intent. When a member of a nondominant group shares something, a culturally humble leader will avoid defensiveness and own their action, even if it had an impact different from what they intended.

The third characteristic follows on the heels of the first two. Once you have listened and believed what people say, validate their thoughts. The Hebraic Jewish leadership in Acts 6 could have easily dismissed the concerns of the Hellenic Jews, claiming that they were being critical or too sensitive. But they didn't do that. They obviously had not seen the problem, or they would have addressed it already, but once they heard about it, they believed it and validated those feelings by springing into action.

It is important in these issues that the church see the progress. These things can often take time to be addressed, but far too often progress is behind the scenes or very slow, and it easily comes across as inactivity, impassivity, or lack of concern. As leaders, if you are validating and taking seriously the concerns of others, let the process be as visible as possible.

The fourth characteristic is respect. If we genuinely love people, we will respect them. Respect is a funny thing, because it can be so conditioned culturally that a group may be actively demonstrating respect to others in their minds, but it comes across as something very different to the recipients. The quickest ways for leadership to demonstrate disrespect to nondominant groups is by making them feel dismissed, patronized, or counterbalanced. Allow me to explain that last idea. Counterbalancing is when we allow a small group to express their opinion, but we don't agree with it, so we immediately seek to counterbalance it with the leadership's opinion. This is often done in a passive-aggressive manner but is far more transparent than we think. And it is toxic.

Disrespect can also come unintentionally, and leaders must be on their guard against this. A few years ago, my wife and I gave a Crossing the Line workshop on culture and race at a church, and it was a great weekend. For the next week, the leaders of the church had already planned a sermon on not complaining. They are goodhearted and loving leaders and had not intended the sermon to be a repudiation of anything in our workshop or to be aimed at the nondominant cultures in the church, but it came across that way to several people. Before that Sunday was even over, we were receiving concerned phone calls and messages. It seemed like an invalidation and disrespect to many members of the nondominant group. Leaders need to be extremely careful not to inadvertently send messages that are different from what they had in mind.

LEADERSHIP QUALITIES

A few months ago, my younger son got me to watch a television show that I had never seen before. It is called *The Office*, and although it went off the air over five years ago, it is now the most-watched show on Netflix. The boss depicted on the show is a buffoon named Michael Scott. Scott seems to think he has the greatest ideas, is deeply respected by his employees, always knows what's going on, and rarely takes input from anyone around him. It makes for a hilarious situation comedy, but he would not be what we could consider a culturally competent leader in any way.

What are some key qualities of a leadership team that will continue to grow in their aptitude? The first is that they are introspective. Good leaders are willing to examine themselves. What are they doing that is good and needs to keep being developed? What do they need to do less of, more or, or stop altogether? Do they make others feel valued and included? Do they create an atmosphere of approachability? For a leader to truly be introspective, they need to be willing to hear from others and seek input. They may not always want to hear it, but it is necessary.

In that vein, good leaders will self-assess culturally and know their own preferences and expressions so that they can begin to consider their level of cultural acumen.

The second characteristic is openness to being wrong. A leader who can never admit when they have made a mistake or have a shortcoming is a leader who will not grow and will certainly never be culturally competent. The very heart of cultural effectiveness is a willingness to make mistakes and learn from them. It is often the most effective way to grow in this area.

The third quality is a hunger to learn. Being all things to all people requires an attitude of lifelong learning. If leaders are not hungry to expand their knowledge base and not intentional about learning through many different methods, they will stunt their effectiveness.

The fourth is being humble about having blind spots. Of course, humility is a presumed quality in a good leader at any level in the church, but specifically, culturally competent leadership groups will be aware that they have blind spots; all humans do. It is a problem when we think we see things clearly and completely. We all have biases, prejudices, and things that we will never see without the help of others. That is true of individuals and of groups. Leadership teams should regularly seek the input of others into matters of diversity and inclusion, which would include those from outside their church, those outside their team, and those from nondominant groups within their fellowship. I wonder what it would look like if leaders willingly gave up their right to always have things go their way. What if they shared power even when they might have reservations because they believed that doing so could be in the best interests of the community? Now that would be interesting, wouldn't it?

The fifth quality is creativity. Diversity demands us to get out of our comfortable little worlds and do things in a new way. This will require a willingness and openness to creative solutions. That's often uncomfortable for those of us in leadership in churches, because it will push us past the way things have always been done and into new and often unchartered territory, which can be terrifying. Secure and creative leaders will be willing to throw new things against the wall to see what sticks and own it when things don't work well. It's okay to have misfires on occasion, but let ingenuity have its place.

The sixth and final characteristic that we will consider is the willingness to distribute power and influence. This is precisely what the leaders in the Jerusalem church did in Acts 6. They were willing to diversify the power and influence in the church by turning one of the most important ministries over to the direction of the nondominant group. How many leadership teams are willing to go beyond merely seeking input from others (as valuable as that is), and actually give them decision-making influence and power in the community? That might even mean that, on occasion, they do something a bit differently than the group of leaders would. Does there still need to be some level of oversight? Most likely. But competent leaders are also willing to let others take some risks and do things that they might not. That's what diversity is all about.

GUIDING THE CHURCH

We were at a church leadership conference a few months ago, and a large group of us separated into about five cars to go from the hotel where we were meeting to the restaurant where we were going to dine together. I was in the third car in line as we dutifully fell into place behind the car that was leading the way. After driving a few miles down a busy street, we pulled into a parking lot that didn't look like it belonged to a restaurant. We soon realized that it wasn't the destination, and we started heading back in the direction we had just come from. After another minute or two, we turned back in the other direction. Keep in mind that having five cars take a U-turn is no small feat. After a little more driving, we started heading back toward the hotel, passing that and going the complete opposite way from our original direction. We finally pulled over in another parking lot to regroup. It was only then that the people in the lead car admitted that they thought they knew the way, but they had no idea where they were going. We eventually got to our destination, but we wasted a lot of time following leaders that did not know where they were headed.

A culturally competent church will have leaders who understand the times and know where the church needs to go. For starters, they must embrace that the mission of the church is to gather the nations. This doesn't mean they will have all the answers, but that they will take seriously the task of being all things to all people and developing and maintaining the diversity of the church. Here are five elements that inclusive leadership will value and implement into the life of the church.

Casting a Vision

A big part of leadership is having a vision for the church. Where are you going and how are you going to get there as a community? The vision must come from the Holy Spirit and God's word and not a worldly perspective, but it should be a careful consideration of how a church community can best embody the multicultural gospel in the context of its locality.

An effective vision for a body will both inspire and challenge people to grow and go beyond where they have been. It will be delivered with passion but not seem reactionary or emotional. It will explain and work toward meaningful solution of problems. It will call for everyone to be part of it and offer ways in which they can do so. And it will demonstrate that God is ultimately the one leading the church toward this destination.

One other word on sharing a leadership's vision with the church: it must be communicated often, clearly, and concisely. Do it only a couple times a year, and it will not become part of the lifeblood of the church. Do it vaguely or ambiguously, and you will lose people. Do it inefficiently, and the church will lose focus. Communicate. Communicate. Communicate. Communicate again. Communicate some more. And when you think you may be overdoing it, you are probably just beginning to get through to people.

Teaching and Training

John Wooden retired from coaching college basketball over forty years ago, yet he is still considered the greatest college coach to this day. Wooden's players will tell anyone who listens that he was first and foremost a teacher and trainer. That is why his teams were so successful. He didn't just give them plays or a system, he trained them in every aspect of life.

It is easy for a leadership team to call the church to racial and cultural diversity and inclusion, but equipping them for the task is an entirely different animal. If you want to know what a church truly values, look at what it spends its time teaching on and training in. There you will find its true treasure. If Paul spent over twenty-five percent of his writings teaching and training the church on the mission of gathering the nations and the task of being all things to all people, then why would we not? I don't think the answer is that we are more adept and skilled at these things than Paul's original audiences were, and so we need less teaching.

Leadership teams need to have frequent training in racial and cultural diversity and sensitivity as well as competence training. In our day and age, I believe it is also necessary to remind people that this is a vital aspect of the gospel. It is not bending to the tastes or trends of the culture. It is preparing us to take the message of the kingdom to those who need it. It is difficult to offer specifics beyond what has been provided through this book, because each church body is a different place with different needs and in a different context. The local leadership will have to discern what should be taught, but it needs to be consistent and something that the entire church leadership is clearly and vocally behind and engaged in.

Honesty and Transparency

Your church has probably not reached the ideal state of diversity yet. I doubt that it has. It may very well have a long way to go. The best policy is to be upfront and honest about that. Share with the church the challenges that you face together. Part of the vision should be a truthful assessment of what you do well and what you don't. If your leadership team is imbalanced and not yet diverse, make it clear that you are aware that this is the case, and explain what you are doing to be a full reflection of God's family of all people at every level of the body. Ask the church for their pressure, patience, and prayer.

Willingness to Take Criticism and Stay the Course

Not everyone will embrace the call to be a culturally competent church. That's just a reality. They may insist on interpreting it as a partisan political position or reflecting worldly values, or have some other justification. Those people are to be loved and brought along patiently and gently, but some may never come around. Listen to critics and other points of view and always be willing to adjust if necessary. But a leadership team needs to be committed to the vision and task of the church within our mission and understand that they will occasionally hear criticism. They will need to stay the course and not let a few detractors derail the direction of the church. Hopefully the critics will see the value and biblical truth of the vision, but they may not. And that must be okay.

Leading and Pushing

A competent church will have leaders that lead the way in competence. Let your growth be evident to all (1 Timothy 4:15). Stagnant leaders will result in a stagnant church. Sometimes you may have to push the church a bit. We all need that from time to time when it involves going beyond our zones of comfort. Knowing when and how hard to push will take constant prayer and guidance from the Spirit but will result in a church that consistently moves toward where God wants us all to be.

FUTURE-FOCUSED

It is important for a church leadership team to not just think about the present but to keep its eye on the future direction of the church. That, of course, is what vision is all about, but there are a few specific aspects of focusing on the future that I want to cover before bringing this chapter to a close.

Revelation 5-Focused

When I was a new disciple, it seemed like there was something fresh each week that the Spirit was calling me to address in my life or character. For a while I stalled in my growth because I started to dispute that I could change in those areas. "That's just the way I am," I argued. I obviously was unaware at the time that there is only one "I AM" and it's not me. I couldn't change because I was more focused on the present than on what I was supposed to become. As churches, we can make the same mistake.

We can often limit our growth in multiculturalism and inclusion because we limit ourselves to what we are. Why add wide-ranging styles of music when we only have a handful of people who connect better through that variety? Why incorporate different languages into the worship service when a large majority speak the same language? Why integrate different approaches to communication and community when this is the way we've always done it? If those become our attitudes, we will never grow.

Instead, we need to keep in mind that the goal is Revelation 5:9. We are a church of every tribe, language, people group, and nation. We are the gathering of all cultures, and that needs to be our target. The leadership group that cares about cultural competency will call the church to keep moving toward Revelation 5 as the vision of what we are trying to develop into. The elements of community life should not reflect who we are as much as who God wants us to become.

Intentionally Diverse

As I write this, social media and news outlets in the United States are flooded with anger over a sweater that Gucci had on their website for their Winter collection. The black sweater is a clever combination face-mask so that it looks like a normal sweater with a puffy neck, but the neck rolls up when you want to cover your nose and the rest of your face below your nose. It has a little circular area around the mouth cut out so that you can breathe, and that is the source of the controversy. The area around the mouth hole is red so that when the mask part is pulled up, it looks disturbingly like an extremely offensive minstrel blackface with the dark face and deep red exaggerated lips. Gucci has been accused of blatant racism, with many calling for boycotts. The company immediately published an apology, vowing to make sure that something like this never happens again, but in many respects, the damage is already done. The anger and frustration mirror the disgust that was generated almost a year ago when H&M advertised a line of children's hoodies with supposedly cute little sayings on them. One of them said, "COOLEST MONKEY IN THE JUNGLE," but had a young black model wearing it in their ads, which was sharply criticized. Both companies have now been accused of blatant racism.

I could be very wrong on this, and I'm open to that possibility, but I have a hard time imagining executives from a company sitting around in a meeting, giggling to themselves as they intentionally plan out racist apparel, sure that it will slip by everyone's notice. Why would they do this? I fail to see the motivation. It just doesn't seem plausible to me. They have been accused of intentional racism, but honestly, I don't think that's the issue. I'm not saying that doesn't exist, and I hope it is not the truth of this situation, although I could be very wrong. My guess is that the cause is much closer to a systemic lack of inclusion at important levels of leadership. There are no decision makers in their inner circles who come from a culture or background that would understand why these things are offensive and hurtful. It's a stunning lack of awareness on their part, yes, but it also speaks volumes that there appears to be no one with the common sense to know why you couldn't have a product like that in this day and age, and it raises the question of why no one with that wisdom and experiences is in a position of power enough to blow the whistle and stop it before it even starts. When you don't have inclusion and diversity at all levels of influence, bad things like this happen.

These corporate examples go beyond lack of diversity, of course, and include a shocking amount of ignorance and insensitivity, but I have to think that if there had been a broader base of power and influence, these distressing cases would have never occurred.

They speak to the dangers that lurk if church leadership teams are not intentionally diverse. There are many other reasons, most of them quite positive, to have diverse leadership, but it does help avoid insensitivities and shallow understanding. The more diverse a leadership is in areas of culture, race, socioeconomic background and status, gender, etc., the stronger it will be. Look at it logically. Which option is more likely to skillfully lead a diverse congregation in a visionary, inclusive, and sensitive manner: a homogenous leadership group or a diverse one?

Does that mean that we should put people onto a leadership team just to fulfill a quota and have diversity for diversity's sake? Absolutely not. But if a group is not diverse already, then it should have a plan to become so and consistently work toward that vision. If the leadership group of a diverse church is not diverse itself, then that speaks to some systemic issues within the body that need to be addressed immediately. No matter how loving and spiritual the leaders are, I can almost guarantee that if the group is not representative of the diversity of the body, there will be blind spots, and there will be groups that feel neglected, misunderstood, underrepresented, or all three.

Teams must also recognize the difference between reasons and excuses. A reason explains why the situation is the way it is without seeking to justify it. It leaves open the possibility of change. An excuse justifies the situation and often closes the door to change, because it denies that change is necessary or possible. If you do not yet have an appropriate representative leadership group, be honest about it, examine the reasons openly, and develop a solution that is spiritual and nonreactive but still urgent. Don't slip into the mode of making excuses, throwing up your hands, and doing nothing or next to nothing and then asserting that disciples who are disturbed by this have bad hearts or are focused on the wrong things.

Everything that we can glean from Scripture demonstrates that as the gospel spread into the kaleidoscopic world, the churches had diverse leadership. Antioch is perhaps the clearest example. Antioch was a diverse city but one marked by ethnic separation. In the church, the dividing walls of race and ethnicity were scaled and torn down. There was such a diverse coming together that it even took Peter off guard when he first visited. But it wasn't just the membership; the leadership was equally inclusive. The list of leaders in Acts 13:1 highlights the broad range of social, ethnic, and cultural backgrounds that were present in the church. If they understood the importance of inclusive leadership, then so must we.

Willing to Right Wrongs

I am unable to give this section the amount of time it deserves, but perhaps in the future someone else will pick up the idea that I present and develop it further. When we are not intentional about inclusion, we will be highly prone to simply reflecting the sins and shortcomings of the society from which we come. Why can it be so difficult for multicultural churches to develop leaders who come from nondominant cultural groups? The answers lie more in the world around us than in the church. We simply mirror the results of centuries of unequal education, access to opportunity, attitudes that favor the dominant group, assumptions that members of the dominant group are more qualified and fit to lead, and so on. There may be other factors as well, but this is usually the biggest one. If your leadership group is not as diverse as it should be, then why not, and what are you going to do about it?

Leadership groups that have yet to reach representative levels of diversity need to ask some tough questions as to why. I can think of five possible reasons. The first is that it is simply random and the result of statistical anomaly. The second is that nondominant groups are underrepresented in leadership due to intentional prejudice in the church. The third is that the individuals in nondominant groups are not as spiritual on average as the dominant group. The fourth is that dynamics of dominant and nondominant cultures have been at play and have unintentionally given advantages within the community to the dominant culture. The fifth is that historic inequities of society have simply been reflected in the church.

If we look at those possible causes, the first seems unlikely as a consistent cause, because that would also result in the occasional random case where a church has much higher representation of nondominant groups in leadership than their percentage in the body, something that is extremely rare. I would hope that we can rule out the second cause and I believe that we can all dismiss the third cause as a ridiculous option.

That would leave us with the fourth and fifth. If dynamics of dominant and nondominant cultures have had an influence, then my hope is that the things we have covered in this book would begin to help us identify and address some of those issues and to be more intentional about developing inclusive leadership.

But it is the fifth cause that will take the most thought and creativity. Is it possible that historic inequities of education, opportunity, and the like do present factors in who we feel might be equipped to lead? Without delving too deeply into that, let's just assume that this is the case in a given country as they tend to see a pattern of underrepresentation in most of the churches in that nation. What are they to do? They could just resign themselves to the situation regarding who is ready to lead, but that would leave them as victims to the forces of the society around them. God will not magically do this for us. He expects us to do the work of reversing the ills of the world within the kingdom.

That would mean that the existing leadership of a church would need to be very intentional about identifying and raising up leaders from nondominant groups so that their multicultural church can be as inclusive in its leadership as in its membership.

Let me give one example to show how this might work. I will use the northern churches of the United States within my family of churches as an illustration. They are wonderfully multiracial and diverse in every way, but many struggle to maintain appropriate numbers of ministry staff and elders from nondominant groups. That is not true for all, but it is impossible to deny that it is a pattern. The reasons are complex, but it seems likely that the inequities in education, wealth, leadership opportunities, and the like have been a contributing factor. Should we simply accept that and hope the imbalance goes away?

What if these churches decided to develop a program to identify young disciples from nondominant groups who could go into a special leadership training track that encouraged them to develop their spiritual gifts and leadership abilities? Included in that track would be special mentoring and available scholarships for ministry schools or seminary. This would not deny opportunity to any other group, especially the dominant group, but would be an addition to existing opportunities to help counteract the historic disadvantages that have been the hallmarks of our society. It would avoid the flaw of many affirmative action programs in the world that carve minority group quotas into a limited number of existing opportunities, which may then result in someone from the dominant group being denied access to the opportunity simply because of the color of their skin. A solution like the one I am proposing would not impose any such negative possibility but only create new opportunities to intentionally cut against the inequities that have been put in place because of the sin of the world.

There are many other creative and probably better ideas that could be developed by church leadership groups, but I offer this merely as a specific example to help groups that find themselves in a similar situation start to think about the possibilities.

Chapter 25

The Culturally Competent Church

In AD 49, the Roman Emperor Claudius delivered a proclamation that had a chilling ripple effect on the small collection of house churches that had popped up throughout the mighty city of Rome. I referred to this incident in Chapter 6, but we return to it briefly here. According to this edict, all Jews living in the city of Rome were banned and would have to leave immediately. Since the Romans made no distinction between the spiritual lives of Jews and Jewish Christians, any ethnic Jew had to leave. It is unknown to what degree this was enforced, but it does seem that most Jewish Christians, or at least most of those who served as leaders in the church, evacuated the city. This apparently caused the churches in Rome to become almost exclusively Gentile almost overnight. That situation lasted for five years, plenty long enough for people to get used to it.

Then in AD 54, Emperor Nero reversed Claudius' decision and allowed Jews to return. Suddenly, the church was not just Gentile anymore. It was once again Jewish and Gentile, which greatly increased the cultural diversity in the church. If we read Paul's letter to the Romans carefully, it becomes apparent that this had kicked up a great deal of cultural and ethnic tension. Was the church a Gentile group now or were they going to be the truly inclusive cultural environment that the community would need to be if it was going to take the gospel to all nations and people groups?

In many ways, the book of Romans is a crash course for the believers in cross-cultural theory and life. After spending an ample amount of time carefully and masterfully laying out the theological basis for why the body of Christ must be a unified family of Jews, Gentiles, and indeed all nations, Paul gives them in chapters 14 and 15 a very practical primer for cross-cultural living in their immediate context. I describe these principles in greater detail in another book but will simply summarize them in list form here.[22]

1. Accept those with a different perspective (14:1–9)
2. Don't judge your brothers and sisters (14:10–18)
3. Pursue peace (14:19–21)
4. Keep some opinions to yourself (14:22–23)
5. Bear with one another (15:1–4)
6. Have the mind of Christ (15:5–6)
7. Accept one another as Christ accepted you (15:7)

8. Remember that this is bigger than any one individual (15:8–22)
9. The mission depends on this (15:23–33)

These principles helped to guide the believers in Rome toward practical implementation of what it meant to be all things to all people on an ongoing basis and how to build that into the life of the church. They continue to disciple and guide us in the twenty-first century and should be implemented into the ethos of churches today, if they are not already.

So far in Section 4, we have considered what it looks like to work toward being culturally competent individuals within a church community as well as working toward a culturally competent leadership group. Now we consider what a culturally competent church will look like in our world today and what they can do to grow in this area.

VALUE DIVERSITY

Some Christians grow suspicious and cautious when they hear talk of diversity in the church. It sounds worldly to them. They fear that progressive dogma is being snuck in through the back door of their beloved church. They love that the body is multiracial but would prefer not to focus on it. It seems compromising to them.

Just because terms or ideas overlap between the world and the church does not mean that they are not biblical. There are numerous groups in the world that are passionate about serving the poor. Does that make it worldly or that it is allowing the world to seep into the church when we talk of the same? You will hear many in secular society speak of loving our fellow man. Must we reject that as letting the world into the church? Of course we cannot, because Jesus commanded it of his followers. The truth is that many of the virtues the world now trumpets come from Christianity, not the other way around. God's mission to gather the nations has been promised since Abraham and been in effect since Jesus. The world has only embraced diversity as a virtue in the last fifty years or so.

We cannot reject biblical truth simply because secular society has mimicked it. The church should not imitate worldly versions of diversity and solutions to division, but the culturally competent church will value diversity and see it as an indispensable reflection of God's grand mission to the nations. That necessitates that something that can be so fragile must be intentionally cultivated and nurtured in the life of a church.

ASSESS CULTURALLY

Benjamin Franklin is often credited with coining the saying "If you fail to plan, you are planning to fail." There is great truth to that statement. Few successes in life simply happen. And even though we serve a powerful God, there are many things in a church that God will not simply do for us. Cultural proficiency doesn't just spring out of a formula of randomness, lack of action, and a dash of hope.

When was the last time your church did any kind of cultural assessment? Are you culturally inclusive? Do existing members feel valued and tied in on a cultural level? Do visitors experience inclusivity, or do they immediately sense the overarching presence of a dominant culture? Do the members feel equipped in cross-cultural communication and conflict? Is there diversity at every level of church leadership? In which of these areas does the church need to grow?

A church that does not regularly assess its cultural competency will most likely not have an effective plan for growth and will do little more than maintain the status quo. I must admit, I am tempted here to offer up a framework for cultural assessment, but I will resist that urge. I believe it is better for a church to wrestle with these concepts and develop their own method of evaluation. The process itself of developing such an assessment is a necessary area of growth for a church community.

REMOVE PRESUMPTIONS

It is easier than we think to make people feel excluded or like they are an "other." When we do not intentionally incorporate diversity at every level, marginalization will happen.

I recently attended a dance at our church for the marrieds ministry. It was a wonderful event that a lot of people had worked hard to put together. One of the games that was played that evening was a version of *The Newlywed Game,* but it was done in teams with three newlywed couples and three "oldy wed" couples. One of the questions innocently asked husbands to consider three superheroes and then guess which one their wife would answer that their husband most resembled. It was a fun game and a funny question, but without the planners ever thinking about it, all three superheroes were white. One of the husbands on the panel was a young black man. He paused for a moment and then repeated a portion of the question, "Which superhero do I resemble?" He jokingly but somewhat uncomfortably pointed out that he didn't resemble any of them.

Do you see how easy it is for an innocent situation to leave someone feeling like they are outside of the norm of this community? Imagine if the question was worded to the men, "Do you most resemble Storm, Wonder Woman, or the Black Widow?" Those are all female characters if you didn't know. How would a man answer that question? It would be awkward, wouldn't it? I only offer that up as an example to frame the exclusion a little more clearly.

It takes a lot of work to think through little things like this, and even if attempts are made, some will fall through the cracks. But I think the call to be all things to all people demands that we do this. Even in contexts where there is a clear majority of one cultural group, great emphasis should be placed on ensuring that the experiences and identity of that group do not become the universal norm or default for everything in the church. There are many different forms of this for which we must keep on the lookout.

PRACTICE INCLUSION, NOT TOKENISM

There is a real danger when speaking of inclusion and diversity. Dominant groups can easily turn to tokenism or make someone feel like they are only there for the optics of looking diverse. When there is true inclusion, people of nondominant groups have the ability and power to influence group behavior, sometimes to a level of discomfort for the dominant group. What is the difference between inclusion and tokenism?

A church that has reached inclusion has diversity as a core value and seeks to implement it at every level of leadership and influence. Tokenism is an attempt to cover over a systemic lack of diversity with a presumption that there is a quick or easy solution such as putting one person of a nondominant culture into leadership, and voilà, problem solved.

Tokenism is typically driven by quotas and mandates, and allows boxes to be checked. It is diversity for the sake of diversity. True inclusion recognizes the deep need for diverse influence and thought to form the authentic identity of your group. It realizes that your church is better and stronger when everyone is valued and their voice is heard.

Inclusion acknowledges the worth of individual contributors and their desirability as leaders. Bringing others into a leadership group is a benefit to the leaders and the church, not just a favor or form of appeasement to a segment of the population. Tokenism values someone more for their diversity than for their spiritual gifts and leadership abilities.

Tokenism expects that people will tweak the status quo when asked but will not make the rest of the leadership group feel challenged or uncomfortable. Inclusion is aware that diversity of thought will mean being challenged and getting out of comfort zones.

Finally, tokenism assumes that individuals of the nondominant group represent the entire group as a unit. Inclusion recognizes that the person has a view that has been conditioned by a different culture, which is valuable, but that they do not and cannot speak for an entire group.

BE DIVERSE IN DIVERSITY

A church that is committed to cultural competency will not become overly focused on one type of diversity and think that covers it. For example, a church might get passionate about increasing the cultural influence and leadership representation of African Americans in their church but completely overlook any inclusion in those areas for Asians, Latinos, or other ethnic groups, or for categories like age and gender. It is important to be diverse in our quest for diversity.

Again, I appeal to the example of Antioch. It seems that the church's ethnic diversity was so mystifying to the racially divided Antioch that they were puzzled by this group of Christ followers. Unable to label them as an ethnic group, the name Christian apparently came about precisely because of their amazing diversity.

VALUE PARTICIPATION OVER TOLERATION

The world trumpets toleration. Let people be themselves. Acknowledge the validity of their way of doing things, and maybe even celebrate it. But the call for God's people to be all things to all people goes beyond that. When appropriate, it will call us to participation in a variety of cultural expressions and inclusion of them into the normal life of the community. Many in the congregation will be hesitant or even resistant to this if it is not taught and revisited often as a thoroughly biblical concept that Paul presents as an important element in bringing people to the life of salvation.

STAY REVELATION-5 FOCUSED

It is easy to focus on simply expressing and celebrating who you are as a group rather than on who you desire to become. Keeping our eyes fixed on the Revelation 5:9 vision of God's people reminds us that God's goal is for us to be diverse. To achieve that and continually grow in it, the church will need to do its best to reflect and embody what we want to be rather than merely who we are. There is no question that doing so will be difficult and even confusing at times. We may not see solutions easily and clearly at first, and it may take substantial creativity and effort of thought, but it will be worth it in the long run.

CREATE A FOCUS GROUP

It is unlikely that the primary leadership group of a church will be able to devote adequate time to strategizing about ways to increase the cultural competency of the church. It's not that it is not significant, nor am I saying that they should just farm that work out to someone else and get on with the important work of the church. It is, after all, a central element of the gospel, so it should never be ignored. True cultural inclusion, however, is a complex process that takes a lot of thought, planning, and effort to implement. In many cases, it will benefit the leadership team to develop and empower a cultural unity and diversity group of some sort that can specialize in cultural competency in communities. They can study it, educate the church, strategize, and communicate with the groups in other churches and organizations for influence and input.

It is important that this group is valued and not simply created as an appeasement or to look good but then hampered in their ability to bring changes into the church. It might be beneficial to have one or more persons from the primary leadership group that also serve on this diversity team to serve as an advocate for the team. To maximize effectiveness, the leaders must commit to taking seriously the recommendations from the diversity group and implementing as many of them as they can. There might need to be advance discussions between the groups at times or modifications to proposals, but the cultural diversity group needs to have strong influence with the church leaders, and the leaders must respect the wisdom and suggestions from the group.

SERVE THE RIGHT KING

Jesus had repeated confrontations with Pharisees over the issue of the Sabbath. His contention was that the Sabbath was a tool under the old covenant to benefit the people, but instead they had exalted it to something to be served rather than serving its intended purpose. Instead of promoting human wellness, it became a burden.

Cultural diversity and inclusion are good things, but they must be kept in their proper place. Jesus is our King, not culture, not diversity, not inclusion, not justice—Jesus alone. It can be very easy to become so focused on cultural issues that they become burdensome rather than a tool to benefit the kingdom. Diversity is important, but it must be kept in proper submission to the King and his kingdom.

How do we know that we have let things get a bit out of hand? One surefire way is if it is causing ongoing anger in the church. I'm not talking about those who balk at changes that bring about more diversity. More to the point is that if those who advocate for issues of race, culture, and the like constantly find themselves irritated, annoyed, angry, or disgusted with those who have yet to embrace or understand their agenda, then it is quite possible that they have made an idol out those things. Competency is a tool to move us toward greater unity. To feel like dividing because some are not moving fast enough or not "getting it" is to lose sight of what we are trying to accomplish and why.

TEACH AND TRAIN

This may go without saying at this point, but I will say it anyway just to make sure. A culturally competent church will teach and train the body in cultural awareness, sensitivity, and competency skills on a regular basis. A one-time workshop is insufficient. A wise leadership will work to find the right balance in their church between not enough and overkill. That said, it is important that this type of training find its way at appropriate levels in kids' classes, teen training, campus teaching, churchwide workshops, the Sunday pulpit, and every area of community life.

MODIFY COMMUNITY LIFE

I once studied the Bible with a neighbor over the course of many months. We spent a lot of time looking at the person of Jesus and the life that he called his followers to, as exemplified in the Sermon on the Mount. They were the best studies I've ever been in, at least for a while. He was engaged in the process and enthralled with the life of Jesus. He would get excited at the Lord's teachings and wrestle with trying to figure out what each small element of each passage meant. He would gobble up assignments for study between our times together and suggest more. He could not get enough of the Scriptures.

But I started to notice something over time. He loved to talk about and learn about Jesus, but there was one big problem. He was quite unwilling to change his life. He would learn about Jesus every day of the week and twice on Sunday, but he would not take the steps to accept Jesus as Lord and King. He would not go through the challenging task of submitting to the life of Christ.

I have been to numerous churches where we have introduced the topics of race and culture and offered ways forward to increase cultural competency, and I have seen many of them make incredible changes. They have humbled themselves to God's word and admitted areas of needed growth. They have taken difficult and sometimes painful steps to align themselves with where they believed God wanted them to go. But I have also taught at churches who loved the material, and then responded by changing absolutely nothing afterward. They were willing to learn about these matters, which is a good thing. But they were apparently quite unwilling to do what they had to do to challenge sacred cows, go after areas of ignorance, and modify the life of the church to work toward competency at all levels.

Most Christians know that the concept of repentance comes from the Greek term, *metanoia*. *Metanoia* is not just about removing certain negative behaviors from your life; it involves a complete transformation of mind and a switching of allegiance. True repentance will result in big changes because it has embraced a radical shift in thinking.

Similarly, if churches are to embrace being all things to all people, it will call them beyond just changing a thing or two and calling it a day. It will involve a radical shift in thinking for many churches. They will be called by this new way of thinking to be willing to change constantly and consistently. They will accept that fear and trepidation will be part of the process of change. But they will stay committed to those "whats" because they remain laser focused on the "why."

A TOUGH QUESTION

I want to end this chapter with a hard question that I get from time to time regarding church life. Is it ever okay for nondominant groups within a church to gather separately or have separate ministries? Although this is not the ideal, I do think that oftentimes circumstances necessitate it for limited periods or specific situations—until a higher level of health is reached.

Let's say that most of the African American women in a diverse church have expressed similar feelings of disaffection and frustration. They consistently point to a lack of the church body to understand or meet the needs they face as African American disciples in their community. Should we let them flounder for reasons of a false sense of unity when they are in spiritual danger? I think not. I would have no problem with the church forming a group that served and met their unique needs until such time as those needs could be met on a more universal scale.

Several teen leaders have told me that there is some value in having separate groups for students from nondominant cultures, in order to help them navigate the specific struggles they face in life and need to talk about, issues that teens from the dominant group have no idea about and can even be insensitive toward. Having their own safe space can help them eventually integrate into the broader community and work toward the goal of inclusivity for all.

Might there ever be a need for a separate service for a second language within a church body? My personal opinion on that is maybe for a limited time or on occasion, but I would rather see a community invest in interpretation devices, offer English as a second language classes regularly, and occasionally even send strong signals of acceptance and support by offering the entire service in the second language and interpreting it into the dominant language.

Someone might then ask if it would be okay for members of the dominant group to meet in an intentionally segregated fashion. I think not. That sends an entirely different message and serves a completely different purpose. When members of the dominant group meet to the exclusion of others, it smacks of segregation and denial of access. When members of the nondominant group are permitted to meet, it signals support, understanding, and empathy.

Chapter 26

Changing a Culture

As I was walking my son from the car to his school for another day of kindergarten, my phone rang. I decided to ignore the ring and call back whomever it was once I had my son inside the building and was on my way back to the car. I barely had time to give him a proper hug before he squirmed off and raced toward the front door to see his friends and get a few moments of play in before class officially started. As I turned to start my journey back down the block to my vehicle, the phone rang again. It had been less than a minute, and I reasoned that if this was the same person, it might be urgent. Looking at the screen told me that it was the same caller, a friend of mine from a church in a different city. I guessed that it wasn't urgent but took the call just the same.

Moments after answering and getting the obligatory greetings out of the way, I asked him how things were going and if he had called for anything specific. "I'm so frustrated right now," he blurted out. He went on to explain how inspired he had been by studying out the topic of the age to come, which I had suggested he do. He was blown away by the early Christians' emphasis on the difference between the present aged marked by sin, evil, violence, and rebellion against God and the age to come, which will be characterized by sin being done away with, no evil, no violence, and living in God's presence for eternity. The thing that really shocked him was the New Testament claim that this period, while only coming fully in the resurrection of believers, was something that we didn't have to just wait for. The New Testament phrase "eternal life" more literally means "the life of the next age." When the Scriptures speak of having eternal life in Christ, they are not just referring to living forever after physical death. They mean that for those who enter Christ, the life of the age to come is available now. We can begin to channel that life of peace, of having no enemies, and of love and forgiveness, right now. We can have the life of the age to come (eternal life), live it out, and show others what it looks like, calling them to take hold of it as well (1 Timothy 6:12).

He was so inspired by all this that he couldn't wait to share it with the small group of single brothers and sisters that he was leading in his church. And that's where the rub came in. "They just don't get it," he pushed out. "I have explained that we can have this life and begin to live it now, to be the people of the coming age, and it goes in one ear and out the other." He continued to share how he taught multiple lessons on what the age to come was and what Scripture taught about having it now and living out this life while still in the present age. And it amounted to a grand total of nothing. He saw no change in the lives of those he was leading, and he was so frustrated that he had basically scolded the entire group in their last meeting and let them have it for their slowness to understand and lack of embracing the life of the coming age.

"Let me get this straight," I responded, "You want them to grasp the enormity of the concept that we enter the age to come when we are baptized in Christ?"

"That's right," he replied.

"And they are just not fully grasping in a few lessons what you spent months studying out yourself?"

"Well, yeah, I guess," he stammered back.

"And just so I am clear," I continued, "you are responding to their inability to understand the life of the coming age by modeling a life of frustration and irritation." Before he could respond, I said, "So you are teaching them about a life of peace, forgiveness, and doing God's will on earth as though you were already in his presence in the age to come by demonstrating the exact opposite values?"

He paused for a long time and finally said, "Ohhh, I think I get what you're saying."

My friend felt initial frustration with how difficult it can be to change the culture of a group. It doesn't happen instantly or easily. It takes effort and perseverance. I'm happy to report that he really did get it. He began to patiently model the life of the age to come as best he could, while continually teaching and reminding them of the enormity of this understanding for our lives of following Christ. The group began to understand and follow his example. He has since moved on to other churches and has become a beautiful living illustration of humility and the embodiment of the life of the age to come, impacting people wherever he has served in the ministry as he has helped them to also take hold of that eternal life.

But the part of that story that I want to reflect on is the difficulty of changing culture in a group. We have covered a lot of ground on cultural topics, and you may see some areas in your life or that of your church that need to transform to become the light on the hill that is all things to all people as God truly desires us to be. To make these types of changes in an existing church is not easy. You cannot just have one weekend workshop, roll out the new vision and values, type them up on a bookmark, hand them out, and then sit back and watch the entire body transform instantly to a culturally competent church. I wish it were that easy. I'm not going to lie to you, it's not. The culture of any group, including a church, is broad, meaning it extends throughout almost every aspect of your group's life. It is also deeply rooted and gets easily wrapped up with identity, which means that even aspects of a culture that have become counterproductive and need changing will be fiercely clung to and even defended. And culture brings stability. The very essence of culture is that it makes life understandable and predictable, so naturally people will tend to react against changes in culture unless they have good reason not to.

Is the culture of a church that consequential, and how do we change it if it needs to be changed?

GETTING PUNCHED IN THE FACE

Boxing champion Mike Tyson once famously quipped, "Everybody has a plan until they get punched in the mouth." There is a great amount of truth in that. Churches can make all the plans, strategies, and programs they want. They can roll out an amazing theme for the year and make as many fresh new starts as they'd like. But if careful attention is not paid to the culture of the church, a hard fist is coming straight for their jaw. Plans and visions without cultural change will add up to minimal, if any, progress.

If we are to develop a consistent church culture that can support the goals and plans of the church, then the core values, the group behaviors, the group language, and our story of who we are and where we are going must all align.

THE FIRST STEP

There are two grocery stores about equidistant from our house, although in opposite directions. They basically have the same food and are similar in prices. Yet there is one that I go to whenever I can, and I avoid the other when at all possible. Why? It's simple, really. One has a nice, comfortable culture and atmosphere to it. The employees are amiable, it's not cluttered, it feels peaceful, and it is very customer friendly. The culture of the other store points in the opposite direction from all those things. Culture and atmosphere are important, whether it be in a grocery store, a coffee shop, or a church family.

But what is the culture of your group? How do you recognize whether it needs to change? Some churches may only need to tweak or improve a few things to continue the journey toward cultural competence. Others may need a complete cultural makeover. But to determine that starts with self-assessment.

I don't believe the starting place is to fill out a questionnaire or survey, add up the points, and then consult the handy-dandy guide provided and alakazam, your personal or church culture has been identified. Culture is much too complex for that. There are a host of problems with these types of surveys. They tend to be superficial and don't get at underlying assumptions or the full breadth of culture. There are many layers to culture, which can make interpreting answers and finding patterns difficult. It is easy to misunderstand or mis-answer questions—which skews the results. It is next to impossible to make group inferences based on individual responses to surveys. These are just a few of the problems.

Rather than specific surveys, the better approach is to provide some basic frameworks of cultural views and allow members of a group to identify where they see the group in that framework. This will start us on the path to identifying where a group is and will need to go. They can then analyze what their most common cultural expressions communicate to others and whether that matches with where they want to be, or instead sends other signals.

Let's look at the stages of cultural sensitivity and multicultural competence as tools to identify where the culture of your church stands.

Cultural Sensitivity

1. **Denial**—At this level there is no recognition of the concept of cultural dynamics and no realization that there is, for all intents and purposes, no culture outside of the dominant one. No one sees a need or has the desire to learn about or include other cultures into the life of the group.

2. **Defense**—We see differences in culture but evaluate other cultures as a threat or in a negative light. Any talk of inclusion will be perceived as an attack on the dominant culture.

3. **Diminishment**—Groups at this stage often minimize the importance of culture. They will see that there are differences and recognize the need for some change but will only be willing to consider minor adjustments that don't demand any true discomfort for the dominant culture. They will embrace special occasions and celebrations or small shifts but will resist more fundamental and systemic changes.

4. **Acceptance**—There is an appreciation of other cultures and cultural expressions that is willing to move beyond superficial

levels and respects them. There is a willingness to add those into church life when possible.

5. **Adaptation**—Recognizes that we must move beyond simple acceptance and addition of other cultural values and expressions. At this stage there is a recognition that the church culture needs to change if true inclusion is to be reached. The dominant group will accept that they must be willing to adapt, become uncomfortable at times, and give over influence to others within the church community.

6. **Amalgamation**—We begin to internalize the things gleaned from other cultures and incorporate them into the community life in meaningful and authentic ways. Diversity in influence is maintained at all levels of authority and leadership within the church, and that diversity is reflected in the activities, culture, and life of the congregation.

Levels of Multicultural Competence

1. **Narrow**—Our way is the only right way to do things. If you want to be here, you will have to adapt to our ways. We don't have a specific cultural expression; we simply follow the Bible.

2. **Ethnocentric**—There are other ways, but our way is best (and most biblical). We welcome everyone here, but they will have to embrace our culture and way of doing things to fit in.

3. **Tolerant**—We believe that our way of doing things is the best for us, but we respect that there are other ways of doing things that are best for other groups. They can join, and we will create subgroups and activities so that they can express themselves in the ways that are best for them. We can both avoid having to make any personal changes or adaptations while maintaining a façade of unity.

4. **Cooperative**—We can learn from each other. We prefer our culture but recognize that there are strengths to yours. We are open to making some changes and modifying our community life to relate to and attract people from other cultures than our own.

5. **Multicultural**—For most expressions and aspects of community

life, there are multiple ways of doing things rather than "a way." We need to incorporate aspects of all those ways and internalize them into church life to send the clear signal that we desire to be all things to all and embrace full inclusion of all people. We are still gospel centered but recognize that God gave humanity many different streams of cultural life for expressing and living out the gospel. God wants us to explore and utilize all of them.

CULTURE CHANGE

The first step toward cultural competency in the church is to identify the major aspects of the church's culture. Self-analysis cannot be rushed and needs to be brutally honest. Often, the opinions that will be most helpful in this identification process are those from nondominant groups within the community and from outside the local congregation.

The second step is to identify changes that need to take place. Does the makeup of the leadership need to shift? Does the music ministry need to be overhauled? Does there need to be more inclusion in planning events? Does the youth ministry seem to appeal to kids of the dominant culture while many from other cultural backgrounds feel rather disconnected? Does the church need to radically embrace the call to be all things to all people in every aspect of church life?

Once again, this step cannot be rushed. It takes time to think through the many aspects of church life and determine which ones need to be reworked in the pursuit of cultural competence.

Start with the end in mind. Take some time to vision cast and create a detailed picture of what a culturally competent church in your context would look like. What would Revelation 5:9 look like, feel like, sound like, be like in your church? Once that is established and agreed upon, you can begin to work backward and determine what needs to change to get there.

You can also consider the cultural sensitivity and multicultural competence principles above and determine which stage your church is at according to those two metrics, so you can discern what it will take to advance to the highest levels.

The third step is to develop a clear vision as a leadership team. Where are you? What needs to change? Where are you going? The vision should be expressible in one sentence but should have a breakdown of specific areas that need to change and what the plan is to execute those changes.

The fourth step is to identify a core group that will champion the efforts at culture change. It does not necessarily have to include the entire leadership team of the church, but key members from that team do need to be in the core group. This team must be diverse in role, age, culture, etc., which will allow them to be inclusive in the way the vision is crafted and communicated within the church body. This group will not just pass along the message but must spread out and serve as models for the desired change. When Paul wanted a church to embrace new cultural ideals, he would either go model the behavior himself or send someone to them to demonstrate the life to which he was calling them (Philippians 2:19–24; Colossians 4:7–8).

BRINGING THE VISION TO THE BODY

The fifth step is to develop the messaging that will communicate the culture change to the church. While the plan needs to be specific and detailed, the messaging should not be. It needs to be clear, concise, and consistent. It needs to utilize memorable language that is easily exportable to the body. The simply communicated vision can be occasionally expanded to include all details, but the compact version should be repeated often until any member could say it in their sleep.

Here is one example:

Our Mission: *To Gather the Nations*
Our Task: *To become all things to all people*
Our Values:
   To Serve
   To Give
   To Love
   To Celebrate
Our Principles:
   Love everyone.
   Value people above your own culture.
   Be gospel driven, not politics powered.
   Embrace cultural humility.

Here is another sample vision of church culture:

Engage the Mission
- Am I advancing our mission as disciples to gather the nations of the kingdom of God?

Share the Task
- Am I doing what I can to become all things to all people?

Pursue Health
- Am I living in a way today that will help me thrive tomorrow?

Embody Reconciliation
- Am I pursuing reconciliation and justice at every level that I can?

Overcome Obstacles
- Am I willing to do what it takes to be the best that I can be for God?

Choose Trust
- Am I believing the best of others and choosing to give the benefit of the doubt?

Grab the Towel
- Am I serving others, or do I expect to be served?

These short vision statements do not embody the entirety of the culture change desired, but they should point to it. One important task for a church is to examine any current vision or mission statements they have and assess whether the current culture of the church supports that vision. Often, our culture and shared life do not match up with the vision statement. For example, a church might publish the vision statement of "being God's family on a mission to all nations," but then lack any meaningful pursuit of inclusion or cultural competency in the life of the church, which would be necessary to support such an ideal. Make sure you are working toward culture changes that will match up with and support the larger church vision.

MOTIVATION

The sixth step is to develop the proper motivation. Very few people wake up each morning looking to make major changes to their core culture and bring upheaval into their life. Culture change is not easy or simple. This is another case where the "why" must be bigger than the "what." For people to embrace the need for a culture change in their beloved church body, they will need to see the motivation, specifically the threat of not making changes. Edgar Schien, an expert in organizational culture, calls this disconfirmation. He describes this as "something that is perceived or felt that is not expected and that upsets some of our beliefs or assumptions."[23] Disconfirmation, Schien says, creates a survival anxiety that leads people to either accept that something negative will happen if change is not implemented or to realize that they are not living up to their stated ideals and goals, which will lead to guilt. Whether it be a bit of healthy fear or guilt, Schien argues that this type of disconfirming motivation must be communicated and understood before true culture change can happen.

This does not have to be negative, but it does need to be honest and realistic. One of the primary obstacles for cultural competency in a church is when the dominant culture is unaware of just how difficult it can be for nondominant members. They hear the stories of those who come and fall in love with the diversity of the church, but they have no idea how many people of different cultures visit the group, feel immediately turned off by the obvious signals of cultural dominance, and never come back. Young people are less and less impressed by simple diversity these days. They are savvy and looking to experience true multiculturalism. The church needs to know the struggles as well as the victories. They need to know what may happen if changes are not made. Multiracial groups are more prone to falling apart over time than staying together. Without an effort toward cultural intelligence, the beloved diversity within the church may slowly disappear.

UNLEARNING

Unlearning old ways is the seventh step. In pursuing cultural inclusion, there will be new concepts, skills, and practices that the community will embrace. This will necessitate unlearning some habits and tendencies as well. It will take time and encouragement. A safe environment needs to be created in the church where people are not afraid to make an occasional mistake. Feeling like you must walk around on eggshells is not conducive to growth. Removing that feeling, of course, does not give license to insensitivity or unwillingness to change.

STAY POSITIVE

The eighth step is to remain positive throughout the process of implementing change. It is easy to attack the old culture of the group and be negative about the current shortcomings, but positivity and encouragement are always far better motivators.

PERSEVERE

As I have stated several times throughout this book, none of this will be easy. The church needs a core team and a leadership group that are committed to change for the long haul. Most culture change will have some opposition at first and some struggles. Much of that depends on the clarity of communication and vision and the level to which the church understands the motivation and disconfirmation. Leaders must be resolved to patiently ride out the bumps with people and get together with those who are struggling or skeptical. You will not convince everyone, but no one should be written off either. Let them give up if they want, but keep fighting for each person to embrace the vision. A group that perseveres will win the day.

WHEN CULTURE CHANGE DOESN'T WORK

There are many elements that can prove to be obstacles to culture change in a group or can completely stall progress.

First is that there is an incongruent or incomplete vision that works on paper but doesn't come together in real life or that doesn't address the issues fully enough to make significant changes. This is often due to a misdiagnosis of the problem. For instance, a church might identify its problem as having a music worship ministry that is not diverse enough, while the real concerns are much deeper than that: there is a significant portion of the membership that is ethnocentric and not open to costly cultural inclusion. The music ministry is revamped, but it is only a superficial change considering the true issues.

Second, there is inadequate explanation or communication. A change of culture must be revisited regularly and communicated often in a variety of ways before people begin to fully grasp their role in the change.

Third, there is resistance or a lack of buy-in from the congregation that is not addressed or dealt with. This is often due to poor communication at the start, but not always. Those who refuse to participate in the quest for cultural competency need to be helped to see the scriptural truths behind it and lovingly brought into step with the rest of the body.

Fourth, the call to culture change from the leaders is at a superficial level that does not involve a deep personal commitment to change. Since culture is not superficial, neither can culture changes be at surface level.

Fifth, advocates for the change fail to keep momentum going. There are many things that can slow the momentum of change. It might be a death in the membership, a holiday season, a conflict, or a loss of focus, but leaders must anticipate and respond to these occurrences and plan to regain momentum and to refocus on the new vision.

THE GREATEST TOOL IN THE QUEST FOR CULTURAL COMPETENCY

My wife has long asserted that the greatest tool we have at our disposal to aid in the growth of cultural competency is the simple dining room table. Eating together is powerful. It is an act that physically changes us as we join in, and the table can be mighty in its ability to bring people together.

Hospitality is not just a good idea; it is a biblical principle and is demanded of God's people (Romans 12:13; Hebrews 13:2; 1 Peter 4:9; 3 John 1:8). Around the table we can laugh, talk, cry, get to know one another, and learn the value of one another's culture.

True change does not come from a lesson, a workshop, or even reading a book. Those might give us tools to help facilitate the change, but the real change comes when we talk to one another. When we get honest and open and listen to each other, miracles happen. The Holy Spirit binds us together in fellowship (2 Corinthians 13:14) and brings about a new body life.

Most often when a diverse church is struggling with cultural togetherness, it is because people have not intertwined their lives together. They are not in one another's homes. They are not communicating at deep levels. They are not sharing the good and bad of life together. When we do that, the goal of learning to become all things to all people becomes much more attainable.

THE VSIRA APPROACH

My good friend, David Jung, who is a minister and conflict resolution expert in Winnipeg, Canada, recently turned me on to the work of Dr. Mary Lippit, an authority on organizational health management. She has proposed a helpful diagnostic for change based on the acronym VSI-RA. According to Lippit, when an organization is undergoing change, the leaders must ensure that all five of the following elements are present and clearly communicated:

1. **Vision**—Why is the change needed, what are the goals for change, and are they measurable and attainable. If there is no clear vision it leads to confusion, which can paralyze a movement for change.

2. **Skills**—It's easy to say how you need to change and the direction you want to head, but you must train people how to get there and provide them with the tools they will need for the job. If this element is absent it will lead to anxiety.

3. **Incentives**—Have you clearly communicated the incentive to

change and the needs that are present that are instigating the change? Without incentives you will experience a lack of buy-in or outright resistance.

4. **Resources**—A successful change in direction or culture will demand resources, whether they be human resources or of the physical variety. Have you planned out the resources you will need to implement the changes you want? Without this element people will grow frustrated and disillusioned.

5. **Action Plan**—The vision is the dream; the plan is putting that dream into reality. It takes time to think this through and have a workable plan, but that all needs to be done before the vision is ever put forward to the group. Without a viable action plan, the result will be false starts with no traction or staying power.

A FINAL WORD

When our family moved from Wisconsin to Minnesota, we were not able to do it all at once. I had some things I needed to finish at our home church in Wisconsin before I moved, so I couldn't make the transition until the beginning of November. Our older son was going to start his senior year of high school in Minnesota and needed to be there at the end of August, so he moved there and stayed with some Christians in the church. At the beginning of September my wife moved into our new place with him. Our younger son was going to stay with me until November but then decided he wanted to get the move over with, so he joined them at the end of September. That left me alone in Wisconsin for a month. The difference without them was conspicuous. The family is just not the same when someone is missing. One by one, their presence was missed as they left. That's the way it is with families. When someone is not there, it has an impact.

In Revelation 5:9, John describes the picture of God's people, his family. It is a picture of the gathering of the nations. People are there from every tribe, language, people group, and nation. That is God's family. That is his plan. This is what it's supposed to look like. In that mission to gather the nations, we find our task: to maintain God's mission by becoming all things to all people. Look at the church you attend. Is the whole family assembled? Are the folks from every tribe there at the table with you each week? How about the different languages, or the people groups? Are all the nations represented in your area there at the family gathering? If not, do you even miss them? God does.

Let's make sure that we are on the mission that God called us to, and as we partake in that mission, let us do everything we can to be all things to all people.

Epilogue

During a dizzying travel schedule that would leave anyone exhausted, the Apostle Paul arrived in Caesarea to stay with Philip for some days. During his visit, the well-known Agabus, who had a prophetic gift, came to visit from Judea. Although accustomed to his prophetic utterances, everyone present had to be a bit surprised when Agabus suddenly grabbed Paul's belt away and used it bind up his own hands and feet. What was he doing, they must have wondered. They didn't have to wait long, as he declared that the owner of the belt faced a dire situation if he continued in his plan to go to Jerusalem. He would be handed over to the Romans.

The disciples must have been relieved, at least for a moment. How good of the Holy Spirit to warn them through Agabus. Paul's life could be spared so that he could carry on with his work spreading the gospel around the world. The joy proved fleeting as it quickly became apparent that Paul had no intention of interpreting this prophecy as a warning. He apparently saw it as a test, one that he would not fail. Their sorrow at his resolve to go to Jerusalem anyway broke his heart but not his determination. He would go.

But why? Why was Paul so adamant about going to Jerusalem? If he wanted to see the apostles, they could come to him. No, that couldn't have been it. Was he homesick? That seems unlikely. Was it to spread the gospel? Jerusalem was teeming with Christians who would continue to do that in the great city.

His primary motivation was seemingly singular. He mentions it explicitly in Acts 24:17. He went there to bring the collection for the poor and famine-ridden disciples in Judea, a collection that had been taken up from the Gentile churches across the Roman Empire.

This collection was of the utmost importance to Paul (1 Corinthians 16:1-4; 2 Corinthians 8:1-9:15; Romans 15:14-32). He knew that carrying around such large amounts of money was an unsafe endeavor (Romans 15:30-31) but was more than willing to do it anyway. He had come this far and now was so close to his goal. And when Agabus warned him of the impending doom facing him in Jerusalem, well, nothing short of a direct refusal from the Holy Spirit was going to stop Paul.

But why was this collection so important? Paul knew that the mission he was on was the call to gather the nations to God's kingdom. This meant both Jew and Gentile coming together as one family; he was passionate about that. But he also well knew what a difficult task it was. There was an ugly past between Jews and Gentiles. There were national, cultural, and identity gaps that would continue to keep them apart. Binding them together as family was no small feat. So for Paul, this collection was huge. The disciples in Jerusalem were in need, and families take care of one another. What could send that signal louder and clearer than Gentile believers whom they had never met giving sacrificially for their needs? Many of the recipients in Jerusalem may have questioned the Gentile conversions for a time or even outright opposed them. And now they were being helped by those same brothers and sisters.

When Paul came to the apostles in Jerusalem to present the message he had been proclaiming to the Gentiles, they approved and then appealed to him to continue collecting money for the disciples in need in Jerusalem (Galatians 2:10). They didn't have to ask twice. Paul was zealous to do so. This was part of being all things to all people for him. This was the gathering of the nations in the real world. For Paul, it seems that this collection was deeply symbolic of all this, but it was more than just a symbol. This was God's plan in action.

Paul was willing to give everything for the gathering of the nations. He was prepared to die for the mission and the ongoing task of being all things to all people. Here is my simple question as we draw this book to a close: How important is it to you?

Resources for Further Learning

Ao, Louis and Penley, David. *Cross-Cultural Leadership: Ministering to a Multicultural Community.* Maitland, FL: Xulon, 2006.

Bauckham, Richard. *Bible and Mission: Christian Witness in a Postmodern World.* Grand Rapids, MI: Baker, 2003.

Brouwer, Douglas. *How to Become a Multicultural Church.* Grand Rapids, MI: Wm. B. Eerdmans, 2017.

Cameron, Kim and Quinn, Robert. *Diagnosing and Changing Organizational Culture.* San Francisco, CA: Jossey-Bass, 2006.

Cartledge, Mark and Cheetham, David, Ed. *Intercultural Theology.* London, UK: SCM, 2011.

Cleveland, Christena. *Disunity in Christ: Uncovering the Hidden Forces That Keep Us Apart.* Downers Grove, IL: InterVarsity, 2013.

DeYmaz, Mark. *Building a Healthy Multi-Ethnic Church: Mandate, Commitments, and Practices of a Diverse Congregation.* San Francisco, CA: Jossey-Bass, 2007.

DeYmaz, Mark and Li, Harry. *Leading a Healthy Multi-Ethnic Church: Seven Common Challenges and How to Overcome Them.* Grand Rapids, MI: Zondervan, 2010.

DeYoung, Curtiss; Emerson, Michael; Yancey, George; and Chai Kim, Karen. *United by Faith: The Multiracial Congregation as an Answer to the Problem of Race.* New York, NY: Oxford University, 2003.

Edwards, Korie. *The Elusive Dream: The Power of Race in Interracial Churches.* New York, NY: Oxford University, 2008.

Ellison II, Gregory. *Fear+Less Dialogues: A New Movement for Justice.* Louisville, KY: Westminster John Knox, 2017.

Elmer, Duane, *Cross-Cultural Conflict: Building Relationships for Effective Ministry.* Downers Grove, IL: InterVarsity, 1993.

Elmer, Duane. *Cross-Cultural Connections: Stepping Out and Fitting In Around the World.* Downers Grove, IL: InterVarsity, 2002.

Elmer, Duane. *Cross-Cultural Servanthood: Serving the World in Christlike Humility.* Downers Grove, IL: InterVarsity, 2006.

Emerson, Michael and Smith, Christian. *Divided by Faith: Evangelical Religion and the Problem of Race in America.* New York, NY: Oxford University, 2000.

Farley, John. *Majority-Minority Relations.* Saddle River, NJ: Pearson Education, 2005.

Fujimura, Makoto. *Culture Care: Reconnecting with Beauty for Our Common Life.* Downers Grove, IL: InterVarsity, 2017.

Georges, Jayson. *The 3D Gospel: Ministry in Guilt, Shame, and Fear Cultures.* [s.l.] Timē Press, 2016.

Hart, Drew. *Trouble I've Seen: Changing the Way the Church Views Racism.* Harrisonburg, VA: Herald, 2016.

Hiebert, Paul. *Cultural Anthropology.* Grand Rapids, MI: Baker, 1983.

Hiebert, Paul. *Transforming Worldviews: An Anthropological Understanding of How*

People Change. Grand Rapids, MI: Baker Academic, 2008.

Lewis-Giggetts, Tracey. *The Integrated Church*. Kansas City, MO: Beacon Hill, 2011.

Lingenfelter, Judith and Lingenfelter, Sherwood. *Teaching Cross-Culturally: An Incarnational Model for Learning and Teaching*. Grand Rapids, MI: Baker Academic, 2003.

Lingenfelter, Sherwood. *Agents of Transformation: A Guide for Effective Cross-Cultural Ministry*. Grand Rapids, MI: Baker Academic, 1996.

Lingenfelter, Sherwood. *Transforming Culture: A Challenge for Christian Mission*. Grand Rapids, MI: Baker Academic. 1998.

Lingenfelter, Sherwood and Mayers, Marvin. *Ministering Cross-Culturally: A Model for Effective Personal Relationships*. Grand Rapids, MI: Baker Academic, 2016.

Lo, Jim. *Intentional Diversity: Creating Cross-Cultural Ministry Relationships in Your Church*. Indianapolis, IN: Wesleyan Publishing House, 2002.

Maurer, Dehner. *The Blended Church: The Emergence of Multicultural Christianity*. Tulsa, OK: Thorncrown, 2010.

Mason, Eric. *Woke Church: An Urgent Call for Christians in America to Confront Racism and Injustice*. Chicago, IL: Moody, 2018.

McNeil, Brenda Salter. *Roadmap to Reconciliation: Moving Communities into Unity, Wholeness, and Justice*. Downers Grove, IL: InterVarsity, 2015.

Okholm, Dennis, Ed. *The Gospel in Black & White: Theological Resources for Racial Reconciliation*. Downers Grove, IL: InterVarsity, 1997.

Otaigbe, Osoba. *Building Cultural Intelligence in Church and Ministry: 10 Ways to Assess and Improve Your Cross-Cultural Competence in Church, Ministry and the Workplace*. Bloomington, IN: AuthorHouse, 2016.

Payne, Ruby. *A Framework for Understanding Poverty: A Cognitive Approach*. Highlands, TX: aha! Process Inc., 2013.

Powell, Mark Allan. *What Do They Hear? Bridging the Gap Between Pulpit & Pew*. Nashville, TN: Abingdon, 2007.

Rah, Soong-Chan. *Many Colors: Cultural Intelligence for a Changing Church*. Chicago, IL: Moody, 2010.

Romano, Dugan. *Intercultural Marriage: Promises & Pitfalls*. Boston, MA: Nicholas Brealey, 2008.

Sayers, Mark. *Disappearing Church: from Cultural Relevance to Gospel Resilience*. Chicago, IL: Moody, 2016.

Schein, Edgar. *The Corporate Culture Survival Guide*. San Francisco, CA: Jossey-Bass, 2009.

Schreiter, Robert. *Constructing Local Theologies*. Maryknoll, NY: Orbis, 2003.

Sechrest, Love; Ramirez-Johnson, Johnny; and Young, Amos, Eds. *Can "White" People be Saved? Triangulating Race, Theology, and Mission*. Downers Grove, IL: InterVarsity, 2018.

Smith, Efrem. *The Post-Black and Post-White church: Becoming the Beloved Community in a Multi-Ethnic World*. San Francisco, CA: Jossey-Bass, 2012.

Wrogemann, Henning (translated by Bohmer, Karl). *Intercultural Hermeneutics*. Downers Grove, IL: Baker Academic, 2016.

End Notes

1. For a fuller description of the history of this time period and multiracial movements, see *United by Faith: The Multiracial Congregation as an Answer to the Problem of Race,* by Curtiss DeYoung, et.al. (New York: Oxford University, 2003), 41–61.

2. The Hebrew term used here is *'Elohim,* which referred to any divine being, including God himself, angels, the divine council pictured in Job 1, and any other beings in the spiritual realm. Typical English translations favor "God" or "angels" here, but I think the larger context of the Old Testament indicates the divine council.

3. For a compelling argument that Luke seems to intentionally echo the language and motifs of Babel in his account of the Pentecost, see: *The Lost World of the Flood* by Tremper Longman III and John H. Walton (Downers Grove, IL: IVP Academic, 2018), 140–142.

4. Ante-Nicene Fathers, Vol. 1, 167, Justin Martyr, The First Apology of Justin, Chapter XIV

5. Matthew Bates, *Salvation by Allegiance Alone: Rethinking Faith, Works, and the Gospel of Jesus the King* (Grand Rapids, MI: Baker Academic, 2017).

6. Jim Lo, *Intentional Diversity: Creating Cross-Cultural Ministry Relationships in Your Church,* (Indianapolis, IN: Wesleyan Publishing House, 2002), 23.

7. This according to the Roman historian Suetonius (c. AD 69–c. AD 122) in his work *Lives of the Twelve Caesars,* in which he mentions the unrest in the Jewish community because of "Chrestos," whom he labels as a troublemaker. While it is not certain that this refers to Jesus Christ, many scholars believe it does, and it fits the facts mentioned in the book of Acts. As a result of this trouble, all Jews were expelled from Rome by Emperor Claudius in AD 49, an expulsion that seems to be referred to in Acts 18:2.

8. There may have been a series of expulsions rather than just one. It is also unclear as to whether the expulsions were total or complete, but it certainly would have affected the Jewish community immensely, including Jewish Christians.

9. Edgar H. Schein, *The Corporate Culture Survival Guide,* (San Francisco, CA: Josey-Bass, 1994, 2009), 13–16.

10. Alexander Nazaryan, *Newsweek Magazine,* "Segregation in America Is as Bad Today as It Was in the 1960s," March 22, 2018; https://www.newsweek.com/2018/03/30/school-segregation-america-today-bad-1960-855256.html, accessed 12/19/18.

11. Alvin Chang, "The data proves that school segregation is getting worse," Vox.com, March 5, 2018, https://www.vox.com/2018/3/5/17080218/school-segregation-getting-worse-data, accessed 12/19/18

12. The definition of a church qualifying as multiracial is that it has no more than 80% of one ethnic or racial group. Thus, the standard to be considered a multiracial church is not a high one.

13. While I am tempted to delve more into issues of politics here, I will save further discussion for a book I am currently developing that is provisionally slated for a 2020 release and is entitled *Crossing the Line: Politics, Nationalism and Kingdom.*

14. For further study on this topic, I recommend *Misreading Scripture with Western Eyes* and *Paul Behaving Badly,* by Randolph Richards and Brandon O'Brien (Downers Grove, IL: InterVarsity); *Jesus Through Middle Eastern Eyes* and *Paul Through Mediterranean Eyes,* both by Kenneth Bailey (Downers Grove, IL: IVP Academic); and *Jesus Behaving Badly* by Mark Strauss (Downers Grove, IL: InterVarsity).

15. For a more thorough examination of the split between middle-class and generational-poverty cultures (as well as wealthy classes), see *A Framework for Understanding Poverty: A Cognitive Approach* by Ruby K. Payne, Ph.D. (Highland, TX: aha! Process, 2013).

16. Jemar Tisby, *The Color of Compromise: The Truth About the American Church's Complicity in Racism* (Grand Rapids, MI: Zondervan, 2019), 175–176.

17. The problem, in my opinion, with the postmodern affinity for moral pluralism is that there is often a lack of discernment as to when that applies and when it becomes no longer valid. In the arena of experiences that differing groups of people have had throughout history, for example, it absolutely stands to reason that there can be very different experiences and perceptions that lead to very different truths from the perspective of that group. These differing perspectives can all contain a portion of truth. But there are arenas in which moral pluralism does not fly. If I'm standing on the road and see a semi truck screaming toward us, but my friend who is facing the other direction does not, it does not hold up to say that we have differing but equally valid truths. There are times when there are certain absolute truths and moral pluralism simply does not work.

18. Campbell Robertson, "A Quiet Exodus: Why Black Worshipers Are Leaving White Evangelical Churches," March 9, 2018, https://www.nytimes.com/2018/03/09/us/blacks-evangelical-churches.html, accessed 1/28/19.

19. Facts and Trends, "10 Traits of Generation Z," September 29, 2017, https://factsandtrends.net/2017/09/29/10-traits-of-generation-z/, accessed 1/29/19.

20. Gordon D. Fee, *The New International Commentary on the New Testament: The First Epistle to the Corinthians* (Grand Rapids, MI: Eerdmans, 2014), 3.

21. Although I would stress that we still need to be aware of the typical dominant and nondominant group dynamics, and those in the dominant group must be willing to adapt, we should be aware that most in the nondominant groups have already been adapting and conceding culturally all along.

22. Michael Burns, *Crossing the Line: Culture, Race, and Kingdom* (Spring, TX; Illumination Publishers, 2017), 206–213.

23. Edgar H. Schien, *The Corporate Culture Survival Guide* (San Francisco, CA: Josey-Bass, 2009), 107.

www.ipibooks.com

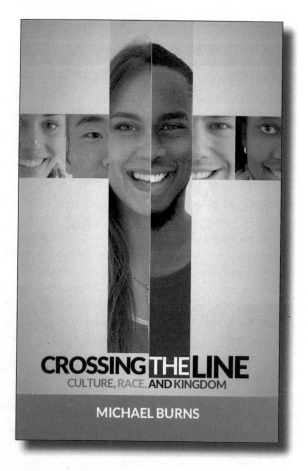

CROSSING THE LINE
CULTURE, RACE, AND KINGDOM

MICHAEL BURNS

In this book, Michael Burns opens the doorway into dialogue and discussion of race and its impact on the culture and Kingdom of God. Issues of racism, race, and culture bring out deep passion and potential conflict in the world; and because disciples live in this world, they affect us, our mission, and our unity. Every potential problem like this, though, can be a pitfall or a platform. It can be our undoing or an amazing opportunity to put the power and wisdom of the true gospel on display.

The real problems that threaten division within the body are not race or skin color as such, but history, culture, perspective, and the solutions that are typically offered by the world. Michael examines these agents of division before delving into the true answers found in God's word. The good news is that perhaps the biggest cause of internal strife and division in the early church was the issue of ethnicity and culture. That means that the New Testament Scriptures are full of principles and teaching that will propel us forward in our search to be the unified people of God that he has called us to be.

Available at www.ipibooks.com